Political Anthropology

POLITICAL ANTHROPOLOGY

An Introduction

Third Edition

Ted C. Lewellen

Foreword by Victor Turner,
Written for the First Edition

Westport, Connecticut
London

Library of Congress Cataloging-in-Publication Data

Lewellen, Ted C., 1940–
    Political anthropology : an introduction / Ted C. Lewellen ; foreword to the first edition
by Victor Turner.—3rd ed.
      p. cm.
    Includes bibliographical references and index.
    ISBN 0–89789–890–7 (alk. paper)—ISBN 0–89789–891–5 (pbk. : alk. paper)
    1. Political anthropology.   I. Title.
GN492.L48   2003
306.2—dc21   2003052889

British Library Cataloguing in Publication Data is available.

Library of Congress Catalog Card Number: 2003052889
ISBN: 0–89789–890–7
    0–89789–891–5 (pbk.)

First published in 2003

Praeger Publishers, 88 Post Road West, Westport, CT 06881
An imprint of Greenwood Publishing Group, Inc.
www.praeger.com

Printed in the United States of America

The paper used in this book complies with the
Permanent Paper Standard issued by the National
Information Standards Organization (Z39.48–1984).

10 9 8 7 6 5 4

CONTENTS

CONTENTS

FOREWORD TO THE FIRST EDITION

Victor Turner
(1920–1983)

In this succinct and lucid account of the sporadic growth of political anthropology over the past four decades, Ted Lewellen traces the development of its theoretical structure and the personal contributions of its main formulators. He makes available to the wider public of educated readers the issues, problems, perplexities, and achievements of political anthropologists as they have striven to make sense of the multitudinous ways in which societies on varying levels of scale and complexity handle order and dispute, both internal and external. He assesses the strengths and probes the weaknesses of successive anthropological approaches to the study of political structures and processes, viewed both cross-culturally and in terms of intensive case studies. The result is a commendable guide to the varied sources of this increasingly important subdiscipline, a guide which, as far as I know, is unique of its kind; his criticisms are sharp, his style genial, and his judgments just. As a student of the first generation of British political anthropologists of the structural-functionalist school, and a teacher of the medial generation of American political anthropologists, I can vouch for the accuracy and balance of Professor Lewellen's conclusions, and applaud the penetration of his criticisms, even when they are directed at positions promoted by those of my own theoretical persuasion.

Professor Lewellen states candidly that he has not written a textbook. Indeed, most textbooks are bulkier and overcharged with disparate materials, mainly descriptive. But this concise book is theoretically fine-honed and minutely integrated. It seems to be the introduction to political anthropology that we have all been waiting for, the prism which accurately segregates the significant constituents. Not only students, but also seasoned scholars will find worth in it. It is at once a summation and a new start.

PREFACE

This book had its origins in 1980 when a sociologist friend who was editing the multivolume *Handbook of Political Behavior* asked me to supply the entry on Political Anthropology. My protestations that I knew no more about the subject than any other budding anthropologist fell on deaf ears. He wanted nothing fancy or even particularly erudite, just a workmanlike overview of the subject matter and theoretical orientation of the subdiscipline. How hard could that be? Barely a year out of graduate school and in need of publications to beef up an emaciated vitae, I finally agreed to do it. I thought I could seek out a few overview books and an encyclopedia article or two on the subject, peruse the most important works in the bibliography, and write it up in short order. This was not to be the case. It quickly became evident that no remotely comprehensive overview book or article existed. There was no shortage of works with "political anthropology" in their titles, but most were theoretically narrow, and those that did attempt some sort of summation were incomplete or hopelessly out of date. The unfortunate reality was that political anthropology existed mainly in widely scattered ethnographies and theoretical writings that had little to do with each other. What Ronald Cohen (1970: 484) had written a decade earlier was still true: "There are, as yet, no well-established conventions as to what [political anthropology] includes or excludes or what should be the basic methodological attack on the subject." There even seemed to be some doubt that there was such a thing as political anthropology: in a 1959 review article, political scientist David Easton charged that political anthropology did not really exist because the practitioners of this nondiscipline had utterly failed to mark off the political system from other subsystems of society.

The *Handbook* entry (Lewellen 1981a), followed in the same year by an article on the anthropological classification of political systems in *Micropolitics,* seemed quite inadequate to the need. The goal of filling in these early outlines, defining the areas that comprised political anthropology, and discovering some coherence in a plethora of viewpoints turned into a fascinating, difficult, and highly rewarding long-term project of which this Third Edition of *Political Anthropology* is the latest installment.

When the first edition was about to go to press, the publisher—realistically fearing a miniscule market—asked that I get a "big name" to write a Foreword. This seemed like an impossible task; there were relatively few superstars in the field, and I did not know any of them personally. On the timeworn principle that you might as well wish for the bakery as wish for the bread, I tried to contact Victor Turner, who was at that time teaching at the University of Virginia in Charlottesville. Turner was not widely identified as a political anthropologist, but his *Schism and Continuity in an African Society* (1957) was—and still is— among the best books ever published in the field, and he was part of the editorial triumvirate that brought out the revolutionary anthology on process theory (Swartz, Turner, and Tuden 1966). My unsolicited manuscript caught up with him in Israel, where he was teaching and researching. I was quite surprised when I received in the mail Turner's Foreword on two single sheets of crumpled onionskin paper typed almost beyond legibility on an ancient typewriter, which Turner apologetically explained he had inherited from Max Gluckman. His enthusiasm for the project probably had less to do with any writing or research skills on my part than with the fact that someone was finally solidifying a field that had previously been amorphous.

I never had the opportunity to meet Turner in person before his untimely death in 1983. However, in many ways he still lives on in the works of contemporary political theorists. Turner did not witness the critical deconstruction that would so severely split anthropology in the 1980s, but he anticipated it with his own emphasis on symbolism and subjectivity, on understanding the worldviews underlying the actors in his ethnographic dramas. I think that he would be right at home with the current synthesis-in-the-making, in which well-sifted postmodern ideas are finding form in the hard-nosed empiricism that Turner himself practiced.

The years have been good for political anthropology. Easton's complaint that political anthropology was unable to mark off the political system from other subsystems of society was, at the time, generally accepted with the humble mortification proper to a young science being criticized by one much older and wiser. It turned out, however, that Easton had construed political anthropology's greatest virtue into a vice. In the societies in which anthropologists have traditionally worked, politics cannot be analytically isolated from kinship, religion, age-grade associations, or secret societies, because these are precisely the institutions through which power and authority are manifested; in many societies and in political subgroups within larger societies, "government" either does not exist or is irrelevant at the local level. The specification of the manner in which the idiom of politics is expressed through the medium of apparently nonpolitical institutions, ideologies, and practices may be the primary contribution of anthropology to the study of comparative politics. Political anthropologists have even carried these insights into the sacred domain of the political scientist by demonstrating that informal organizations and relationships may be more important than are formal institutions, even in such modern governments as those of the United States and China (Britan and Cohen 1980; Weatherford 1981). Postmodern concepts of subtle forms of authority that inhere in knowledge, discourse, and gender have broadened the purview of political anthropology to consider power in all its forms. A new anthropology of globalization is inevitably and profoundly political, demanding analysis not only of how global structures impose themselves at the local level, but also of how these impositions are resisted and opposed.

Unlike the situation in the early 1980s, political anthropology is now a full-fledged and respected member of the anthropological community of subdisciplines, and there is no lack of overview books on the subject, as well as general anthologies (Cheater 1999; Gledhill 2000; Kurtz 2001; McGlynn and Tuden 1991; Shore and Wright 1997; Vincent 1990, 2002). Each assumes a different perspective on the material, so that they are less competitive than complementary.

For readers of previous editions, this Third Edition will be both familiar and new. I have left the earlier chapters relatively intact. These are "historical" chapters in the sense that they deal with subject matter and theories that are important in the development of political anthropology, but have been displaced or sidelined in contemporary research. Classification of political systems is seldom argued any more (although in my opinion the old typologies are a lot better than the present tendency to lump everything under the rubric "ethnicity"). Once-dominant struc-

tural-functionalism has seen its day. Process theory is very much alive
and kicking, but has been overshadowed over the last decades by postmodernism. The material on gender has been expanded, and the chapter
devoted to the world system has been extended to include globalization,
which I believe represents a wave of the future for political anthropology.
Two entirely new chapters have been added: one on contemporary theory,
especially postmodernism, and the other on the politics of ethnicity and
nationalism.

This book is written for anyone seeking a relatively painless overview
of one of anthropology's most fascinating areas of specialization. I emphasize "painless" because this is not a scholarly monograph or an exhaustive summary. Rather, I have tried to write the type of introduction
to the subject that I would have welcomed as a student in a class on
political anthropology—a book that provides the background necessary
to understand more focused ethnographic and theoretical accounts, as a
stage setting might provide the context and meaning for a play's action.
Although this book may be read easily by undergraduates, professionals
(including those outside the field of anthropology) should not be fright-
ened off; I am offering here mostly other people's research and, although
the mode of presentation may be simplified, many of the ideas are both
complex and insightful. If this book does no more than convey enough
of the excitement of this discipline to direct readers to the "real thing,"
I will be satisfied.

Work on the Third Edition of *Political Anthropology* was supported
by the Irving May Chair in Human Relations at the University of
Richmond.

Chapter 1

THE DEVELOPMENT OF POLITICAL ANTHROPOLOGY

Although political anthropology as a specialization within social anthropology did not appear until as late as 1940, and did not really kick in until after World War II, this is also true for most anthropological subject specializations. From its beginnings as a scientific discipline in the latter half of the nineteenth century to the middle of the twentieth century, anthropology was relatively unified. The early evolutionists admitted no boundaries to their comparative method and blithely roamed through the world and through the farther reaches of history examining any subject that met their eye. Franz Boas, the Father of American Anthropology, was equally ready to analyze Eskimo art, Kwakiutl economics, or immigrant craniums. What lines were drawn were theoretical: a person was an evolutionist, a historical particularist, or a structural-functionalist, but there was little sense that a person might be a political anthropologist, an ethnolinguist, or an ecological anthropologist. The ideal of a holistic anthropology only began to break down through the 1940s as increasing data and increasing numbers of professional anthropologists forced specialization. The development of political anthropology was part of this general process, which continues today, with ever-smaller subspecialties being delineated. However, the comparative study of politics in "primitive" societies dates to the very beginnings of anthropology.

A cannon squad in revolutionary Mexico. True revolutions, involving structural change in the state system itself, have been rare in Latin America. Courtesy of the Library of Congress.

THE NINETEENTH-CENTURY EVOLUTIONISTS

Darwin's influence dominated the development of cultural anthropology in the second half of the nineteenth century just as it dominated biology. Much of the evolutionary theory emerging from this period was as primitive as the societies it sought to make sense of: evolutionary schemas were rigid and simplistic, there were endless arguments over whether the earliest societies were matriarchal or patriarchal, ethnocentrism ran rampant as Christianity and the Aryan race were seen as the apex of human progress, and customs were torn out of their cultural context and compared indiscriminately by armchair anthropologists who had never seen the savages that were their subjects. However, it is easy to forget how perceptive many of these studies were. Whatever their faults, the evolutionists laid the foundation for modern scientific anthropology.

Prior to this period, the tradition that reached back to Plato and ran through Aristotle, Hobbes, Rousseau, and most philosophers of politics until (but not including) Marx was that government and politics were products of civilization, and lower stages were characterized by anarchy. One of the earliest to challenge this view with hard evidence was Sir Henry Maine, who, in *Ancient Law* (1861), postulated that primitive society was organized along the lines of kinship, was patriarchal, and was ordered by sacred proscriptions. Evolution was in the direction of secularization and organization based not on kinship but on territory—"local contiguity"—which formed the basis for political action.

Maine's important insight that kinship could be a primary sociopolitical structure was developed by Louis Henry Morgan in *Ancient Society* (1877). Morgan had studied the Iroquois Indians of New York State firsthand and had been fascinated by their kinship terminology, which was very different from that used in Western European countries but similar to that employed in other parts of the world. His description and categorization of kinship systems was itself a lasting contribution, but before these could gain recognition they had to be couched in the type of theoretical framework popular at the time. Morgan developed an evolutionary sequence based on mode of subsistence, the stages of which he termed savagery, barbarism, and civilization. These grossly connotative terms actually translate rather well into their modern equivalents—societies based on hunting-gathering, horticulture, and developed agriculture. Morgan, like others of his time, began with the postulate of the psychic unity of mankind—the belief that there was a common origin and parallel development all over the world—though he was unable to follow the idea to its inherently antiracist conclusions and assumed that the Aryans were naturally "in the central stream of human progress" (Morgan 1877: 533).

With his considerable sophistication in the analysis of kinship, Morgan was able to elaborate Maine's inchoate ideas. Social organization began with the promiscuous horde that developed into kin-based units, organized along sexual lines: intermarrying sets of male siblings and female siblings (this was an early insight into cross-cousin marriage). In emphasizing the role of exogamy, he touched on the conception of intergroup bonds formed through marriage that would become the alliance theory of French structuralists three-quarters of a century later. Progressive restriction of marriage partners led to the development of gens (clans) that joined to create increasingly larger units up to a confederacy of tribes. Sociopolitical structure at this level is egalitarian and is based on sets of interpersonal relations. (With the exception of the "promiscuous horde," this is not a bad description of the Iroquois confederacy, although there is little reason to generalize to a universal evolutionary process.) The specialization of the political sphere does not appear until the full domestication of plants and animals creates sufficient surplus to lead to urbanization and private property. True government, then, is based on territory and property.

Morgan is subject to most of the criticisms directed by later generations at the evolutionists (except, of course, that he was no armchair anthropologist, having studied the Iroquois firsthand), yet much of his thinking has been absorbed into modern anthropology, especially in relation to politics. Although anthropologists no longer distinguish kin-based from territory-based groups, Morgan's emphasis on kinship as a primary medium of political articulation at the subsistence levels of hunting-gathering and horticulture was justified. Equally important was Morgan's discovery of the gens as a corporate lineage in which decision making was confined within a group tracing common ancestry through either the male or the female line. Another lasting insight was his recognition of the egalitarianism of primitive society and the lack of a concept of private property. These latter ideas contributed to Morgan's most significant influence: they formed the basis for Frederick Engels's *The Origin of the Family, Private Property and the State* ([1891] 1972), the Marxian view of the evolution of capitalism.

THE REACTION

Early twentieth-century anthropology was characterized by two fundamental changes: the rejection of evolutionary theory and methodology, and a widening hiatus between the anthropologies of the United States and of England and France. In the latter countries, the immediate repudiation of evolutionism was relatively mild, but there was a significant shift in new directions. This shift was based on the work of Emile Durkheim—in France leading to an increasingly cognitive structuralism that would culminate with the works of Claude Lévi-Strauss; in England leading to an emphasis on social facts (and a corresponding disregard for the psychological aspect of culture) and a theoretical point of view dominated by the ideas of function and structure. Durkheim had little influence on U.S. cultural anthropology, whereas Franz Boas's historical particularism dominated. Boas was absolute, and often vehement, in his repudiation of the comparative method and of the vast generalizations that had emerged from it. He emphasized detailed descriptive studies of particular cultures. Theory did not disappear altogether, but orientations such as diffusionism took on a very particularistic turn, with field anthropologists spending years collecting the most minuscule facts of daily life and charting them on enormous trait lists (one suspects this type of inquiry declined through sheer boredom). Although English anthropologists were turning increasingly to the study of kinship, not much was accomplished in terms of the political dimension, aside from an occasional reference to Durkheim's mechanical and organic solidarity. In the United States, there was little in the way of theory that would separate out the political for analysis.

A major exception was Robert Lowie's *The Origin of the State* ([1927] 1962). In order to find a framework to deal with the political, Lowie reached back to outmoded evolutionary theory. Fittingly enough, he started by rejecting the unilineal evolution of his predecessors; there was no evidence that all societies pass through similar stages of development. Maine's and Morgan's contention that primitive political order was maintained solely through personal relations was also rejected. Rather, the territorial bond, which Morgan saw as a characteristic of civilization, was universal, and thus formed a bridge between primitive political organization and the state. In an earlier book, *Primitive Society* (1920), Lowie had recognized the political importance of associations in uniting otherwise disparate groups and he saw these as forming the basis of the state because they weakened the blood ties of kin groups. Now he modified this view, showing how associations can also be as "separatistic" as kin relations. Thus associations, which are because of their nature neither centralizing nor disruptive, require a supraordinate authority in order to achieve higher-level integration.

Georges Balandier's (1970) contention that specific, explicit political anthropology developed during the 1920s is true only to a point. Here we find certain lasting ideas: that all societies recognize territory, that increases in population and in conflict lead to states, that class stratification is a key element in movement up the evolutionary ladder toward the state, and that the central element of the state is a monopoly of coercive power. Although these concepts were not developed in a systematic causal model, Lowie clarified a number of issues, asked some crucial questions, and presented anthropology with a fascinating challenge.

Unfortunately, the challenge was not taken up. The evolutionary phrasing of Lowie's book, despite his denials of unilineal development, must have seemed sadly anachronistic to his peers who had thought themselves done with this evolutionary nonsense once and for all. The beginning of political anthropology was also its end—until 1940.

THE BRITISH FUNCTIONALISTS

In England during the 1930s, two brands of functionalism vied for dominance: the psychobiological functionalism of Bronislaw Malinowski, and the structural-functionalism of A. R. Radcliffe-Brown. Malinowski, often considered the founder of modern fieldwork techniques for his extensive research in the Trobriand Islands, sought to interpret cultural institutions as derived from certain psychological and biological needs. Although he contributed little to political anthropology per se, his studies of law, economics, and religion—as observed in ongoing, rather than historical, society—cleared the way for the type of specialization that would later become commonplace. Malinowski's participant-observation method became the model for an entire generation of British fieldworkers whose intense analyses of African societies would establish political anthropology as a legitimate subdiscipline. However, it was Radcliffe-Brown's structural brand of functionalism that would ultimately come to predominate in England, where academic chairmanships at Oxford, London, or Manchester were close to the equivalent of theoretical fiefdoms. For Radcliffe-Brown, a society was an equilibrium system in which each part functioned to the maintenance of the whole (the obvious organic analogy was not avoided). Thus, there was a sense that societies were to be described from high above, to be mapped to show how their various elements intermeshed. As we shall see, this approach is more atemporal than static, that is, it does not really postulate an unchanging society or a society without conflict, but rather its focus is on those norms, values, and ideal structures that form the framework within which activity takes place.

Feeding this theoretical orientation, and feeding upon it, was the concentration of British research in colonial Africa. Much of the purpose of such research was to instruct colonial authorities on the social systems under their control, and this affected both the emphasis and the image of social anthropology. On the one hand, there was little recognition that the societies that anthropologists were studying were severely changed by colonialism, and by the Pax Britannica imposed by English guns. Also, there was a tendency to study chiefdom and state systems, some of which, like the Zulu, had been integrated partially as a reaction to the British threat.

These two trends, structural-functionalism and the African experience, came together in 1940 in a work that, at a single blow, established modern political anthropology: *African Political Systems,* edited by Meyer Fortes and E. E. Evans-Pritchard. In their introduction, the editors distinguish two types of African political systems: those with centralized authority and judicial institutions (primitive states), and those without such authority and institutions (stateless societies). A major difference between these types is the role of kinship. Integration and decision making in stateless societies is based, at the lowest level, on bilateral family/band groups and, at a higher level, on corporate unilineal descent groups. State societies are those in which an administrative organization overrides or unites such groups as the permanent basis of political structure. This typology was later criticized as much too simplistic, but the detailed descriptions of how lineages functioned politically in several specific societies were lasting contributions. Social equilibrium was assumed, so that the major problem was to show how the various conflict and interest groups maintained a balance of forces that resulted in a stable, ongoing social structure. The integrating power of religion and symbol were also noted, especially the role of ritual in confirming and consolidating group values.

African Political Systems' introduction and eight ethnographic articles established the problems, the theoretical foundation, the methodology, and the controversy for more than a decade of research into the politics of preindustrial societies. The original typology was increasingly refined. A. L. Southall, in *Alur Society* (1953), challenged the assumption that segmentary systems—those in which authority was dispersed among a number of groups—were always uncentralized; he provided an example of a society in which segmentary lineage organization existed side by side with a centralized state. Others questioned segmentation as a factor in classification at all, because even centralized governments are seg-mented. Nor could lineages be the basis for all stateless societies, because age-grades, secret associations, and ritual groups could cross-cut lineage divisions for purposes of political action. Jumping off from Fortes's and Evans-Pritchard's bare suggestion of types (the two editors did not seem to think that their typology was universal, or even very important), clas-sifications were increasingly refined until political taxonomy became vir-tually an autonomous field of research. The static structural-functionalist paradigm maintained itself through a number of studies as the old guard—Evans-Pritchard, Raymond Firth, Daryll Forde, and Meyer For-tes—held, contemporaneously or successively, the princely academic chairs of British anthropology. This is not to say that the situation itself was static; there was constant ferment, as Malinowskian or Radcliffe-Brownian emphases alternated, and as conflict and change increasingly imposed themselves with the rapid demise of African colonialism.

THE TRANSITION

By the 1950s, after a decade of gradual chipping away, the edifice of structural-functionalism was showing cracks in its very foundation. There was little sense yet of a complete repudiation of this paradigm, but there was a quite self-conscious sense that fundamental modifications were being made.

A major contribution in this direction was Edmund Leach's *Political Systems of Highland Burma* (1954), which signaled the shift to a more process-oriented, more dynamic form of analysis. In the Kachin Hills area of Burma, Leach found not one but three different political systems: a virtually anarchic traditional system, an unstable and intermediate sys-tem, and a small-scale centralized state. The traditional system and the state were more or less distinct communities made up of many linguistic, cultural, and political subgroups, all somehow forming an interrelated whole. This whole could not be supposed to be in equilibrium; there was constant tension and change within and between the various subsystems. In order to make sense out of all this, Leach felt it necessary "to force these facts within the constraining mold of an *as if* system of ideas, composed of concepts which are treated *as if* they are part of an equi-librium system" (Leach 1954: ix). This was no more than the people themselves did, for they also had an ideal cognitive pattern for their society, expressed in ritual and symbolism. In reality, however, the peo-ple were hardly constrained to follow their own, and certainly not the anthropologist's, *as if* conception of their behavior. These ideas are similar to the mentalistic structuralism of Claude Lévi-Strauss (whom Leach would later help introduce into English-language anthropology), and there are suggestions of the cognitive mapping later to become central to American psychological anthropology. The immediate importance for the study of politics, however, was in the clear differentiation of abstract political structure from the on-the-ground political reality. Almost as crucial, Leach finally got political anthropology out of Africa and broke it free from the relatively cohesive, single-language societies to which it had been confined.

Meanwhile, Max Gluckman was also breaking new ground. In his chapter on the Zulu in *African Political Systems,* in *Custom and Conflict in Africa* (1956), and in *Order and Rebellion in Tribal Africa* (1960), Gluckman developed the theme that equilibrium is neither static nor stable, but grows out of an ongoing dialectical process in which conflicts within one set of relations are absorbed and integrated within another set of relations: cross-cutting loyalties tend to unite the wider society in settling a feud between local groups; witchcraft accusations displace hostilities within a group in a way that does not threaten the system; apartheid in South Africa, while radically dividing white from black, ultimately unites both groups within themselves. The Roman maxim "divide and conquer" is cleverly restated as "divide and cohere." Politically, this is especially evident in African rituals of rebellion in which the king must periodically dress as a pauper or act the clown, is symbolically killed, or is subjected to open hatred and obscenities from his people. For Gluckman, such rituals are not merely catharsis; they are the symbolic reassertion of the priority of the system over the individual, of kingship over any particular king.

At this stage, both Leach and Gluckman are transitional figures, still rooted in the structural-functionalism of the 1930s and 1940s, developing ever more clever arguments in defense of equilibrium theory; yet at the same time they are taking a giant step toward a new paradigm. Gluckman, as founder and chairman of the anthropology department at Manchester University, was to see his ideas extensively elaborated by his students, known collectively as the Manchester School, a phrase that came to represent a new orientation to society based not on structure and function but on process and conflict.

THE NEO-EVOLUTIONISTS

Without a doubt, England dominated political anthropology during its first two decades. Meanwhile, in the United States, an incipient and quite different political anthropology was fermenting. Evolutionism, long banned by Boasian edict from the proper study of mankind, began a slow and not entirely respectable resurgence through the writings of Leslie White and Julian Steward. White (1943, 1959) developed a complex sequence leading through agricultural intensification to private ownership, specialization, class stratification, and political centralization. Much of this was elucidated at such a high level of generality that it left White open to the charge of merely resuscitating nineteenth-century unilineal theory, and Steward's (1965) use of the term *multilinear* evolution for his own theory only served to validate an unnecessary dichotomy. Actually, no serious evolutionist has ever held a truly unilineal theory (Harris 1968: 171–73). However, the situation was not clarified until the unilineal/multilineal dichotomy was replaced with the complementary concepts of general evolution and specific evolution, the higher level referring to evolutionary processes such as increased specialization or intensification of production, the lower to the historic sequence of forms (Sahlins and Service 1960). This clarified, evolutionary anthropology was free to move, unfettered by a heavy load of semantic, rather than substantive, difficulties.

Thus, in contrast to their English colleagues, American political anthropologists started with the idea of change on a panoramic scale in a context that was fundamentally ecological and materialist. White measured evolution in terms of energy efficiency and saw technology as a prime mover. Steward's cultural ecology focused on the cultural core, the subsistence and economic arrangements that largely determine social structure and ideology. The differences between British and American anthropology were vast, but can be overemphasized. For example, one of the earliest American political ethnographies, E. Adamson Hoebel's 1940 study of the Comanche Indians, was neither evolutionary nor materialist. Throughout the 1940s and 1950s, and into the 1960s, there was a strong current of structural-functionalism in the United States. However, that which was particularly American was quite different from that which was particularly British, to the extent that there was often little communication between the two.

Political evolution became almost synonymous with political classification. The two major evolutionary works of the period, Elman Service's *Primitive Social Organization* (1962) and Morton Fried's *The Evolution of Political Society* (1967), were more taxonomic and descriptive than causal; the emphasis was on the characteristics of different levels of sociocultural integration, rather than on the factors that triggered evolution from one level to another. Causal theories were hardly lacking, but these were derived from archeology rather than from cultural anthropology. Many notable archeologists devoted their careers to the processes involved in the evolution of state societies. These two trends, the archeological and the cultural, which originally ran parallel, came together in Service's *Origins of the State and Civilization* (1975). Although political evolution remained an ongoing field of study, it soon lost its position as the major focus of American political anthropology; process and decision-making orientations quickly crossed the Atlantic from England.

PROCESS AND DECISION MAKING

Max Gluckman had tentatively experimented with the analysis of "situations" involving individuals, in contrast to the usual ethnographic focus on group norms and social structures. Elaborating on this experiment, Victor Turner, in *Schism and Continuity in an African Society* (1957), followed a single individual through a series of social dramas in which personal and community manipulations of norms and values were laid bare. To Gluckman and Leach's emphasis on process and conflict was added a new element: individual decision making observed in crisis situations.

The belated discovery that the world is in motion stimulated an enthusiastic disavowal of structural-functionalism, almost equal to that which had temporarily obliterated evolutionism at the turn of the century. Structure and function became unfashionable terms, to be replaced by process, conflict, faction, struggle, and manipulative strategy. As Janet Bujra (1973: 43) succinctly expressed it, "For the early functionalist, the assumption was that social unity was the normal state of affairs, whereas conflict was a problematic situation which could not easily be incorporated into their theoretical framework. More recent studies of political behavior, however, seem to indicate that it is conflict which is the norm, and it is the existence of social unity which is more difficult to explain." The fact that conflict and accord, unity and disunity, might be two sides of the same coin, as Gluckman emphasized, was temporarily forgotten.

The change from structural theory to process theory had its correlate in the dissolution of the false stability imposed by colonialism in Africa. With the rise of postcolonial nation states, and the incorporation of tribal societies within larger political organizations, new problems presented themselves. No longer could "primitive" politics be treated as though it existed in a closed system; the wider sociopolitical field replaced the more restricted concept of political system. On the other hand, the intensive study of particular situations gave rise to the more restricted concept of political arena, wherein individuals and political teams vie for power and leadership.

Although many of these ideas come together in such works as Swartz, Turner, and Tuden's "Introduction" to their edited volume *Political Anthropology* (1966) and Balandier's (1970) book of the same title, it would be a mistake to consider the process approach as a coherent theory. Many ethnographies that emphasize process continued to focus on the level of norms and institutions. The decision-making approach, often referred to as action theory, was a somewhat separate subdivision of the less cohesive process orientation.

Process theory opened the way for a cross-Atlantic dialogue that was muted, at best, during the heyday of structural-functionalism. American leaders of political anthropology such as Marc Swartz and Ronald Cohen, who had shown only passing interest in evolution or evolutionary typology, joined the British in what constituted a truly international trend.

WOMEN, WORLD SYSTEMS, AND WEAPONS OF THE WEAK

Although earlier perspectives and theoretical approaches continued throughout the 1980s and into the 1990s, three strong new trends were evident. Perhaps the most important development was the emergence of a distinctly feminist anthropology. Although not specifically political, virtually all of the writers in the field were examining the relative *power* of women. Not only was the supposition of universal male domination challenged, but so were other anthropological assumptions, such as the Man-the-Hunter model of physical evolution. In addition to the expected cross-cultural statistical comparisons, two important theoretical schools developed within feminist anthropology—one analyzing the cultural construction of gender and the other, based on Marxist theory, examining the historical development of gender stratification. More recently, postmodern influences have refocused feminist studies away from concerns with male domination to analyses of identity and the ways in which power is subtly infused through every aspect of culture and discourse.

Eric Wolf's *Europe and the People Without History* (1982) brought the World System perspective and so-called dependency theory into the mainstream of anthropology. Wolf contended that all, or virtually all, cultures can be understood only in relation to the expansion of European capitalism over the last centuries. In a closely related development, many researchers began to counter the natives-as-victims approach—which fo-

cused on the destruction of tribal cultures by the spread of Western civilization—with a new emphasis on the ways in which indigenous peoples
fight back, often quite subtly, against the dominant state, either to maintain their group identity or to create for themselves niches of independence and pride. Political scientist James Scott's *Weapons of the Weak*
(1985) demonstrated how peasants resist—through gossip, slander, petty
arson, and thievery—the marginalization that comes with large-scale capitalist agriculture.

POSTMODERNISM AND GLOBALIZATION

The 1980s and well into the 1990s was a period of ferment within
anthropology. In what came to be referred to as a "crisis of representation," critical theorists challenged many of the underlying assumptions
of anthropological research and writing. Classical works of Boas, Malinowski, and Radcliffe-Brown were subjected to intense and unflattering
scrutiny, castigated as imbued with unacknowledged subjectivism, colonialism, and Western bias. At the same time, postmodernism rejected
the ostensible Enlightenment assumptions and values of anthropology,
repudiating all grand theories as well as anthropology's scientific pretensions. Drawing its inspiration and vocabulary from French philosophy
and literary studies, postmodernists sought to redeem the marginalized
discourses of the "subaltern other." The struggle between postmodern
and traditional anthropologists bifurcated the profession, splitting academic departments and leading to struggles over the editorship of major
journals. At the turn of the new century, a synthesis of sorts seems to
be emerging, in which selected postmodern insights are being developed
within a strongly empirical framework. For political anthropology, the
reconceptualization of the nature of power by Michel Foucault and others
is requiring new modes of research and analysis.

Globalization, although inchoate in anthropological studies, may turn
out to have an even greater impact than did postmodernism. The increasing flow of trade, finance, culture, ideas, and people brought about
by the sophisticated technology of communications and travel and by
the worldwide spread of neoliberal capitalism is forcing radical revi-
sions in anthropological conceptions of culture, locality, community,
and identity. The local and regional adaptations to these flows and the
resistances against them are already becoming the stuff of a new political anthropology. Power in a globalized world is both more diffuse
and more locally concentrated as decision making simultaneously shifts
upward from states to multinational corporations and the World Bank

and downward to community-level nongovernmental groups and ethnic organizations.

The challenges of the future will be considerable for political anthropology, but as I hope this book will show, the subdiscipline is working from a substantive base.

SUGGESTED READINGS

Kurtz, Donald V. *Political Anthropology: Paradigms of Power* (Boulder, Colo.: Westview, 2001). The author uses the term "paradigm" to mean the general agenda and strategy of a research community at any particular historical time. This overview assumes a paradigmatic approach to political anthropology, including structural-functionalism, the processual approach, political economy, political evolution, and postmodernism.

McGlynn, Frank, and Arthur Tuden, eds. *Anthropological Approaches to Political Behavior* (Pittsburgh, Pa.: University of Pittsburgh Press, 1991). This collection of 16 essays from the journal *Ethnology* is designed as a supplementary reader for the classroom. The essays come from many different periods in the history of political anthropology and represent a wide range of cultures.

Vincent, Joan. *Anthropology and Politics: Visions, Traditions, and Trends* (Tucson: University of Arizona Press, 1990). An exhaustive and erudite history of political anthropology from the nineteenth century to 1990. Vincent rejects as ethnocentric the genealogical method of tracing the discipline through a family tree. She attempts to include virtually everybody who ever wrote on the subject. The results are impressive, and sometimes difficult.

Vincent, Joan, ed. *The Anthropology of Politics: A Reader in Ethnography, Theory and Critique* (Malden, Mass.: Blackwell, 2002). The editor starts with an essay on the Enlightenment as a hegemonic system of Western thought that has pervaded the development of political anthropology, and thus the first section is devoted to Enlightenment authors. The 35 essays that follow are grouped as classics, studies of imperialism and colonialism, and the present period of "cosmopolitics."

Wolf, Eric. *Pathways of Power: Building an Anthropology of the Modern World* (Berkeley: University of California Press, 2001). Eric Wolf, who died in 1999, was one of the towering figures in anthropology during the second half of the twentieth century. Through over 40 years of research and writing the intimate connection between culture and power was a central concern. This collection, which covers the entire span of his writings, reveals the evolution of his ideas.

Chapter 2

TYPES OF PREINDUSTRIAL POLITICAL SYSTEMS

No anthropologist lays himself more open to the charge of Bongo-Bongoism than he who dares to classify; whatever generalization is made, some researcher will be able to protest, "Ah, but in the Bongo Bongo tribe they do it differently." It is safe to say that when it comes to creating typologies of social systems, such aberrant tribes abound. British anthropologist Edmund Leach (1961) once relegated virtually all attempts at anthropological classification to the lowly status of butterfly collecting, on the grounds that the resulting typologies made no more sense than, say, grouping together all blue butterflies. Contemporary postmodern theory has been even more inimical to classification, viewing it as the imposition of the rationalist Enlightenment compulsion to scientifically pigeonhole everything. A large antidevelopment literature has rejected classification on the grounds that it is a means by which a hegemonic West asserts power over the designated groups. In addition, current trends in globalization theory are not any more sympathetic to traditional typologies; the emphasis is on fluidity, hybridity, and change rather than the static structures designated by systems of classification.

This said, classification has been a major focus of research since the beginnings of political anthropology; indeed, the foundational book, Fortes and Evans-Pritchard's *African Political Systems* (1940), begins with a typology. Most introductory textbooks in cultural anthropology continue to employ the classical band-tribe-chiefdom-state designations.

Traditional Eskimo society was comprised of families and egalitarian bands that fluctuated in size according to the seasonal availability of food. Courtesy of the Library of Congress.

Lumping all such groupings within the overgeneralized terms "ethnic" and "nation" has become more politically correct today, but it is questionable whether this is an improvement.

The reality is that no matter what designations and differentiations are employed few will be completely happy; this is no more than we might expect when something as historically unique as society is confined within a set of neat categories. However, a system of classification emerged between 1940 and 1980 that gained general terminological acceptance, providing a common vocabulary of political difference. This classification, shown in Figure 2.1, has been somewhat vindicated by cross-cultural testing. It is based on means of political integration, access to leadership positions, and methods of group decision making. Allen Johnson and Timothy Earle (2000: 36) have recently developed a different, and in many ways better, classification that sets the key socioeconomic levels as family group, local group, and regional polity, with subcategories in each class (acephalous local group, big man collectivity, chiefdom). However, even in such a recent typology there is a great deal of overlap with the classical designations shown here.

Classification is possible because a society is no more just a collection of individual human beings than a house is just a conglomeration of lumber, bricks, and nails. Two houses built of different materials but to the same floor plan will obviously be much more alike than two houses of the same materials but very different designs (e.g., a town house and a ranch house). Similarly, we would not expect to find the same architecture in the arctic and in the tropics, or among the pastoral Nuer of Africa and the modern industrial Swedes. In short, a house is defined in terms of its systemic properties, not its individual components, and that system will be influenced by its physical environment and the level of technology of the people who designed it.

This analogy can easily be strained, but it helps to keep some such idea in mind when dealing with any type of anthropological classification. If the traditional Bushmen of the Kalahari Desert of Africa are to be placed in the same political category (bands) as the nineteenth-century Shoshone Indians of Utah, it must be on the assumption that a hunting-gathering adaptation to an arid environment gives rise to particular social characteristics, such as egalitarian groups with no formal leadership and a system of economic exchange based on sharing. The relationships are causal, to be sure, but it is more difficult than one might think to determine exactly how one element of a system causes another. Does the arid environment, and thus the relative scarcity of food and water, cause low population densities and consequently a flexible small-group type of so-

Figure 2.1
Preindustrial Political Systems

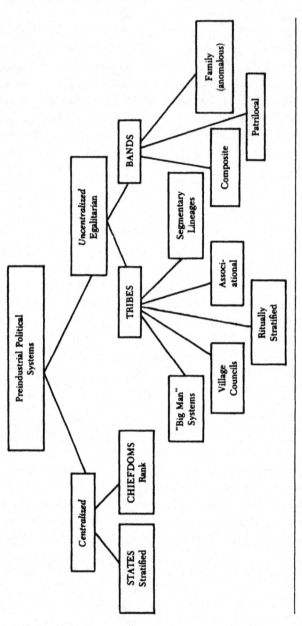

Sources: Eisenstadt 1959: Fried 1967; Service 1971.

cial organization? Perhaps. However, a cause is usually thought of as being active, whereas the environment just sort of sits there. In addition, the relationship between society and environment is one of constant feedback; people not only adapt to their surroundings but also change their physical and social worlds to meet their own needs. In other words, when classifying social systems, it is often more productive to think in terms of structural relationships in the sense that one element logically implies another. A useful typology, then, would be one that delineates systems— that is, units in which the parts are so structurally interrelated that from the specification of one element one can predict other elements.

However, it cannot be too strongly emphasized that interrelations of social traits—for example, chiefdoms with unilineal kinship—represent only statistical probabilities. To return to the house analogy, it is possible to legitimately class ranch houses together, but an enormous range of variation of particulars within the general style is to be expected. In contrast to strictly materialist theories of culture, environment and technology do not seem so much to *determine* social structure and ideology as to *limit* the range of possibilities.

Table 2.1 suggests some of the social and economic characteristics that may reasonably be associated with each major political type. Any such chart must be approached with caution. First, no society should be expected to match all the characteristics of its type, any more than one would expect to discover some perfectly average American man who is five foot ten, 39 years old, married, has some college experience but no degree, and earns $37,057 a year (U.S. Census Bureau 2002). Second, what this chart really shows is cultural complexity, and therefore it should not be assumed that politics is the primary determinant simply because the major headings are band, tribe, chiefdom, and state; if this book were about kinship, the headings might just as well be bilateral, patrilineal, matrilineal, and cognatic. Third, it must be kept in mind that certain characteristics are better predictors than are others. Statistically, the strongest predictor on the chart is *population density* (which is not included, because increasing densities from band through state may be assumed). Fourth, a chart of this kind, by its very nature, implies that each of these types is quite distinct from the others, whereas in reality they form points along a continuum. Fifth, it should neither be assumed that a higher level of cultural complexity leaves behind all the characteristics of lower levels (reciprocity, e.g., is a significant means of exchange in all societies), nor that cultural complexity is simply additive (bilateral systems of kinship appear at both the simplest and most complex levels, but are replaced by unilineal kinship at the intermediate

Table 2.1
Preindustrial Political Systems: An Evolutionary Typology

	Uncentralized		Centralized	
	Band	Tribe	Chiefdom	State
Type of Subsistence	Hunting-gathering; little or no domestication	Extensive agriculture (horticulture) and pastoralism	Extensive agriculture; intensive fishing	Intensive agriculture
Type of Leadership	Informal and situational leaders; may have a headman who acts as arbiter in group decision-making	Charismatic headman with no power but some authority in group decision making	Charismatic chief with limited power based on bestowal of benefits on followers	Sovereign leader supported by an aristocratic bureaucracy
Type and Importance of Kinship	Bilateral kinship, with kin relations used differentially in changing size and composition of bands	Unilineal kinship (patrilineal or matrilineal) may form basic structure of society	Unilineal with some bilateral; descent groups are ranked in status	State demands suprakinship loyalties; access to power is based on ranked kin groups, either unilineal or bilateral
Major Means of Social Integration	Marriage alliances unite larger groups; bands united by kinship and family; economic interdependence based on reciprocity	Pantribal sodalities based on kinship, voluntary associations, and/or age-grades	Integration through loyalty to chief, ranked lineages, and voluntary associations	State loyalties supercede all lower-level loyalties; integration through commerce and specialization of function
Political Succession	May be hereditary headman, but actual leadership falls to those with special knowledge or abilities	No formal means of political succession	Chief's position is not directly inherited, but chief must come from a high-ranking lineage	Direct hereditary succession of sovereign; increasing appointment of bureaucratic functionaries
Major Types of Economic Exchange	Reciprocity	Reciprocity; trade may be more developed than in bands	Redistribution through chief; reciprocity at lower levels	Redistribution based on formal tribute and/or taxation; markets and trade
Social Stratification	Egalitarian	Egalitarian	Rank (individual and lineage)	Classes (minimally of rulers and ruled)
Ownership of Property	Little or no sense of personal property	Communal (lineage or clan) ownership of agricultural lands and cattle	Land communally owned by lineage, but strong sense of personal ownership of titles, names, privileges, ritual, artifacts, etc.	Private and state ownership increases at the expense of communal ownership

Law and Legitimate Control of Force	No formal laws or punishments; right to use force is communal	No formal laws or punishments; right to use force belongs to lineage, clan, or association	May be informal laws and specified punishments for breaking taboos; chief has limited access to physical coercion	Formal laws and punishments; state holds all legitimate access to use of physical force
Religion	No religious priesthood or full-time specialists; shamanistic	Shamanistic; strong emphasis on initiation rites and other rites of passage that unite lineages	Inchoate formal priesthood; hierarchical, ancestor-based religion	Full-time priesthood provides sacral legitimization of state
Recent and Contemporary Examples	!Kung Bushmen (Africa) Pygmies (Africa) Inuit (Canada, Alaska) Shoshone (U.S.)	Kpelle (W. Africa) Yanomamo (Brazil, Venezuela) Nuer (Sudan) Cheyenne (U.S.)	Precolonial Hawaii Kwakiutl (Canada) Tikopia (Polynesia) Dagurs (Mongolia)	Ankole (Uganda) Jimma (Ethiopia) Kachari (India) Volta (Africa)
Historic and Prehistoric Examples	Virtually all Paleolithic societies	Iroquois (U.S.) Oaxaca Valley (Mexico) 1500–1000 B.C.	Precolonial Ashanti, Benin, Dahomy, Scottish Highlanders	Precolonial Zulu (Africa) Aztec (Mexico) Inca (Peru) Sumeria (Iraq)

Sources: Abrahamson 1969; Carniero 1970; Eisenstadt 1959; Fried 1967; Levinson and Malone 1980; Lomax and Arensberg 1977; Service 1971.

levels). Finally, special mention must be made of the case of religion, in which a strong relation is found between cultural complexity and religious organization, but little or no relation is found with regard to belief (which is why magic, animism, polytheism, and monotheism are not mentioned on the chart). If these *caveats* are kept in mind, the chart provides a useful summary of the characteristics of preindustrial political systems.

UNCENTRALIZED SYSTEMS

Many of the groups traditionally studied by anthropologists possess little that could be called government, at least not in the sense of a permanent political elite. In most nonstate systems, power is fragmentary and temporary, dispersed among families, bands, lineages, and various associations. Wider political groups may be formed temporarily to counter some threat, such as warring neighbors, but these groups will break apart when the problem has been overcome. Thus these social systems can best be viewed not as permanent, centrally organized societies, but rather as fluid groups that, over short or long periods of time, sometimes seasonally and sometimes almost randomly, coalesce into larger tribal units that then disintegrate into smaller units, which may themselves be divisible. Although politics is constant in such societies as individuals seek support for leadership positions, public decisions are made, and territory is defended, it is not manifested in either a monopoly of coercive force nor in any form of centralized economic system based on taxes or tribute. There may be great differences in individual status, but there is little in the way of class stratification. Thus, these systems, although only egalitarian in any real sense at their lowest level (that of hunters-gatherers), appear more democratic in decision making and access to leadership than do more centralized groups.

Bands

A major conclusion deriving from a 1965 Conference on Band Organization was that the term band, although still useful, was regularly applied to groups as diverse as those with an average size of 25, as well as those with 300 to 400 members, rendering the term virtually meaningless. It was also argued that the usual defining qualities of bands—seasonal scheduling, lack of centralized authority structures, and hunting-gathering economy—were not sufficiently restrictive to make these units automatically comparable (Damas 1968). However, in those few societies lacking agriculture, domesticated food animals, or dependable year-round fishing, there would seem to be only a limited number of cultural options available. Similarities in the social and political structures of such widely separated groups as the Canadian Eskimo and Australian Aborigines suggest that dependence on wild foods, the consequent nomadism, and seasonal redistributions of population fix the adaptive possibilities within relatively narrow limits. For this reason, the band may have been a normal mode of social organization in Paleolithic times. The band form is extremely rare today; therefore, this classification is more historical than contemporary.

Bands are typically small, with perhaps 25 to 150 individuals, grouped in nuclear families. Although there is a division of labor along age and sex lines, there is virtually no specialization of skills, with the result being that the unity of the wider group is, in Emile Durkheim's term, "mechanical"—that is, based on custom, tradition, and common values and symbols, rather than on an interdependence of specialized roles. A strict rule of band exogamy forces marriage alliances with other bands, and this wider group is typically also united by bilateral kinship (traced equally through both parents). Lineages, in the sense of corporate descent groups holding territorial rights, would not be sufficiently flexible for the constant fluctuations of hunting-gathering societies.

Morton Fried (1967) categorizes such groups as egalitarian in terms of economy, social organization, and political structure. Distribution of food and other needed goods is at the simplest level of sharing; bonds are established within the band and between bands on the basis of ongoing reciprocal relations. Political organization is also egalitarian to the extent that decision making is usually a group enterprise, and access to leadership positions is equally open to all males within a certain age range. Leadership, which is temporary and shifts according to the situation, is based on the personal attributes of the individual and lacks any coercive power. A headman or leader in a hunt cannot really tell anyone what to do, but must act as arbiter for the group, and perhaps as expert advisor in particular situations.

This least complex of political structures may be further subdivided into patrilocal, composite, and anomalous bands. The patrilocal type is based on band exogamy and a marriage rule that the woman lives with her husband's group. This type was so widespread that Elman Service (1962: 97) regarded it as "almost an inevitable kind of organization." Indeed, it has the advantage of band stability, because each group is constantly replenished over time by new members coming in from outside; but it also is capable of forming wide-ranging alliances through marriage and possesses considerable flexibility. The composite band was viewed by Service as the result of the collapse of originally patrilocal structures that were rapidly depopulated from disease and war after having come in contact with civilization. It is a group that lacks both band exogamy and a marriage residence rule and, therefore, is "more of an expedient agglomeration than a structured society." In the anomalous category are the traditional Basin Shoshone and the Eskimo, both of which had social structures so fragmented that they have been characterized as typifying the family level of sociocultural integration.

The !Kung Bushmen

The Nyae Nyae region of the Kalahari Desert in southwest Africa covers about 10,000 square miles, in which there are a number of small waterholes but no rivers or streams or other surface water except for some shallow ponds during a brief rainy season. Within this area, about 1,000 !Kung Bushmen (the ! represents a "click" in their pronunciation) lived[1] in 36 or 37 bands. Although at the lowest level of technological development, relying on digging sticks and poison-tipped spears and carrying all of their meager possessions with them during their constant treks in search of food and water, they had adapted well to the extremely hostile environment. About 80 percent of the food was supplied by the women, who daily collected nuts, fruits, tubers, roots, and various other field foods. The remainder of the !Kung subsistence was supplied through hunting, which was exclusively a male occupation. Various species of large antelope provided most of the meat, although occasionally a buffalo or a giraffe was also killed. About 15 to 18 such large animals were killed by a single band in a year, and the meat was shared by the entire group.

Although there was no separate political sphere among the !Kung, a number of political problems had to be dealt with, such as the defense of territories, the protection and allocation of water, and public goals with regard to band movements and collective hunts. Each band claimed a territory that had to have a permanent source of water at a reasonable distance from sufficient vegetable foods for day-to-day consumption. Within such a territory would be sporadic fertile areas, such as groves of mangetti nut trees, clumps of berries, and special places where tubers grew in particular abundance; these were considered "owned" by a band and were jealously guarded. Incursions into another band's territory occasionally occurred, especially during hunting expeditions, in which case violence might be threatened; but true wars were unknown.

Headmanship was passed on from father to son. The existence of hereditary political positions seemingly defies the principle that all adult males in a band have equal access to leadership. However, the headman's authority was largely limited to control of field food and water; he planned the utilization of these various resources and had charge of the group's movements from one area to another within the territory. Most of this was firmly established by custom, and important decisions were arrived at by group consensus, so that the headman position was, to some extent, symbolic. Visitors had to ask his permission to partake of food or water within the band's territory, but custom dictated that all reasonable requests be granted. Headmanship brought responsibility without reward, and because it was the !Kung ideal that no individual should stand above another, such positions were seldom actively sought.

The hereditary headman might or might not be the actual leader of the band. If he was too young or lacked leadership abilities, this role might fall to someone with more of the personal qualities of leadership, so that the position became nominal. Also, effective leadership shifted according to the situation; a person might be an exceptional hunt leader but have little authority over public decisions, such as when and where to move camp (Marshall 1967).

The Eskimo

Despite the vast territory inhabited by the traditional Eskimo—from Siberia to Greenland—they have been described as remarkably alike in their political and social organization. Environmental determinist arguments are especially tempting, for the Eskimo lived in possibly the most hostile humanly habitable regions on Earth. Their food resources—mainly fish, caribou, and seal—were seasonal and widely scattered, which would logically lead to low population densities, nomadism, and extremely fluid social organization based on small subsistence groups. The basic unit was the extended family, which could take advantage of bilateral kinship relations to join with other families in temporary bands or even villages as food supplies waxed and waned during the year. A household might comprise a family of 12, which subsisted alone part of the year but joined groups of up to 270 at other times. Leadership outside the household was elementary; even villages sometimes lacked a headman, and what minimal influence might be possessed by an individual rested with the local shaman, whose authority was neither coercive nor uniting. Along the coast, the owner of a whaling boat had unrestricted authority over his crew during a voyage, and might, by the prestige of his wealth, maintain a loose chieftainship over a community; but even in this case, group unity was maintained not by government, but by conventionalized reciprocal obligations among kin. As with the !Kung, maintenance of order derived from the power of custom and public opinion (Weyer 1959).

Although this textbook view of the Eskimo was probably reasonably accurate for a majority of groups, there also existed a much greater diversity of social and political forms. Bilateral kinship was in some places replaced by corporate patrilineages; men's associations sometimes overrode kinship relations as decision-making bodies; there were large permanent settlements in some areas; and there were wide differences in types of leadership, from virtual chiefdoms to an absence of authority beyond the head of the family. Some of this variation was undoubtedly secondary, deriving from long contact with agents of Western civilization, such as explorers, whaling crews, traders, and missionaries. However, such diversity does suggest that the hunting-gathering adaptation permits a broader range of sociopolitical variation than is accounted for in conventional typologies (Damas 1968).

Tribes

"If I had to select one word in the vocabulary of anthropology as the single most egregious case of meaninglessness," wrote Morton Fried (1967: 154), "I would have to pass over 'tribe' in favor of 'race.' " The comparison is apt; like race, the concept of tribe is used to refer to a vast range of entities that have almost nothing in common with each other.

There are three basic objections to the concept of tribe: (1) it does not encompass a discrete group of societies that share common qualities; (2) it is not sufficiently different from other types, such as bands and chiefdoms; (3) it suggests a degree of social integration, or at least boundedness, that is often nonexistent (Helm 1968).

Why, then, is the term in use at all? There are both logical and empirical reasons. First, the term is a recognition that in sociopolitical complexity and evolutionary development, there must be a form that bridges the gap between hunting-gathering bands and centralized systems. Second, cross-cultural studies do reveal features in common to at least many of these groups.

Tribes are uncentralized egalitarian systems in which authority is distributed among a number of small groups; unity of the larger society is established from a web of individual and group relations. Because these groups rely on domesticated food sources, they are more densely populated and usually more sedentary than are hunting-gathering bands. As with bands, there is little political or economic specialization, except for a division of labor along age and sex lines, and there is no religious professionalization. However, according to Elman Service (1962), the defining quality of the tribe—that which separates it from the band—is the existence of pan-tribal sodalities that unite the various self-sufficient communities into wider social groups. A sodality is simply a formal or informal association, such as a family group, a college fraternity, or the Boy Scouts. In tribal societies there are two types of sodalities: those that are derived from kinship, and those that are not. Kinship sodalities include lineages—groups tracing descent through either the male line (patrilineage) or the female line (matrilineage)—and clans, which are groups of lineages tracing common descent to an often-mythical ancestor. Nonkin sodalities include a host of voluntary and involuntary associations.

If tribes are viewed in terms of the types of sodalities that unite them, or in terms of who makes the decisions for the group, a number of subtypes immediately emerge. Even in cases in which other forms of sodalities are evident, kinship will almost invariably be an important element of social integration. One form of political organization based on kinship is the segmentary *lineage*—especially common in Africa—in which a number of autonomous village groups can join together in ever-larger units for ritual purposes or to counter some threat. Many tribal societies are integrated by *associations,* which cross-cut kinship divisions. In age-set systems, the group initiated together at puberty will form a continuing sodality that takes on different functions as it passes through certain age levels—for example, if the group is male, they will form a warrior society as young men, and will become the governing body of the community as elders. In other tribes, such as the American Plains Indians, voluntary societies of warriors, clowns, or police may serve important integrating and decision-making functions. Although tribal societies do not have hierarchies of full-time religious professionals, religion may be extremely important, especially if it is tied to some sort of ancestor veneration, as is often the case in unilineal groups. In these societies, *ritual stratification* may be a key element of integration, as those responsible for major rituals assume decision-making leadership even in secular matters. In some tribes, *village councils* of elders will make public decisions, usually through a process of discussion leading to consensus. Finally, throughout Melanesia certain big men attain significant political authority through wealth, generosity, and courage in war. Although these leaders may exercise chieftainlike authority, their position is inherently unstable, because it is dependent on their ability to buy followers through gift giving and loans. A bad crop, an inability to gather sufficient pigs for a lavish feast, or failure in battle can quickly shift authority to a contender with better luck or skill.

It is tempting to think of such a breakdown of subtypes as fairly covering the range of possibilities, but there are tribes that include elements from more than one subtype, and others that do not fit any of these forms. Why this endless profusion of subtypes? Perhaps the basic problem is in attempting to define tribe in political terms at all. Unlike band, chiefdom, and state, the concept of tribe really does not—and cannot—refer to a particular type of political organization, because there seem to be few structural, or systemic, limits on the variety of forms. Ronald Cohen's characterization of this midrange group of societies as noncentralized "polities based on domesticated plants and animals" may be the best we can do and still allow for the range of variation, and even then, we are faced with certain rather glaring anomalies. The American Plains Indians, some of whom lacked domesticated plants or food animals (their subsistence was almost entirely based on the buffalo), certainly had more complex integrating institutions than did those found in hunting-gathering bands.

The Kpelle

Just how complex all this can get is illustrated by the Kpelle of West Africa. Their larger cultural group was fragmented into a number of self-sufficient communities, each with a hereditary "owner of the land," but also with a council of elders that made decisions by consensus. Complementing the political power of these groups was the men's secret society—secret in the sense that its symbols and rituals were not to be revealed to outsiders. This society, the Poro, held a supernatural political power that cut across lineage and small chiefdom boundaries and could thus unite the Kpelle into larger groups. Actually, the Poro extended far beyond the Kpelle, including a host of cultures in Nigeria, the Ivory Coast, Liberia, Sierra Leone, Ghana, and Portuguese Guinea. It arbitrated in local wars and even united entire countries for common action in times of emergency. Thus, we find the centralization and hierarchy we expect from chiefdoms, the segmentary organization and pantribal sodalities common to tribes, and at least three of the subtypes—associational, village council, and ritually stratified—combined in the Kpelle (Fulton 1972; Little 1965).

The Yanomamo

The Yanomamo are a horticultural group living in scattered villages in Venezuela and northern Brazil. As described and analyzed by Napoleon Chagnon (1968), these people were traditionally extremely aggressive and warlike, which derived partially from a shortage of marriageable women. Polygamy was mainly reserved for the older and wealthier men, and there was a marriage rule that gave older brothers first right for brides. In addition, a broad definition of incest restricted a male's sexual access to a very small proportion of the women in the village. The result was that within villages, brothers were pitted against brothers, adultery and accusations of adultery were common, and hostility levels were high. The maintenance of order in such a situation would seem to demand a strong headman, but, as with bands, the headman had no coercive authority. Within the village, the men were kept from killing each other by a system of conventionalized violence: taking turns hitting each other with the fist on the side or chest, or striking each other on the head with long poles. The political leader's function in these battles was to maintain the level of violence within the rules— that is, just this side of lethal.

Because young men had to go to war to capture wives, and every killing of a member of one's own group had to be avenged, raiding other villages was routine. In a situation of constant war, intervillage politics was a matter of survival. Unlike many horticultural tribes that participate in warfare almost as a game, the Yanomamo were deadly serious; it was not unknown for entire villages to be overrun, with all the men killed or dispersed and all the women taken captive. In order to maintain a balance of power, a village sometimes needed to form alliances with former enemies. This took place in three stages: first, ritual exchange of goods; second, mutual feasting; and finally, exchange of women as wives. Such alliances were tenuous, and might be broken with impunity, especially in the early stages.

In many ways, the Yanomamo would appear to be a typical tribe: their social organization was certainly more complex than that of nomadic hunter-gatherers; their villages were permanent and relatively stable (they tended to fission after reaching a certain size), there was no centralized coercive leadership, and there was equal access to headmanship positions among the men of the village. However, these obviously tribal people seemed to lack the one thing Service held to be the defining quality of tribes, namely, pantribal sodalities. It was true that lineages extended beyond village boundaries, but they did not unite villages. In fact, because of the hostilities created within lineages through competition over women, bonds of marriage were often stronger than were patrilineal bonds. There were no pantribal associations, and military alliances united only two or a few villages. Certainly no political structure integrated the entire Yanomamo group or even a large proportion of it.

The Nuer

The Nuer of southern Sudan, described by E. E. Evans-Pritchard (1940a, 1940b), provide a classic example of the segmentary lineage solution to the problem of tribal unity. About 200,000 Nuer lived in villages, cultivating maize and millet during the rainy season, herding cattle in almost constant nomadism during the dry season. Their social system was fluid in the extreme, and individually they had a reputation for being fiercely independent. Although they lacked centralized authority, or any formal authority at all beyond the village level, they were able to join together in large groups to counter an external threat. Evans-Pritchard characterized the Nuer as "an acephalous state, lacking legislative, judicial, and executive organs. Nevertheless, it is far from chaotic. It has a persistent and coherent form which might be called 'ordered anarchy.' "

The smallest corporate economic unit was the household, comprised of several patrilineally related men and their families. A group of these households might be clustered as a hamlet within a village. As one of these hamlets grew through the processes of birth, adoption, and immigration, it would inevitably fission, creating another group that might form a hamlet in a nearby village. These hamlets comprised a minor lineage, and several of them, spread between many villages, made up larger and larger units: major lineage; maximal lineage; and, finally, clan. A clan might include thousands of people and be spread throughout all Nuerland, creating a network of social ties that these highly mobile people could call upon as needed. Because clans were exogamous, marriage alliances established hundreds of small bonds with other clans.

Parallel to the segmentary lineage system, but not identical with it, was a territorial system. Each clan "owned" a certain territory that was, however, open to members of other clans; in fact, the owner clan did not form an aristocracy and might actually populate only a small portion of its territory. However, those moving into a village attempted to establish relations with an owner lineage through being adopted into it or through marriage.

War and feuding were almost constant. By means of a process of complementary opposition, increasingly larger territorial groups could be united for such purposes. For example, two sections might be fighting with each other, but they would become allies if another group attacked either or both. To counter an even larger threat, all three former antagonists would join together. The political unity of the Nuer had to be defined situationally as increasingly larger units were assembled according to need, and then dismantled when the threat was gone.

The complementary opposition solution to the problem of tribal integration, shown in Figure 2.2, was especially adaptive for a tribe that intruded into an already occupied territory. This was the case with the Nuer, who had within historical times expanded into the land of the Dinka. Such a system, extremely flexible yet capable of forming a powerful united force, channeled expansion outward and released internal pressures in warfare against other peoples (Sahlins 1961).

CENTRALIZED SYSTEMS

As noted previously, a valid typology should designate systems, so that within any single category the determination of one or a few variables will predict others. The category of centralized political systems encompasses societies in which power and authority inhere in one person or a small group. This is true by definition. By extension, however, it is possible to predict that these societies will tend to be more densely populated than are bands and tribes, will be stratified by rank or class, will have specialized social and occupational roles, will utilize more productive technology, will have economies based on centralized redistribution, and will be more stable in terms of ongoing sociopolitical groupings. Morton Fried emphasizes the basic inequalities of these systems relative to uncentralized systems: recruitment into political positions is no longer equal but may be based on membership in a certain class or in an elite lineage. Although unilineal descent groups may exist and even hold a great deal of local power, politics is no longer manifested mainly through kinship; political specialization appears with full-time politicians and an attendant bureaucracy.

Chiefdoms

With respect to social integration, the chiefdom level transcends the tribal level in two major ways: (1) it has a higher population density made possible by more efficient productivity; and (2) it is more complex, with some form of centralized authority. Unlike segmentary systems in which political units coalesce and dissolve according to the situation,

Figure 2.2
Nuer "Complementary Opposition"

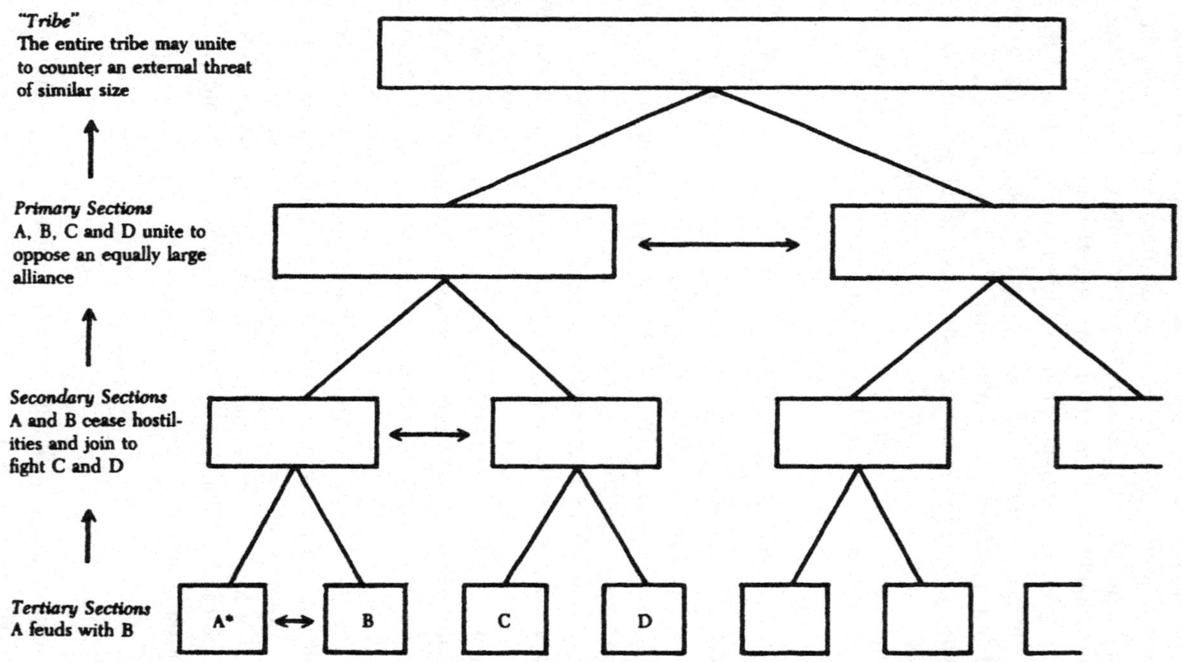

"Tribe"
The entire tribe may unite to counter an external threat of similar size

Primary Sections
A, B, C and D unite to oppose an equally large alliance

Secondary Sections
A and B cease hostilities and join to fight C and D

Tertiary Sections
A feuds with B

A*   B   C   D

*Each box in the bottom row represents several allied villages.

chiefdoms have relatively permanent central agencies of government, typically based on collection and redistribution of an economic surplus (often including a labor surplus).

The position of chief, unlike that of headman of a band or lineage, is a position of at least minimal power—that is, the chief has access to a certain amount of coercion. The chief may be the final authority in the distribution of land, and may be able to recruit an army. Economically, he is the center and coordinator of the redistribution system: he can collect taxes on food or goods, some of which will be returned to the populace, creating a new level of group solidarity in which a number of specialized parts depend on the smooth functioning of the whole. Even if the chief's position is not directly hereditary, it will only be available to certain families or lineages. Although actual class stratification is absent, every individual is ranked according to membership in a descent group; those closer to the chief's lineage will be higher on the scale and receive the deference of all those below. Indeed, according to Service (1971: 145), "the most distinctive characteristic of chiefdoms, as compared to tribes and bands, is . . . the pervasive inequality of persons and groups in the society."

However, the chief by no means possesses absolute power. The aristocratic ethos does not carry with it any formal, legal apparatus of forceful repression, and what obedience the chief can command may derive less from fear of physical sanctions than from his direct control of the economic redistributional system. The chief's lineage may itself become exceptionally wealthy, but ultimately loyalty is purchased by constant bestowal of goods and benefits. Although there may be the approximation of a bureaucracy, offices beneath that of chief are not clearly differentiated, and when pressures build up, these lower bureaucrats can break away from the parent body and set up an opposition government. Thus, a chief walks a narrow tightrope between conflicting interest groups and maintains his position through a precarious balancing act.

Although definitions of tribe have often been accused of being so general as to be meaningless, the above description of the chiefdom level of political integration, derived largely from Elman Service (1971), has been accused of being too specific. According to Herbert Lewis (1968), Service has logically deduced this model according to what should exist between the tribal and state levels, then joined it with the specific model of Polynesian political structure, and proposed this hybrid as a general evolutionary type. Lewis points out that many groups that appear to have chieftainships are not stable at all; they oscillate back and forth from centralized leadership to egalitarianism as strong leaders come and go.

Such looseness in categories, however, should be assumed without another long disclaimer.

Precolonial Hawaii

The eight islands of aboriginal Hawaii were under the domination of a number of rigidly stratified hereditary chiefdoms. The paramount chiefs were believed to be descendants of the gods and were so charged with *mana*—supernatural power—that even the ground they walked on could not be touched by lesser mortals. The chiefly personage was thus surrounded by an elaborate set of taboos, the breaking of which could mean a sentence of death. The chiefs were supreme economic, military, and ritual leaders, although most of these functions were delegated to a group of noble administrators and war leaders who formed the upper strata of society. There were two other levels below these administrators: lesser nobles and commoners. Each individual belonged to one of these strata, and the nobles were also ranked according to the order of their birth and their nearness to the high chief. The higher nobles, or lesser chiefs, were accorded a great deal of deference; for example, commoners had to throw themselves face down on the ground as they passed. In order to keep the chiefly line pure, the heir to the position of high chief was supposed to be the firstborn son of the chief and his firstborn sister (a form of incestuous endogamy that is also found in ancient Egypt and Inca Peru).

Lesser chiefs controlled allocations of land and water—the latter exceedingly important, because much of the productive land was irrigated. They also, de facto, controlled the communal labor of commoners. Tribute was paid to the high chief by the upper-level nobles, who collected from the lower nobles, and so on, down the line to the commoners. This tribute—or some of it—would be used in public works, mainly irrigation canals and warfare. Nobles also subsidized a group of professional craftsmen from the tribute till.

What kept these polities from attaining the status of states was partially the lack of differentiation of the political sphere; these were hereditary theocracies in which authority was still relatively undifferentiated from religion and kinship. Also, although a chief might hold life and death power over his subjects in some regards, the central governing unit by no means held a monopoly on this power, which was distributed among a number of lesser chiefs; nor was there any legal structure to administer such force. Finally, these governments were far from stable. Warfare was constant, and chiefdoms were regularly overthrown, in which case the entire noble class would be replaced by the conquering group (Davenport 1967; Seaton 1978; Service 1975).

The Kwakiutl

Indian societies of the Northwest Coast of North America are usually categorized as chiefdoms, although these groups do not fit the ideal pattern as neatly as do the Hawaiians.

The Kwakiutl Indians of Vancouver Island were never studied in their aboriginal state; by the time Franz Boas began his fieldwork among them in 1885, they had already had almost a century of contact with white traders, missionaries, sailors, and Indian agents, and had been decimated by disease. At that time, their plane of living, based on hunting and fishing and virtually devoid of domesticated food supplies, was among the highest in North America as measured by material possessions— houses, canoes, utensils, tools, and art objects such as carved masks and totem poles.

The Kwakiutl were divided into about 25 villages, each of which was comprised of two to seven *numayma,* or tightly cohesive units made up of one to several extended families. *Numayma* were stratified in terms of prestige within the village, and each individual was ranked within his *numayma.* Ranks, which were obtained mainly through heredity or marriage, were intricately elaborated by titles, crests, and ceremonial privileges.

Such prestige positions were by no means rare; out of a population of about 1,500 individuals, there were 650 named positions, some of which were held by more than one person at the same time. These social positions were maintained through the medium of the *potlatch*—an elaborate feast in which an enormous amount of goods was distributed to all present. One could also insult a rival by destroying goods in his presence, but these rivalry potlatches, although dramatic, were not as common as is often believed.

The Kwakiutl obviously suggest many elements of the classical chiefdom: a strong system of ranking, specialized leadership roles based on heredity, permanent agencies of government, and redistribution. However, the fit is far from perfect. First, there was no integration beyond the village, and precious little within it, because most political integration was focused in the *numayma.* The highest-ranking chief in the village would supposedly have some extra authority, but in practice, the *numayma* was the day-to-day political entity, which means that politics was manifested through kinship, as in tribal society. Also, it is debatable that the potlatch really represented a system of redistribution. No one in Kwakiutl society was sufficiently wealthy to give a potlatch without both calling in debts and borrowing. The potlatch was the center of a complex economic system based on an intricate web of loaner-debtor relationships. Although an invited *numayma* might not be directly involved in such debts, it was expected to reciprocate the potlatch, preferably with greater abundance. Also, the main article distributed at a potlatch was the Hudson Bay blanket, which could hardly be eaten and so was most valuable as a sort of currency used for further loaning and borrowing. Thus, the potlatch suggests a system of reciprocity (common to bands and tribes) and not the centralized redistribution that is supposedly a defining quality of chiefdoms. In other words, the Kwakiutl, and perhaps all the cultures of the Northwest Coast, would seem to represent a blending of elements of both tribes and chiefdoms (Codere 1950, 1957; Drucker and Heizer 1967).

THE STATE

For Elman Service (1971: 163), the distinguishing quality of the state, that which separates it from the chiefdom, "is the presence of that special form of control, the consistent threat of force by a body of persons legitimately constituted to use it." Morton Fried (1967), on the other hand, emphasizes stratification: the state has special institutions, both formal and informal, to maintain a hierarchy with differential access to resources. This stratification goes beyond the individual and lineage ranking found in less complex societies; it involves the establishment of true classes. For Ronald Cohen (1978a, 1978b), the key diagnostic feature of the state is its permanence. Unlike lower order forms of political organization, the state does not regularly fission (i.e., break up into a number of smaller groups) as part of its normal process of political activity.

States are generally large, complex societies, encompassing a variety of classes, associations, and occupational groups. Occupational specialization, including a full-time political bureaucracy, unites the entire group in a web of interrelated dependencies. Because of the vast range of individual and class interests within a state, pressures and conflicts unknown in less complex societies necessitate some sort of rule of impersonal law, backed by physical sanctions, for the ongoing maintenance of the system.

The Precolonial Zulu

The Nguni family of Bantu-speaking peoples included about 100,000 pastoralists and shifting cultivators living in about 80,000 square miles of southeastern Africa. The basic residence unit was the patrilineally extended family. The largest permanent political unit was the clan, although several clans might temporarily form a tribe. Actually, these were classic chiefdoms, as described above.

During the early years of the nineteenth century, most of these independent chiefdoms were united through conquest into the powerful and highly militaristic Zulu state. To a great extent, this relatively undeveloped state owed its continuing unity to the threat of the Boers and British who were pushing at the edges of its territory (the British conquered the Zulu in 1887). Regiments of conscripted soldiers, belonging to the king alone, were stationed in barracks concentrated in the capital. The king not only had the power to command military and labor service, but also collected "gifts" from his subjects, which made him the wealthiest man in the kingdom. In turn, he was expected to be generous in providing food and other goods for his people. He had a council of advisors whose recommendations, ideally, were followed. He was also the ultimate appeals court for cases referred from the lower chiefs' courts, and he reserved to himself the right of passing death sentences (although the chiefs did not always respect this reservation). Individuals and clans were stratified according to their genealogical closeness to the king.

Thus, although inchoate and short lived, the Zulu state displayed many of the attributes of more complex states: it united a large number of disparate groups under a central authority; it claimed, at least in theory, a monopoly on the use of force; its power was allocated through a complex bureaucracy; and it maintained government by objective law.

However, much of the old chiefdom stage remained—so much so that the people themselves seemed to think of the state as a glorified chiefdom. The state was essentially a collection of clans that were still relatively independent. Loyalties were inevitably divided between chief and king, with the people often siding with the local group. Chiefs retained day-to-day rules, including the right to use force to put down rebellions as long as the king was informed. The idea persisted that a bad king could be overthrown, just as could a bad chief, as long as the individual and not the system was changed; in fact, kingly succession was largely a matter of assassination or rebellion. Also, although there was definite social stratification, it was much the same as that of the Hawaiians (individuals and clans ranked according to their genealogical closeness to the king). In addition, occupational specialization was not much more developed than in the prestate period. In short, although definitely a state with regard to unification of a number of formerly autonomous groups under centralized government, the precolonial Zulu encompassed many of the aspects of the chiefdoms upon which it was based (Gluckman 1940; Service 1975).

The Inca

At the beginning of the fifteenth century, a powerful chiefdom in the Cuzco Valley of Peru began the military expansion that would create the largest of the pre-Columbian New World states. At its climax, the Inca empire extended 2,700 miles from Central Chile to the present-day border of Ecuador and Colombia, an area that was united without the use of animal transportation (although llamas and alpacas were used as cargo carriers). Contemporary characterizations of the Inca as a communist, socialist, or welfare state do little justice to this unique adaptation to the ecological, social, and historical conditions of the Andes.

The Inca empire was integrated as much by a system of economic redistributions as it was by military force or political centralization. Food production was greatly expanded, not through technological innovation, but through the increasingly efficient organization of labor—for agricultural terracing, for example, or in the construction of extensive irrigation systems—and through transferring entire communities to formerly underutilized areas. Throughout the empire, land was divided into thirds to provide for the common people, the state religion, and the secular bureaucracy. After 1475, there was increasing state ownership, especially of lands newly developed for cultivation or pasture.

Three bureaucracies were supported by this economy. At the top was the central bureaucracy, comprised of ethnic Inca nobles and others who had attained the status of Inca through their contribution to the state. This Cuzco-based bureaucracy consisted of a Royal Court (made up of 11 minor lineages, each with its own palace); a royal advisory council; and more or less specialized agencies to administer the judiciary, the military, education, transportation, and communications. A parallel, and to some degree separate, religious bureaucracy administered a state religion that was fairly open in the sense that it was quite capable of incorporating the gods, idols, and rituals of the conquered tribes. As much as one-third of the Inca's entire gross national product was devoted to religious ceremony. Finally, a provincial bureaucracy encompassed about 80 regional groups through a hierarchy of local chiefs called *curacas*.

The existence of such sophisticated bureaucratic structures might give the impression that the Inca state had completely overridden and replaced earlier forms of social organization; yet over millennia, and through the

risings and fallings of civilizations, the basic unit of Andean social structure remained the *ayllu,* a lineage-based community in which land was
held in common and redistributed according to need. The *ayllu* was
highly self-sufficient, unified by common territory and by complex in-
terrelationships of social and economic reciprocity. Each *ayllu* had its
own leader, who lacked coercive authority. The *ayllu* cared for its own
infirm and aged and achieved public building and maintenance goals
through cooperative labor. Many *ayllus* were united into larger tribes and
confederacies for trade and defense.

Conquest by the Inca left this fundamental social structure intact, and
many state governmental forms and practices were based on those of the
ayllu. For example, the system of conscripted labor by which the Inca
built their phenomenal roads (one road was almost two-thousand miles
long), public buildings, and agricultural terraces was a direct extension
of traditional *ayllu* collective labor patterns. Even at the highest levels
of government, the *ayllu* form was the model: each new Inca emperor
began a new royal *ayllu* consisting of all his male descendants. According to John Murra (1958), the widespread belief that the Inca polity was
divided into groups based on a decimal system is but a literal reading
of a census taker's shorthand (records were kept on knotted ropes); the
actual division of the empire was the traditional one of *ayllu,* tribe, and
confederacy. Thus, despite its complexity, the Inca state does not represent a quantum leap in social organization, except in sheer magnitude;
rather, it was a drawing together of a number of intact traditional units
(Mason 1957; Murra 1958; Shaedel 1978).

CLASSIFICATION TODAY

The classification described in this chapter, although still widely employed, has come under attack from a number of different directions.
When these categories were first developed starting in the early 1940s,
there was still a sense of autonomous, primordial cultures that had existed unchanged for very long periods of time. This was reinforced by
the structural-functional paradigm that dominated anthropology for about
two decades and that tended to view societies synchronically, that is, as
outside of time (see chapter 5). In reality, as later colonialist, postcolon-
ialist, and world-system perspectives would reveal, the primordial tribe
was often more an artifact of anthropological theoretical blinders than a
reality. Beginning with capitalist expansion out of Europe in the sixteenth
century, virtually all cultures, even the most isolated, had been radically
changed, many forced into tributary production, driven deeper into de-

serts or jungles, or transformed by disease and traded metal implements (Wolf 1982). The term "tribe" has been recognized as not only nebulous but also pejorative, connoting primitivism and subordination. Because all such groups are increasingly being integrated into the state, forcibly or just through the random processes of development, the all-purpose terms "ethnicity" and "nation" have come to replace earlier classifications. Another issue has been the increasing hybridity not only of individuals but also of societies; the territorial, linguistic, and cultural boundaries that were assumed by earlier generations of anthropologists have, to a great degree, broken down. Globalization has increasingly led to more fluid categories such as transnational, creole, and diaspora communities.

The value of any typology depends as much on what is done with it as on the criteria used in forming it. The traditional classification outlined in this chapter is quite general, and more recent types such as ethnicity and nationalism are even more so. Specialists will require more precise classification, and may develop any number of subtypes. Peasants, for example, have been subdivided into multiple categories (Wolf 1996), and newer research suggests the need for a category of postpeasant (Kearney 1996). The specialist in a single culture area, such as the Arctic, might focus on the *variety* of adaptive strategies and thus be fully justified in rejecting any typology at all. Many postmodernists have rejected all classifications, on the grounds that anthropology is a science of *difference,* and grouping disparate societies together based on arbitrary criteria does more harm than good. However, as long as anthropologists need to talk to each other and be understood, some form of common classification will be necessary.

NOTE

1. Except for very current research, all ethnographic examples are presented in the past tense. Virtually all traditional cultures are undergoing significant change.

SUGGESTED READINGS

Cohen, Ronald, and John Middleton, eds. *Comparative Political Systems* (Austin: University of Texas Press, 1967). Although this anthology seems random in its selection, it does provide studies of a wide range of political types. Among those groups represented are the !Kung, Eskimo, Nambikara, Mapuche, and Inca. The list of authors of these 20 articles reads like a *Who's Who* of cultural anthropology through the mid-1960s: Claude Lévi-Strauss, Robert Lowie, John Murra, F. C. Bailey, and S. N. Eisenstadt, among others.

Fried, Morton. *The Evolution of Political Society* (New York: Random House, 1967). Fried classifies political systems in terms of an individual's access to power. This gives him the basic categories of egalitarian, rank, and stratified, each of which is described in detail.

Johnson, Allen W., and Timothy Earle. *The Evolution of Human Societies: From Foraging Group to Agrarian State* (Stanford, Calif.: Stanford University Press, 1987). A highly readable evolutionary approach that provides an alternative typology to the conventional one presented in this chapter. Each socioeconomic level (family, local group, big man collectivity, chiefdom, archaic state, and nation-state) is described in detail with examples.

Levinson, David, and Martin J. Malone. *Toward Explaining Human Culture* (New York: HRAF Press, 1980). This is an admirable attempt to collect in a single short volume much that has been learned about cross-cultural regularities from statistical studies using the Human Relations Area Files. Many of the chapters are valuable in providing quantitative data to support or refute speculation on the classification of political systems.

Service, Elman R. *Primitive Social Organization: An Evolutionary Perspective* (New York: Random House, 1962). This is the book that established band, tribe, chiefdom, and state as the basic levels of sociocultural integration. Despite its subtitle, the book is largely descriptive and makes little attempt at suggesting causes of evolutionary change.

Ancient Egypt was one of the world's six primary states; that is, those that developed uninfluenced by previous states. Its rise may have been partially in response to population pressure within a narrow strip of land circumscribed by desert. Courtesy of the Library of Congress.

Chapter 3

THE EVOLUTION OF THE STATE

About 5,500 years ago, on the fertile floodplains of the Tigris and Eu-phrates Rivers in what is today Iraq, there developed a type of society unique to its time. After millennia in which humans have gradually turned from migratory foraging toward seasonal settlements based on a few domesticated plants and animals, and then toward year-round farm-ing villages, there came into being the world's first true cities, and with them a novel form of political organization. Previously, society had been structured according to kinship networks; now there appeared a perma-nent administrative bureaucracy that demanded loyalties transcending lineage and clan. Local chiefs relinquished much of their authority to a ruling class who had the power to gather the agricultural surpluses and call forth the labor necessary to create large-scale irrigation projects and monumental architecture. Fortified cities, such as Uruk and Ur, boasted populations of upward of 40,000 "citizens." A full-time caste of priests presided over a complex temple religion. Craft specialists manufactured the obsidian knives and gold and silver figurines that would tie vast areas together through webs of trade. The state had been born.

Today, when national populations are counted in the hundreds of mil-lions and power is so concentrated that the word of a president can send huge armies scurrying to any part of the globe, it may be difficult to realize the significance of the 13 or so small city-states collectively known as Sumeria. Just as it is legitimate to speak of an agriculture revolution or an industrial revolution to suggest quantum changes in human social complexity, so too can one speak of a state revolution. Various authorities might argue the defining characteristics of the early state, but none would demean its importance; for it was a new kind of society—a seed bearing the genetic code for the giant nation-states of the modern world.

The Mesopotamian state developed through a long series of adjustments to a particular environment and a specific set of social problems. In retrospect, however, the process seems almost inevitable, for similar adaptations are found leading to similar sociopolitical structures in Egypt, the Indus River Valley of India and the Yellow River Valley of northern China, Mesoamerica, and Peru. These "primary" states are illustrated in Figure 3.1. Although these six states appeared hundreds or even thousands of years apart (see Figure 3.2), and there was minimal commerce between a few of them (such as India and Mesopotamia), each seems to have originated independently of the others. This poses a problem: if the state evolved autonomously not once but six times, can fundamental processes be discovered that were common to all?

Although far removed from the state, the rudiments of human social evolution can be found in human's closest animal relatives. Among higher primates characterized by marked sexual dimorphism (differences in size and musculature between sexes)—such as baboons and gorillas, is found strong male dominance, specialization for defense, and various patterns of ongoing family organization. Some primate species reveal extremely complex elaborations of social structure. Cynocephalus baboons, for example, live in stable groups of 40 to 80 individuals, and these bands exhibit clear hierarchies of status and considerable specialization of function among both males and females. Hamadryas baboons forage in small one-male groups, but join together in troops of several hundred for sleeping. Some primates pass on significant learned skills from generation to generation and reveal remarkable cooperation in rearing the young, collective defense, grooming, and sexual behavior. However, only the genus *Homo* has extended such basic primate adaptations by cultural means. The most significant of these are symbolism, through which humans communicate and embellish both individual and group ideas, and sharing (reciprocity), which underlies the division of labor, creates the potential for increasingly elaborate social organization, and ties kinship groups together.

More than 99 percent of human's two- to three- million-year sojourn on Earth has been spent in small bands—flexible, egalitarian, nomadic groups comprised of several extended families. Because contemporary

Figure 3.1
Primary States

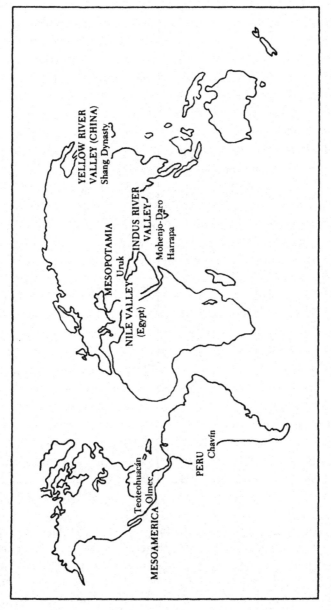

Figure 3.2
Chronology of Primary State Development

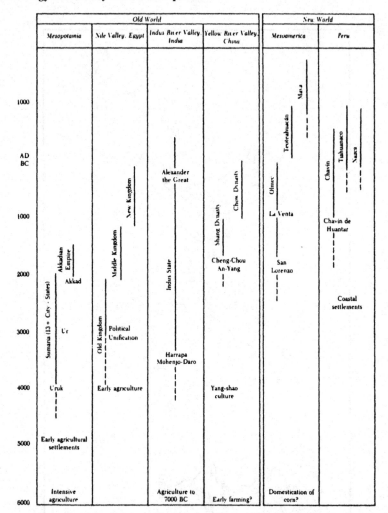

Sources: Claessen 1978; Fagan 1978; Jolly and Plog 1979; Pfeiffer 1977; Wenke 1980.

hunting-gathering peoples occupy only the most marginal environments, care should be taken with regard to generalizing their social organization to remote ancestors who lived in more hospitable places and climes. Yet archeological evidence from Paleolithic times suggests little elaboration on the basic band form. One reason that this structure may have persisted for so long is that it was an evolutionary dead end. The hunting-foraging adaptation requires an almost perfect ecological balance, in which populations must be maintained below the food supply; thus, there would have been little selective pressure for change. What requires explanation is not why such an excellent adaptation should have lasted so long, but rather why a few groups of people—very few, at first—abandoned it for more complex forms of subsistence and society.

Radically new types of social structure appeared only with the sedentary lifestyles and greater population densities brought about by the domestication of plants and animals. It should not be supposed, however, that this revolution was sudden, or that it immediately led to the formation of the state. Agriculture and animal husbandry apparently developed independently in a number of areas throughout the world, but only a few of these went on to evolve states. In the Tehuacán Valley of Mexico, the period of development from hunting-gathering bands to agriculturally based states was more than 7,000 years (Flannery 1968). In other areas of primary-state development, too, centralization of government was long preceded by sedentary agriculture, permanent villages, and even extensive irrigation works.

American and Dutch anthropologists have tackled the problem of the origin of the state with enthusiasm (the British and French tend to ignore evolutionary questions). Until recently, such theorists carefully distinguished the six primary states from secondary states (those that developed out of or through contact with already existing states). Because virtually all theories focused on the former, evidence was exclusively archeological. Today, some researchers have abandoned the primary-secondary distinction for a typology that allows for the inclusion of recent states, such as the Ankole of Uganda, as long as they remained pristine. We will examine some of this important research later, but first we must look at the classical theories of state origins.

INTERNAL CONFLICT THEORIES

The doctrine that the state evolved through class struggle is implicit in many of the writings of Karl Marx. However, these ideas were not fully worked out until Frederick Engels' major work, *The Origin of the Family, Private Property and the State* ([1891] 1972), which was published after his mentor's death. According to Engels, who borrowed heavily from American evolutionary anthropologist Lewis Henry Morgan, the earliest form of social organization was communistic: resources were shared equally by all and there was no strong concept of personal possession. Technological innovation gives rise to surplus, which allows for a class of nonproducers to develop. Private ownership is simply a concomitant of commodity production. Once established, private property stimulates an inexorable chain of cause and effect that leads to an entrepreneurial class—owners of the means of production and buyers and sellers of human labor. This, in turn, results in differential access to resources, and thus to vast discrepancies in individual wealth. In order to protect its interests against the masses of active producers, who understandably want to share in their own production, the elite must erect a structure of permanent centralized force to protect its class interests.

Given its time, this analysis is sophisticated and subtle. In it is found the perception that the primary means of economic exchange in band and tribal society is reciprocity, and that more complex systems involve concentrations of wealth and redistribution through a central agency, be it chief, king, or bureaucracy. Engels artfully applies Marxian materialism to long-term social evolution; the basic causes of change are held to be technological and economic, not ideational. There is also a clear recognition that social stratification is one of the defining qualities of the state.

Unfortunately, as Elman Service (1975: 283) has observed, "there is absolutely no evidence in the early archaic civilizations themselves, nor in archeologically- or historically-known chiefdoms and primitive states, of any important private dealings—e.g., evidence of capitalism." Indeed, the very concepts of communism and capitalism seem absurd when projected onto band and chiefdom societies, so different from modern industrial states.

Morton Fried (1967), who bases his evolutionary typology of political systems on the degree of individual access to resources and positions of prestige, offers a variation on the class-conflict model. Once true stratification exists, Fried notes, the state is already implicit because the maintenance of a class system requires that power be concentrated in the hands of an elite. By its very nature, this creates conflict within the society. Differential access to resources and the exploitation of human labor create pressures that are quite unknown in less complex societies. Conflict arising out of social stratification should not be thought of as the cause of state formation; rather, such conflict is merely a prior condition for the development of the state. Incipient social stratification is so unstable that a society that finds itself at such a stage must either disintegrate to a lower level of organization or continue its process of centralizing political power. In other words, once classes begin to separate themselves from hierarchies based on individual or kinship status, power must be fairly rapidly assumed by the privileged elite if the true state is to come into existence.

EXTERNAL CONFLICT THEORIES

In the Biblical version of social evolution, the development of cities is a direct result of Cain's primordial murder of his brother Abel. This idea, that states are born in blood and war, was given scientific respectability with the emergence of Social Darwinism in the latter half of the nineteenth century. Herbert Spencer, chief spokesman for the more violent interpretations of evolutionary theory, applied the idea of survival of the fittest mainly to individuals, but it took little imagination to extend this concept to societies. The stronger, more militaristic organizations would inevitably prevail over weaker groups, uniting them under a powerful centralized government with a monopoly on the use of force. Militarism alone, even without warfare, would be sufficient; merely the existence of an external threat that required a large standing army could push a loosely structured society in the direction of strong centralized leadership. Implicit or explicit in such theories, of which Spencer's was one of many, is the idea that state government is modeled on military organization in terms of its hierarchical structure and centralized control of physical force.

A nineteenth-century tendency to oversimplify and overgeneralize is evident in these theories, which are based on a gross misunderstanding of physical evolution. Darwin's rather prosaic idea that the mechanism of evolution is differential reproduction (parents with the most surviving offspring pass on more traits) was transliterated into the law of tooth and fang, with imagery of big tigers devouring little tigers with much sound and fury. When applied to society, such a theory could—and did—provide the philosophical justification ("Law of Nature, you know!") for colonialism, imperialism, monopoly capitalism, and every other form of exploitation.

As we shall see, cross-cultural research does support the hypothesis that war and conquest are important factors in the development of some states, but there are two important objections to the theory that war is the *primary* cause: (1) a society can marshal forces only according to available levels of population and organization and, thus, warfare might be better viewed as a function rather than a cause of a given level of social integration; and (2) warfare among tribes and chiefdoms is more likely to prevent state formation than to cause it, because groups will simply disperse when threatened by a power greater than themselves (Price 1979; Service 1971).

This latter point is a salient consideration in Robert Carniero's (1967, 1970, 1978) theory of environmental circumscription. Because warfare is virtually universal and usually has the effect of dispersing people rather than uniting them, conflict could only lead to centralization in particular situations. After examining primary-state development in both the Old and New Worlds, Carniero notes that a common denominator is that they are all areas of circumscribed agricultural land; that is, they are bounded by mountains, sea, or desert. When there is no such circumscription, population pressures on the environment can be expanded outward, and losers in a war can resettle in a new area. This is not possible in cases in which the only arable land is surrounded by unproductive land. Population pressure must then be resolved by unification and by increases in productive capacity (both characteristics of the state), and losers in a war—lacking means of escape—must submit to their conquerors. Amazonian Indians waged frequent wars for revenge, the taking of women, personal prestige, and the like; but these wars never resulted in widespread conquest by a central power because new areas of forest could always be found in which to start a new village. However, the riverine valleys of coastal Peru—surrounded by sea, desert, and mountains—offer no such options. As the small, dispersed villages of the Neolithic grew and fissioned, the narrow valleys became increasingly crowded. Intensification of agriculture, through terracing, for example, would only solve the problem temporarily. Revenge warfare would turn to warfare over land, with one group trying to increase its productive capacity at the expense of others. However, for the weaker in these conflicts, there would be no place to escape that could provide even minimal subsistence; submission to a dominant force was the only viable survival strategy. In this way, a number of independent chiefdoms would be brought under a single hierarchical military government.

Circumscription need not be strictly physical; it can also be social. The Yanomamo of the Venezuelan jungle are not physically circumscribed, but village fission and expansion into virgin territory is easier for those at the periphery of the tribal group than for those near the center. According to Carniero's theory, we would expect that central villages, surrounded by other warring villages, would tend to be larger and have more powerful headmen than do peripheral villages, and this is indeed the case. Although the Yanomamo are far from the state level of cultural integration, the socially circumscribed villages do exhibit greater tendencies toward centralization.

Carniero subsumes these processes under the principle of competitive exclusion, derived from evolutionary biology. This principle states that two species occupying and exploiting the same portion of the habitat cannot coexist indefinitely; one must ultimately eliminate the other. In applying this idea to societies, Carniero observes that throughout history, chiefdoms have been united into states and states have gone to war to create larger states, with competition and selection increasingly moving toward larger and larger units. In plotting the decreasing number of autonomous political units in the world from 1000 B.C., Carniero predicts the political unification of the entire planet by about the year 2300. (However, the breakup of the Soviet empire and the tendency for the world community to intervene to halt interstate wars suggests that there may be countercurrents working against sheer hugeness.)

POPULATION AND IRRIGATION

From about 23000 B.C. until 2000 A.D., world population has grown from an estimated 3.5 million to over 6 billion and from a density of 0.1 persons per square mile to 124 per square mile (Campbell 1979: 462–63). The correlation between this increase in population and the rise of the state has been noted by virtually all evolutionary cultural anthropologists. Robert Carniero (1967) plotted the relation between population density and social complexity in 46 societies and found a significant statistical correspondence between the two variables. Although the correspondence held, at least loosely, for arithmetic density (i.e., the average number of people per square mile over an entire territory), a much stronger relationship is found when economic density alone is considered. Economic density is the relation between population and sources of production. For example, in Egypt, the vast majority of people are concentrated in a narrow strip of arable land on either side of the Nile.

According to the early nineteenth-century economist Thomas Malthus, population is negatively checked by disease, famine, and war as it threatens to outgrow the food supply. However, if this were the only principle operating, population growth would have stabilized at a much lower level than today's. Certainly, one possible response to population pressure on food supply is exactly the opposite of the Malthusian checks; the food supply itself may be increased through some sort of intensification of production, often involving the development of a new technology or the refinement of an existing one. Irrigation, terracing, fertilization, using animal labor, cultivating more types of crops, and exploiting previously unused lands can significantly increase the carrying capacity of a given territory. The resulting increases in population density require more complex forms of social and political organization. This correspondence between population and social evolution was most extensively elaborated by Ester Boserup (1965). In a slight variation on the theory, Michael

Harner (1970) argues that population pressure is not only directly responsible for some form of intensification of food production, but also leads to unequal access to resources and subsequently to increasing social stratification.

The importance of irrigation to state formation was recognized as early as the writings of Marx and Engels, who noted that a major difference between small-scale agricultural communities and state societies was that the latter required the support of extensive irrigation systems. More recently, Julian Steward (1955) has emphasized irrigation as the fundamental mechanism of state development, because water control permitted sufficient agricultural intensification to create large population densities, and the construction of massive hydraulic systems required new levels of social organization, power, and coordination of labor.

It was Karl Wittfogel (1957) who elaborated the hydraulic theory in such detail that his name is now associated with it. Neolithic farmers in the areas of primary-state development, such as Egypt or the riverine valleys of Peru, were dependent on flood irrigation; their fields were watered once a year and new soil was deposited by the annual flood. Flood irrigation is quite variable, however, and even in the best of times it provides only one crop per year. Slowly, farmers began to exercise control of the floods with dikes and reservoirs, preserving and taming the precious water that could then be released as needed through a network of canals. Early irrigation systems were small and primitive, involving only the labor of a few neighboring farms, but as the productive capacity of the land increased and the human population burgeoned, irrigation works grew in size and complexity. A group of specialists emerged to plan and coordinate the construction of these systems, and later to control the flow of water. This group, whose hands now quite literally held the very life of the community, developed into an administrative elite that governed despotic, centralized states.

This model has fared surprisingly well. Irrigation seems to have been important in all of the primary states. The lowland Maya of the Yucatan Peninsula in Mexico were believed to be an exception until recent aerial photographs revealed that this civilization, too, was reliant on elaborate irrigation systems. However, the hydraulic theory should not be interpreted in too rigid a cause-and-effect manner: in some areas, complex irrigation systems long preceded state development, whereas in others (such as Mesopotamia) large-scale water control systems only developed well after state development. Furthermore, in the American southwest and other areas, large hydraulic systems existed for centuries without political centralization. Finally, the theory has only the most tenuous application to secondary states, many of which possessed the most rudimentary irrigation.

These objections may be beside the point. Marvin Harris (1977) has noted that Wittfogel's theory is not really about the origin of the state per se, but rather about the development of certain types of managerial systems. To postulate centralization of despotic power around the management of water supplies is not to deny the importance of population density, trade, warfare, environmental circumscription, and other factors that have had key roles in the increasing integration of society.

Harris, in *Cannibals and Kings* (1977), incorporates population pressure, hydraulics, and environmental circumscription into a complex argument in which social organization and ideology are viewed as the results of a society's technological adaptation to its physical environment. Harris begins by noting the main objection to population pressure theories; namely, that populations usually tend to stabilize comfortably below the carrying capacity of the land. Indeed, all societies have cultural means of supplementing Malthusian checks on population. Hunting-gathering groups maintained relative population equilibrium for tens of thousands of years, and the few such societies that survive today depend on balancing population to food supply. In all preindustrial societies, such practices as female infanticide, two- or three-year long taboos on sexual intercourse with a woman after she has borne a child, and prolonged nursing (which delays ovulation) serve to keep population in balance with food production. It is only in modern times that population has been allowed to grow unchecked. If population equilibrium was the norm in most premodern societies, then *why* would population increase to the point where it would force more complex forms of social organization?

Harris's explanation to this question is that during the Pleistocene Era, which lasted until about 10,000 to 15,000 years ago, hunting bands had come to rely on an abundance of large game, and populations had stabilized at levels made possible by such resources. At the end of the Pleistocene Era hundreds of big game species became extinct, for reasons still not entirely understood, with the result that people had to rely increasingly on alternative sources of food. Wild plants susceptible to domestication had always been available but had been rejected for cost-benefit reasons: without population pressure, hunting and foraging was more expedient for expending a minimum of calories. Now, plant domestication raised the carrying capacity of the land, allowing populations to increase. Population would tend ultimately to stabilize, but over time—perhaps hundreds of years—a gradual and inevitable decrease in productivity occurs as agricultural land loses nutrients and game is overhunted to supply animal protein. In other words, pressure is created not only by population growth, which might be quite slow, but also by a natural decline in the productivity of the land.

In tribal societies, populations are often controlled through a "male supremacist complex" that develops out of constant warfare. A premium on masculine fierceness diminishes the value of women, so that female infanticide—certainly one of the most effective means of population control—becomes virtually normative (some societies have institutionalized the killing of the firstborn, if it is a female). Agriculturalists have another option: instead of reducing population, they can increase their workload or add a new technology to augment production. This leads to agricultural surpluses, which are collected and redistributed by "big men" who use their role to gain and maintain status and power. These redistributive chiefs—often war chiefs as well—take on the role of a centralized coercive force. At this point, Harris brings in both Carniero's circumscription theory and Wittfogel's hydraulic theory to show the conditions under which centralization will continue until the state is formed.

To Harris the initial kick for this whole process is population; but, in a reverse on the Boserup theory, he sees a relatively stable population adapting to a diminution of food supplies. A major element of the theory—one not too auspicious for the future of civilization—is that any form of productivity will gradually lead to depletions of primary resources, with the result that all societies must sooner or later face the alternative of collapsing or moving to a new level of intensification. Once the domestication of plants and animals becomes the basis for subsistence, there can be no long-term stabilization.

Harris's argument, although appealing, is open to challenge. State development occurred so long after the end of the Pleistocene Era—thousands of years—that the relationship is tenuous at best. Population pressure on resources cannot, in every area that became politically centralized, be related to declines in productivity. Also, Boserup may be more correct in placing her emphasis on population growth rather than resource depletion. Even relatively minor changes in nutrition can radically alter the size of a population. Food supplies are quite elastic and can easily be affected either by a redefinition of usable food resources or by slight changes in technology. As Harris and others have pointed out, population growth may indeed need explaining, but not very much explaining.

THE INSTITUTIONALIZATION OF LEADERSHIP

In *Origins of the State and Civilization* (1975), Elman Service proposes an integrative theory. After an extensive review of the rise of the six archaic primary states and a number of modern primitive states, he rejects all conflict theories. Warfare and conquest, he points out, are too universal in human experience to count as causes of a particular form of social organization, and "the only instances we find of permanent subordination from war are where government already exists" (Service 1975: 271). Arguments based on irrigation or other forms of intensification admit too many exceptions. In ancient Peru, for example, agricultural intensification was achieved through canal irrigation 1,500 years before the first truly urbanized state. The idea that population pressures create conflicts that can only be solved by centralized government is rejected partially on the grounds that such pressure could just as well lead to increased sharing.

These negative conclusions derive from a particular reading of the data; they would hardly be convincing to an ardent proponent of any of the theories rejected. Indeed, although it is conflict theory that is specifically rebutted, implicitly what is being rejected is cultural materialism. What Service has done is to shift the argument from ecological determinants to strategies of decision making.

Service traces a logical development from the basic inequality inherent in human society to formalized and centralized inequality. In all societies, even the most egalitarian bands and tribes, certain individuals stand out by reason of their exceptional talent, intelligence, strength, or beauty. Although it is completely natural to confer status upon such people, the resulting inequalities remain individual, rather than class-based, and do not confer privilege or wealth. Certain circumstances tend to favor centralization of effort—for example, when a variety of local ecological niches forces specialization of production and symbiotic trade, or when collaborative work on public projects requires a division of labor. Such circumstances also favor centralized redistribution, which will naturally be handled by the exceptional people of the society (such as the Melanesian big men, who are usually war chiefs). Because such centralization offers obvious benefits, there will be a snowball effect leading to increasing concentration of administration. This enhancement of leadership, although economic, is not based on ownership, as Engels would have it; rather, it is "the result of a form of dependence that in primitive society results from generosity, from favors given" (Service 1975: 293).

Such leadership is unstable because it depends on an individual who may get sick, die, or simply run out of luck, and there is no normal method of succession. In order for a society to maintain the benefits of centralization, temporary charismatic leadership must be transformed into a permanent hierarchy. When this stage is reached, then a chiefdom has developed—the first true institutionalization of power, which is also an institutionalization of inequality. As this power center grows, so does the need of the newly developed ruling class to protect its privilege. One method of doing so, aside from the use of force, is to legitimize the power elite by connecting it with the supernatural, by giving it divine sanction. The use of force, then, far from creating the state, actually represents a temporary failure of the state to function responsibly by providing such benefits as protection, redistribution, and coordination of trade. Thus, "political evolution can be thought to consist, in important part, of 'waging peace' in ever wider contexts" (Service 1975: 297).

It should be evident that this is not merely a shift of emphasis from population pressure, irrigation, or environmental circumscription, but rather a shift in the kind of theory offered. The "considerable exaltation" a leader's successes could produce "in the minds of his followers" (Service 1975: 291) would be of little relevance to Robert Carniero or Marvin Harris, who view whole social systems as reacting in survival terms to material environmental determinants. Service's theory shifts the weight of argument from environment to cognition; that is, to the people's perception of accruing benefits. Service also uses models based on cooperation and integration, whereas most other theories have held conflict and instability to be the fundamental conditions out of which the state develops.

Service's point of view is refreshingly innovative, yet conflict and integration are definitely not mutually exclusive; all societies are involved in both, alternately and simultaneously. Similarly, societies are materialist and cognitive at the same time. Each perspective offers much in the way of explanation, but to claim exclusivity for one or the other is rather like claiming that a glass of water is half full rather than half empty.

SYSTEMS THEORIES

Few anthropologists today would hold to a single-cause model of the evolution of states. (It should be pointed out that those theories regularly referred to as unicausal—Carniero's, Wittfogel's, and Boserup's—are really singular only in emphasis.) All involve interactions between such factors as population, environment, technology, and irrigation. Synthetic models, like that of Marvin Harris, make these interactions more explicit. However, all such models are based on the idea that given certain preconditions, particular causes will lead to particular effects in a more or less sequential manner.

Unlike theories that designate specific causes, systems models are based on sets of principles, drawn mainly from physics and biology. These include negative and positive feedback, initial kick, system self-maintenance, and system self-development. *Negative feedback* is the process by which a stable system minimizes any deviation from equilibrium. For example, in a hunting-gathering society, an increase in the birth rate will be balanced by higher infant mortality rates if the population threatens to overgrow the food supply. *Positive feedback* is just the opposite: a small deviation may set in motion a process of increasing change. If the response to population growth is intensified agriculture, the result will be further population growth that will in turn generate more intensification, and so on until some limit is reached. The initial kick that transforms a negative feedback system into a positive feedback system may be very small. Kent Flannery (1968) hypothesizes that in the Tehuacán Valley of Mexico, the processes leading to the development of civilization were set in motion when nomadic foraging bands began to take care of a few edible wild plants. Over generations, this human intervention caused genetic changes that allowed for increased dependence on these semidomesticated foods, and this led to more sedentary lifestyles and larger populations, which in turn increased dependence on domesticates. This chain of events led eventually to the people settling into year-round farming villages. Stable societies are self-maintaining insofar as they are constantly making small adjustments to changes in the physical and social environment. Once positive feedback processes are set in motion, a society becomes self-developing as population growth, agricultural intensification, urbanization, and political centralization feed on one another in constant circular causality. It should be noted that this is almost the exact reversal of the Newtonian principle that every action must have an equal and opposite reaction; with positive feedback, the most minute initial kick can, over the long run, lead to massive change. It is no longer necessary to explain the origin of the state as the effect of some equally momentous cause.

A number of different systems theories of political evolution have been developed. Some of these focus on environment and technology, whereas others employ a decision-making perspective. Common to all, however, is the idea that societies respond adaptively to many conditions.

The goal of explanation, then, is not to pinpoint one or two factors that cause change in all cases, but to specify the processes by which social systems will alter their internal structures in response to selective pressures. As Ronald Cohen (1978b: 142) puts it, "The formation of a state is a funnel-like progression of interactions in which a variety of prestate systems, responding to different determinants of change, are forced by otherwise irresolvable conflicts to choose additional and more complex levels of political hierarchy." The opposition between force and benefit theories, between materialist and cognitive paradigms, and between conflict and integration models becomes blurred, because a systems model can incorporate these various perspectives simultaneously.

One such approach has been developed by Clifford Jolly and Fred Plog (1979). In their specific example of the Valley of Mexico, population growth was the initial stimulus, but theoretically any other stimulus that put exceptional stress on the equilibrium system would have been sufficient to cause significant change. Several options were available, given such stress: to reduce the population through infanticide or other cultural means, to disperse the larger settlements, to migrate to new areas, or to intensify agricultural production. Of these alternatives, only the latter would have led to the formation of the state. There are several conditions under which the option for intensification might be chosen: agricultural land might be circumscribed so there would be no place to disperse; farmers could drift into intensification without realizing it, perhaps through a slight new technology such as small irrigation canals; or the people might be forced by a conquering group to pay tribute and thus to increase production. In any case, once the option is chosen, it will lead by a series of feedback loops to nucleation, stratification, differentiation, and centralization. *Nucleation* (roughly synonymous with urbanization) will become necessary for large cooperative labor projects; in turn, as people concentrate in relatively small areas, pressure on local resources will be aggravated, requiring further intensification of food production. Economic *stratification* develops as more productive farming techniques amplify slight environmental differences, so that a person possessing even marginally better agricultural land will become richer relative to his neighbors. These forces also promote *centralization* of decision making, because such concentration is more effective for planning large-scale projects and organizing labor. Farming becomes more *differentiated* as entire fields are turned over to a single crop in order to increase the efficiency of plowing and irrigation. A surplus of food ensures that some do not need to work as farmers at all, and this permits the development of craft *specialization*. Finally, each one of these factors stimulates the others. The model developed by Jolly and Plog is shown in Figure 3.3. This model uses many of the same elements as the so-called unicausal and synthetic theories. However, a major difference between this model and that of, say, Marvin Harris is that Jolly and Plog are much less specific about the actual train of events. The processes with which they deal, such as nucleation and differentiation, are abstract and can involve stresses deriving from any number of sources. Society is viewed not as a row of dominoes falling in a predictable pattern, but as a flexible, adaptive system making constant internal adjustments to various stresses. These adjustments modify the environment, which requires further adaptations of the social system in a self-developing process.

THE EARLY STATE: THE CROSS-CULTURAL EVIDENCE

The Early State (1978), edited by Henri J. M. Claessen and Peter Skalník, brings together cross-cultural data on 19 formative states, ranging from Egypt in 3000 B.C. to the contemporary Kachari of India. The distinction between primary and secondary states is ignored. This omission is both deliberate and legitimate. So much emphasis has been placed

Figure 3.3
Systems Model of State Development

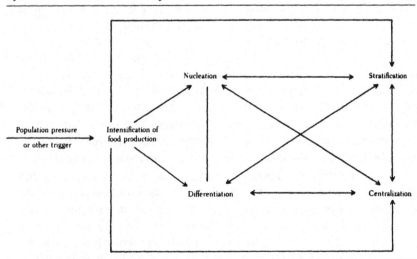

Source: Jolly and Plog 1979: 365, based partially on Logan and Sanders 1976.

on primary state development that the rich evidence of social evolution provided by other historical states—even those that developed with a great deal of autonomy—has been too often neglected. However, because most of the theories discussed here were originally applied almost exclusively to primary states, it is difficult to appraise Claessen and Skalník's evaluations, based as they are on evidence drawn from a different set of societies.

In any case, this massive work offers a wealth of data and conclusions from a wide range of social systems that fall within the authors' definition of "the early state" as "a centralized socio-political organization for the regulation of social relations in a complex, stratified society divided into at least two basic strata, or emergent social classes—viz. the rulers and the ruled—whose relations are characterized by political dominance of the former and tributary obligations of the latter, legitimized by a common ideology. . . . " (Claessen and Skalník 1978: 640). This definition, which summarizes many of the regularities found in the sample, supports the view that class stratification is a primary quality of the state, but it is not necessarily a cause, because differential access to material resources may exist long before the state comes into existence. Indeed, social stratification together with an economy that is capable of producing a surplus are considered predisposing factors without which the early state is impossible.

Four factors are singled out by the authors as directly causal: (1) population growth and/or population pressure, (2) war or the threat of war, (3) conquest, and (4) the influence of previously existing states. Most early states seem to have developed out of a combination of these, interacting with each other and appearing in no particular sequence. Wittfogel's (1957) hydraulic theory is not supported, since less than half the sample was clearly dependent on extensive irrigation systems. However, both Carniero's environmental circumscription model and Boserup's (1965) population pressure theory would be supported, but only if assimilated into some sort of systems model in which these factors are viewed not as primary causes, but as elements interacting with many other elements. In Table 3.1, the characteristics of 21 early states are outlined.

Although no previous book has gone so far in classifying the early state or in delineating its common elements, the conclusions regarding the genesis of this form of political organization seem anticlimactic. As the scope of theory broadens from the primary states to the scores of systems that can be classified as early states, fewer generalizations would be expected to hold for the entire sample, and the influence of preexisting states is probably powerful, subtle, and immeasurable. There has been

Table 3.1
Typology of 21 Early States

	Inchoate	Typical	Transitional
Examples (and period covered in sample)	Ankole (Uganda) 1650–1900 A.D. Hawaii 1700–1850 A.D. Norway 900–1100 A.D. Tahiti 1700–1800 A.D. Volta (Upper Volta and Ghana) 1400–1900 A.D. Zande (Sudan) 1750–1850 A.D.	Angkor (Cambodia) 1150–1300 A.D. Axum (Ethiopia) 25–625 A.D. Egypt 2950–2500 B.C. Inca (Peru) 1425–1532 A.D. Kachari (India) 1800 A.D. Mongolia 1200–1325 A.D. Scythia (Ukraine) 400–725 A.D. Yoruba (Nigeria) 1400–1900 A.D.	Aztecs (Mexico) 1425–1521 A.D. China 250 B.C.–225 A.D. France 900–1100 A.D. Jimma (Ethiopia) 1825 A.D.– Kuba (Zaire) 1850–1900 A.D. Maurya (India) 1100–1275 A.D.
Trade and Markets	Of limited importance.	Developed at the supralocal level.	Fully developed and of great importance.
Mode of Succession to Office	Predominantly hereditary.	Hereditary and by appointment.	Mainly by appointment.
Ownership of Land	Private ownership rare. Mainly communal ownership of land and livestock.	Private ownership of land limited, but increasing ownership by the state.	Private ownership of land important for both aristocracy and common people.
Judicial System	No codification of laws and punishments. No specialized formal judges.	Incipient codification of laws and punishments. Formal judges and general (nonspecialized) functionaries who decide cases.	Codification of laws and punishments complete. Administration of justice in the hands of formal judges.
Taxation	Irregular voluntary tribute and occasional labor.	Regular tribute. Major works undertaken with aid of compulsory labor.	Well-defined taxation system with complex apparatus to insure regular flow.

Source: Claessen and Skalník (eds.) 1978.

progress, of course. The search for a single dominant cause has been abandoned in favor of theories that stress the systemic interaction of many causes. One wonders, however, if systems approaches have really added that much to our understanding, because they mainly combine forces and processes that have been known for a long time. Essentially, what the systems theorists have done is raise the model of the evolution of the state to such a high level of abstraction that it is no longer easy to find exceptions to every generalization. Because of the resulting loss in specificity, one feels the need to fill in blanks in the model and re-establish the sense that what is being discussed are real human beings—living, dying, warring, and struggling to make it against the odds. The generalizations must be taken back to the archeological digs, to the sad pottery shards and broken amulets and old walls of lost civilizations; back to the nascent states of Africa and India where kings and peasants contended in an eternal game of conflict and accord. Theory must hold a middle position in anthropology, for ultimately everything begins and ends in the field.

SUGGESTED READINGS

Claessen, Henry J. M., and Peter Skalník, eds. *The Early State* (The Hague, The Netherlands: Mouton, 1978). This massive work (nearly 700 pages) begins with 4 chapters on the theory of state origins, then offers 20 chapters on individual states, and closes with 4 chapters synthesizing these specific studies and making cross-cultural comparisons. The book deliberately avoids the distinction between primary and secondary states and, therefore, cannot deal with some of the most basic theories of state formation.

Cohen, Ronald, and Elman R. Service, eds. *Origins of the State: The Anthropology of Political Evolution* (Philadelphia: Institute for the Study of Human Issues, 1978). The introduction and first chapters provide brief overviews of the major theories of state formation. Two other articles are especially valuable: Henry Wright's "Toward an Explanation of the Origin of the State," which puts many of the major theories in easy-to-understand flowchart form; and Robert Carniero's application of the principal of competitive exclusion (from evolutionary biology) to state formation.

Diamond, Jared. *Guns, Germs, and Steel: The Fates of Human Societies* (New York: Norton, 1999). This Pulitzer Prize-winning best-seller is a sweeping prehistory/history of the emergence of civilization. Rejecting racial explanations for different trajectories and rates of social evolution, Diamond seeks out causes in culture, disease, and military might. His discussion of human's unique ability to exterminate species and destroy entire ecosystems is depressingly convincing.

Earle, Timothy. *How Chiefs Come to Power: The Political Economy in Prehistory* (Stanford, Calif.: Stanford University Press, 1997). The intense interest in chiefdoms derives from the fact that they are a transitional form, from uncentralized to centralized systems. Thus, understanding the evolution of chiefdoms is crucial to understanding the evolutionary state. This book offers detailed examination of the development of chiefdoms in Denmark, Hawaii, and the Andes, focusing on the roles of the economy, military power, and ideology.

Haas, Jonathan. *The Evolution of the Prehistoric State* (New York: Columbia University Press, 1982). A clearly written and comprehensive theoretical overview that attempts to consolidate the conflict and integrative approaches. The author contends that once the foundations of centralization have been laid, the crucial variable becomes the increasing *power* of individuals and elites in controlling basic resources.

Upham, Steadman, ed. *The Evolution of Political Systems* (New York: Cambridge University Press, 1990). This volume is not concerned with the evolution of states but with the processes of change leading to "middle-range" polities, such as chiefdoms. The authors challenge various models of state development, without, however, emerging with a coherent theory to replace them. The 10 articles range from the broadly theoretical to specific studies of the Sausa of Peru and the Iroquois.

A traditional Zulu chief drew much of his political legitimacy from the consent and approval of the lineage ancestors. Courtesy of the Library of Congress.

Chapter 4

RELIGION IN POLITICS: SACRED LEGITIMACY, DIVINE RESISTANCE

It may not be true, as Georges Balandier (1970: 38) has contended, that the sacred is *always* present in politics; but it is seldom far away. As Myron Aronoff (1985b: 1) observes, "Religion and politics have been inextricably interrelated since the dawn of human culture and civilization." Viewers of the classic propaganda film *Triumph of the Will*, made at the 1934 Nazi Party Conference in Nuremberg, might justifiably wonder whether they are watching a political rally or a religious ceremony. An implicit sacredness underlies the Declaration of Independence and the Constitution of the United States, and offers a divine legitimacy to political succession. In modern-day Ireland, political conflict may be indistinguishable from religious conflict. However, in preindustrial societies, the boundaries of the various subsystems—political, kinship, economic, religious—are far less clearly demarcated than in more complex and specialized societies. An African candidate for headmanship who calls on ancestor spirits for support no more considers himself resorting to the supernatural than would a senatorial candidate in the United States who accepts a campaign contribution from a major corporation.

The role that religion plays in politics is difficult to correlate with specific types of religion, such as shamanistic or priestly. Among some Eskimos, the shaman was the most powerful of men by virtue of his access to the spirit world; among the tribal Hopi of the American southwest, political power is articulated through ceremonies, dances, and religious sodalities; modern Saudi Arabia is an internationally powerful nation-state, intimately based on Islam. On the other hand, it would be equally easy to provide examples of hunting-gathering peoples (the !Kung), tribal groups (the Yanomamo), and states (the Peoples Republic of China) in which religion plays relatively little part.

The role of religion and the supernatural in supporting a particular political regime is manifested mainly in three ways: (1) the government may be directly based on religion, as in a theocracy; (2) religion may be used to legitimize the ruling elite; and (3) religion may provide the underlying structures, beliefs, and traditions that are manipulated by aspirants to power. However, it should not be assumed that religion only reinforces existing political structures; religion can also be a powerful force of opposition. Religion may be the binding force of identity politics, as is seen in Northern Ireland, in Christian fundamentalism in the United States, and in Islamic nationalism.

SACRED LEGITIMACY

There is no clear-cut dividing line between a theocracy and a secular state. Because virtually all preindustrial states claim at least some degree of divine legitimacy and even the most religiously oriented of administrations must solve a number of very secular problems—defense, trade, and development of roads and irrigation networks—the amount of religious emphasis is a matter of degree, not of kind. Even in most cases in which religion plays an extremely important role, the secular and priestly bureaucracies are usually kept separate, as was true, for example, for the Inca and the Maya. Although the priests may have enormous power, it is not power that would normally be expended on the mundane functioning of the government. Divine kings may, like the Pope, express their divinity only on certain specific occasions and in limited contexts. Jacobus Janssen (1978) argues that this was true of the Egyptian pharaohs, who guaranteed and maintained the cosmic order (*Ma'at*) while at the same time were subject to that order; their persons were taboo, but they were incapable of working miracles; they were omnipotent but subject to the gods and forced to rule through purely mundane means. People in states that are not as highly segmented as our own seem to have little problem dealing with the simultaneity of the human and the divine, the sacred and the secular.

Lucy Mair (1962) notes two requisites for kingship in Africa: the support of a loyal following, and some claim on the part of the would-be king to a special relationship with supernatural beings. In other words, a king requires both secular support and sacred legitimacy. The first will derive from the individual king's personality and abilities and from his rightful claim, within traditional rules, to the throne; he must attain legitimacy through linking himself by myth to a supernatural ancestor responsible for the origin of the group or for some crucial event in the mythological history.

The Shilluk of the Sudan believed in a semidivine cultural hero who, through an Exodus-like epic adventure, established them as a unique people, set up the first villages, and founded the basic divisions of their society. This deathless hero, Ny'ikang, simply disappeared, and his spirit entered into each succeeding king. The Shilluk were the only contemporary group chosen by James George Frazer, in his classic *The Golden Bough* ([1890] 1900), to support his theory that the king represented the fertility of the land and cattle. According to Frazer, the king had to be killed in a ritual manner before he became old, so that the mystic potency would always remain with a virile leader. Although it is true that many such kings died young, in battle or through assassination, the belief that the king was ritually killed was itself part of Shilluk mythology. However, Frazer, although overemphasizing the symbolic value of fertility, did hit on an important element of African kingship: the symbolic identification of the king's person with the welfare of the whole society (Mair 1962).

Religious ritual also has important political functions. The periodic reenactment of legitimizing myths unites the entire community in a sacred bond that transcends private interests and day-to-day conflicts, while reinfusing the society with the mystical power of the world of the ancestors. In some uncentralized societies, religious ceremony was the major source of tribal integration. For many of the Plains Indians, for example, it was only for two weeks during the summer Sun Dance that the entire tribe came together as a unit. It was at this time that the council of chiefs would meet and make group decisions, and when Medicine Bundles, which brought both mystical and secular power to their owners, exchanged hands.

Manipulation of Religious Symbols among the Lugbara

The supernatural is much more than a simple set of passive beliefs that form an unchanging backdrop for political action. Such beliefs are subject to the manipulation both of individuals who compete for power and those who are called to support (or withhold support from) the competitors. This is clearly exemplified in the political system of the Lugbara of Uganda. This group, which had a classic segmentary lineage system, lacked any formal government whatsoever prior to the colonial period. The smallest effective unit of society was the local patrilineal kinship group, consisting of a cluster of families, and in lieu of kings or chiefs, authority was vested in an age-set system. As members of the age-grades of youth and big youth grew older, they came in conflict with their elders over land and authority. Because violence was not permitted among kinsmen, generational conflicts had to be worked out by mystical means. If one of the parties in the conflict were to fall sick and the oracles showed that his opponent had conjured the ancestors to wreak illness, the conjurer would gain power by having his authority affirmed. On the other hand, if it were believed that the dead had been invoked merely to gain or maintain status, rather than to benefit the lineage, the invoker could be accused of being a witch, and therefore lose status. These two interpretations were only narrowly different, but could have the effect of either legitimizing or destroying a person's authority. Thus, there was room for manipulation of the belief system not only by the individuals involved, but also by the public and the guardian of the oracle making the decision. Conflicts between local groups were not susceptible to this sort of resolution, because ghost invocation and witchcraft were thought to be ineffective beyond the minimal lineage. Dueling, feuding, and outright warfare were common means of conflict resolution; but accusations of sorcery were often employed between close neighbors who wished to avoid open violence. In any case, all political authority was primarily supernatural, because it was controlled by the dead ancestors and the power of sanctions derived from the same source (Middleton 1960, 1966).

Symbolism and Ritual in Secular Politics

It is comforting to assume that such sacred legitimacy is an anachronism of "primitive" societies. However, even secular politics, in which religion is not immediately evident, is often replete with the emotional fervor that marks the realm of the sacred. David Kertzer (1988) observed that despite modern man's illusion of political rationality and of making decisions based on the weighing of objective evidence, symbolism pervades virtually every aspect of modern politics. However, because symbolism, by its nature, is unconscious and has a taken-for-granted quality, there is a tendency to treat symbols as though they were things. Government, party, and state are really symbolic constructions, not the concrete entities that most people suppose. Indeed, such organizations take their continuity only through symbols; only the symbols remain constant, whereas the people making up the organization are regularly changing.

There are three properties to true symbols, according to Kertzer. The first is *condensation of meaning.* The ideas of the United States as a physical entity, as "one nation under God," as a repudiation of European tyranny, as patriotism in warfare, or as freedom and democracy (themselves ill-defined symbols) are all funneled into a single point in the Stars and Stripes. Secondly, symbols are *multivocal,* that is, they encompass a wide variety of different meanings. A single symbol, such as the Christian cross, may mean very different things to different people. Finally, true symbols are possessed of *ambiguity,* so that they can never be fully and completely defined; they have no precise meaning.

Ritual is "action wrapped in a web of symbolism"; it is highly structured and is often enacted at emotionally charged times and places (Kertzer 1988: 9). It is through ritual, and through the individual's participation in it, that the ordinary citizen makes the crucial emotional bond with the otherwise unthinkably huge and often impersonal state. Symbols make power sacred. A Fourth of July celebration, a national political party convention, the inauguration of a president, the bicentennial of the Constitution—all provide the symbolic form through which the state can be emotionally embraced. Rituals need be neither positive nor routinized. The assassination of President Kennedy, the explosion of the space shuttle Challenger, the Iranian hostage crisis, and certainly the terrorist attacks on the World Trade Center and the Pentagon were all national-level events that provided a gut-level override of party loyalties and conflicting ideologies and drew people together in an emotional bond of shared tragedy. A major conflict, such as the U.S. wars with Iraq and Afghanistan, is certainly real enough and tangible enough to the people who are fighting, but for the people left at home, it becomes a powerful symbol of national courage, unity, and pride.

It is this commonality of the nature of symbol and ritual that makes it difficult to distinguish the sacred from the profane in politics.

RELIGION AS RESISTANCE

It is a truism that official or dominant religions tend to support those in power. Obviously, however, this is not always the case; all or virtually all religions and cults begin in opposition to some sort of dominant power; it is only when the religion has become standardized, routinized, and achieved a critical mass of followers that it passes from protest to support. Christianity, which originated in Roman-occupied Israel and op-

posed what its followers perceived as an overly routinized and hypo-
critical Judaism, did not itself attain dominant status for half a
millennium. Over the last two centuries, religion has often emerged as
a primary form of "antisystemic protest" against the rapid changes
wrought by the spread of world capitalism. The Islamic resurgence of
the last decades may be read in this light, as a protest against capitalism
and secularism (Robbins 2002: 337–63).

Revitalization Movements

Religion may substitute for direct political action in cases in which
natives have been rendered politically impotent by an alien power or
they do not understand the nature of their situation. In such cases, a
revitalization movement may arise as "a conscious, deliberate effort on
the part of some members of society to create a more satisfying culture"
(Wallace 1985: 319). Such movements are an almost predictable response
to Western expansion, although they can be expected in any situation in
which cultures at totally different levels of technological sophistication
or different levels of raw power come into contact. Incipient Christianity,
arising within a situation of conquest by Rome, possessed all the elements of a revitalization movement.

There are many types of revitalization movements. A *millenarian*
movement looks forward to an apocalyptic transformation of the society
through supernatural means. The Ghost Dance that swept through the
Plains tribes during the last quarter of the nineteenth century was based
on the teachings of Wovoka, a Piute living in Nevada, who prophesied
that whites and Indians alike would be destroyed in a holocaust. Only
those Indians who performed the Ghost Dance and led pure lives would
inherit a world in which the buffalo would return to the plains and the
people would live in peace and security in a halcyon society based on
traditional Indian ways (Mooney [1869] 1973). (The religion ended trag-
ically when hundreds of Sioux who had escaped their reservation to
practice the Ghost Dance were rounded up and gunned down by the U.S.
Cavalry at Wounded Knee, South Dakota.) In a *messianic* movement, it
is a messiah that will bring about this transformation. In the mid-1700s,
a Seneca Indian named Handsome Lake had a series of revelations in
which he envisioned a new faith that combined elements of both traditional religion and Christianity and was more adaptive to the reservation
context within which the Indians found themselves. Through a rigid pro-
scription of liquor and an emphasis on family, the new religion was able
to bring the Seneca and other tribes of the former Iroquois confederacy

back from cultural collapse. Today, the Handsome Lake religion remains strong among the Iroquois, and its founder is considered a great prophet (Wallace 1972). In *nativism,* the goal is to purge the society of unwanted or alien elements, and in *revivalism* the aim is to reinstitute a former era of happiness. Most movements combine several of these elements. The so-called Vailala Madness, which swept parts of New Guinea in the early decades of this century, showed strong nativistic and revivalistic tendencies. After whites and their negative influences were totally expelled, believers would return to a Golden Age in which they would live with their ancestors (Wallace 1985).

The Vailala Madness was a *cargo cult,* a type of revitalization movement that sought to gain access to Western trade goods ("cargo" in Pidgin English) by magical means. When colonization or invasion by an industrialized power brought a massive influx of manufactured goods—cars, radios, processed food—natives sought some explanation for these wonders within their own cultural understandings. Because the whites were never seen manufacturing these goods but only receiving them, often by airplane or ship, it was assumed that foreigners had some magic at their disposal, perhaps the secret words that they endlessly wrote on pieces of paper. Perhaps it was white rituals, such as walking up and down in military formation carrying rifles, or sitting around a table in suits and ties, that brought the cargo. Perhaps a rough airport, carved out of the jungle, or a mockup of an airplane would attract the cargo from the skies. Perhaps the cargo was really created by the ancestors, and the whites had only usurped the magical formulas to attract goods really meant for the natives. There were numerous variations, all quite logical from the point of view of the natives, who were desperately trying to make sense of a situation that would otherwise be chaotic and incomprehensible. Unfortunately, cargo cults could sometimes end in tragedy. In New Guinea in 1946, in response to wartime occupation of the islands, natives slaughtered their pigs, their main source of subsistence, in the belief that Great Pigs would appear from the sky at the millennium, which would be announced on mock radios attached to bamboo and rope "antennae" (Worsley 1985).

According to Anthony F. C. Wallace (1985), revitalization movements pass through a number of stages, although not all movements complete the cycle. The first stage is a premovement phase in which society is in a steady state without strong stresses or pressures for radical change. Gradually, as a consequence of alien invasion, famine, acculturation pressures, or whatever, individuals experience psychological stress and the culture becomes increasingly distorted as crime rises, alcohol or drug abuse becomes normative, and leaders are corrupted. A movement phase begins with the formulation of a new code of living by a prophet, often as the result of a vision. The revelation is disseminated to disciples who spread it among the masses until some sort of organization of believers becomes necessary. The new faith must adapt to its environment, either defeating vested interests or making modifications in the original doctrine to allay hostility and suspicion. When a significant number of people, or the whole population, has adopted the new doctrine, a cultural transformation will be affected, bringing the culture into a more harmonious alignment with the conditions that precipitated the movement. Finally, in a postmovement phase, the movement will become routinized as a mainstream religion or political party, and a new steady state will have been achieved.

Revitalization movements are basically attempts, often unsuccessful, to adapt to new conditions, and, despite the religious trappings, they are basically political. The prophet's vision may be seen as a pivotal point in the history of the culture, at once combining external and internal factors, past and future, tradition and inevitable change. Over the past two centuries most such movements have arisen in the context of domination by Western powers; therefore, they may be seen as a first form of political protest, a cry of pain and accusation in the absence of the knowledge, organization, or power to confront the occupiers on their own terms.

In the words of an African adage: "At first we had the land and you had the Bible. Now we have the Bible and you have the land" (Lanternari 1963: 20). Indeed, many revitalization movements, including the Handsome Lake and peyote religions in the United States, borrowed heavily from missionization, using the apocalyptic vision of Christian fundamentalism against the usurpers of their lands, their freedoms, and their cultures. Once routinized, however, a religion may become a focal point of protest within the rules of Western political systems (e.g., when African American Christian sects took the lead in the civil rights struggles of the 1960s) or the emergence of secular organizations, such as trade unions and native councils, may consign such religious movements to political irrelevancy.

Revitalization movements do not emerge only among tribal peoples, however. The stress and chaos of modern industrial society is sufficient to impel many individuals and groups to seek religious transformation. As analyzed by John Hall (1985), the tragedy of the People's Temple, in which 900 people died in an orchestrated mass murder and suicide in Guyana in 1978, was a revitalization movement that actually achieved its apocalypse. The following example, which follows all of the stages set forth above, reveals the emergence and routinization of a messianic movement in modern Israel.

Gush Emunim—Revitalization in Modern Israel

According to Myron Aronoff (1984a: 63), Gush Emunim ("bloc of the faithful") began as "a spontaneous, charismatic, loosely organized, extraparliamentary pressure group on the margins of the political system" and evolved into "a well-organized and functionally differentiated network of related institutions that were incorporated within the present national ruling establishment." This transformation from fervent religion to routinized semisecular political party was possible because Gush Emunim articulated a new sense of purpose and meaning within a situation rent with chaos and despair.

As described by Aronoff, the framework for the subculture from which Gush Emunim would arise was provided by the establishment, in 1953, of a state religious school system under the control of the National Religious party. Virtually all of the leaders and supporters came out of this system of high school yeshivot, which combined both secular and religious instruction. This group created a virtual subculture within Israel, distinguished by the knitted skull caps that all members wore. The founder leaders were all graduates of the advanced Yeshivat Merkaz Harav, which they attended after fulfilling their military obligations; and all were disciples of the late Rabbi Zvi Yehuda Kook, who saw himself as interpreter of his father's teachings. Kook, who was heavily influenced by the mystical Kabalah, was an unlikely candidate for charismatic leadership. He was difficult to comprehend and often barely articulate, but his ideas, especially as they were modified and elaborated in the concrete politics of Israel, provided a new faith that inflamed his young followers.

Although Gush Emunim never developed a complete ideology, it proclaimed a sort of neo-Zionism, a revivalistic return to the historic vision of Zionism that had languished with the establishment of the Israeli state. Formerly sacred creeds had been corrupted by secularism, and these creeds needed to be reinterpreted according to new realities. It was the duty of Jews to "liberate" all of their ancestral lands. In fulfilling this historically inevitable aspiration, Jews would reclaim all that was great, heroic, and beautiful from their past. The territories acquired in the wars of June 1967 and October 1973 thus became the focal points of the movement. There could be no withdrawal from any occupied territories, no sacrifice of any part of the Holy Land.

The event that provided the political opening for Gush Emunim was the chaotic and morally ambiguous October 1973 war, which led to widespread doubt and agony among the people and a crisis of confidence in the government. The liberal Labor party, which had dominated Israeli politics almost since the nation's inception, found itself under severe challenge from a conservative backlash. It was within this atmosphere of confusion and general malaise that Gush Emunim commenced its active protest.

As a newcomer to the political scene, the movement was not constrained by the established rules of political order. The leaders believed that it was their duty to operate outside of the legal system. Democracy was acceptable only as long as it subscribed to the proper Zionist framework. Toward its goals, Gush Emunim developed a pattern of protest against retreat from the occupied territories or accord with Israel's enemies. Demonstrations, including mass rallies and marches, opposed both the Camp David Accords and Egyptian President Anwar Sadat's historic visit to Jerusalem. A major "Movement to Stop Retreat from the Sinai" involved marches and attempts to establish settlements in the occupied desert. When the government went ahead with plans to return the Sinai to Egypt, Gush Emunim followers broke into abandoned houses there and obstructed efforts to forcibly remove them. When such tactics threatened a backlash among the majority of Jews—who saw the pact with Egypt as a first step toward security and peace—Gush Emunim launched a policy of "victimization," designed to ensure that future settlements on the occupied West Bank and in the Golan Heights and Gaza Strip were not abandoned. Settlement became the primary strategy for retaining occupied territories, and a central tenet in Gush Emunim ideology. In 1976, a suborganization, Amana, was established to promote the settlement of the occupied territories.

All of these activities were opposed by the Labor government. However, in 1977, Labor was replaced by the conservative Likud party, which shared much of Gush Emunim's hawkish ideology and which was allied with the National Religious Party from which Gush Emunim had originally emerged. With a like-minded government in power, the stage was set for the routinization of the former opposition movement, which now gained access to many government ministers and members of the Knesset. With routinization inevitably came bureaucratization: the once loosely structured group was organized into sections for promoting settlements, lobbying, and political party activities. Gush Emunim was gradually incorporated into the normal institutional framework of Israeli society and politics.

Noting that Gush Emunim involved aspects of millenarian and messianic movements, Aronoff (1984a: 81) observed that such "political-religious revitalization movements provide serious critiques of contemporary political and cultural systems. They offer dramatic alternative definitions of reality, symbolic systems of cultural meaning, and political agendas that they seek to impose in place of those that are currently dominant."

Pentecostalism and Antimemory in Malawi

The study of postcolonialism has become a cross-cultural discipline in itself, closely allied to and sharing many of the tenets of postmodernism: a rejection of grand theories or metanarratives, a concern with subjectivity, an emphasis on the creative construction of memory, and a focus on the discursive aspects of culture (see chapter 10). Anthropological post-colonial studies of religion in Africa have tended to stress an invention-of-tradition approach to precolonial or colonial nostalgia, in which historical memory is selectively and creatively constructed in order to provide legitimacy for postcolonial governments and to accommodate the transition from rural traditionalism to urban modernity. Rijk van Dijk's (1998) analysis of Christian Pentecostalism in Malawi goes against this trend, revealing religion as a form of resistance against such attempts to fashion legitimizing histories.

In 1989, Dennis Tembo, a preacher in the Living Waters Church of the *Abadwa Mwatsopano* Pentecostal movement was picked up by officials of the dictatorial government of President Hastings Banda and taken to a meeting with the head of security. Much to his surprise, instead of being beaten or imprisoned, he was ensconced overnight in a lush bedroom and the next day was returned home, where for several weeks he was the recipient of a series of luxurious gifts. It only gradually dawned on him that he had been chosen to marry the daughter of one of the state security staff. Such arranged marriages are normal in Malawi culture, but Tembo resisted. Bypassing his elder kin, he turned to the leader of his church for advice, who told him to refuse the marriage, return all of the gifts, and move away from the area until any insult resulting from his actions had been forgotten. Tembo promptly followed his mentor's advice.

This small social drama is replete with meaning that can only be interpreted within the context of the politics and religion of contemporary Malawi. When Banda became president in 1966, he sought to provide a cultural and historical foundation for his brutally corrupt government.

He did this by celebrating rituals of nationhood designed to unite the country's multiple ethnic groups, establishing a national language, and resuscitating a precolonial political culture based on matrilineality and strict age hierarchy, in which the young were unquestionably submissive to their elders. Marriage was central to these goals because under the matrilineal system, young men were obliged to pay a bride price in labor to their wife's kin and to accept multiple obligations to village societies and local chiefs. This structure and set of values was carried over to the national level, providing Banda and his government with power and authority previously reserved to village elders. The youth of the country, many of whom had strayed from this cultural ideal during and after the struggle against colonialism, were organized into two large government youth organizations, the paramilitary Malawi Young Pioneers and the League of Malawi Youth. By the late 1980s, "Malawi had been transformed into one of the most highly supervised countries on the African continent, with state power represented in virtually every corner of society through an astoundingly intricate network of informants, training camps, teachers, roadblocks, checkpoints and party membership. . . . " (van Dijk 1988: 173). Officially sanctioned religions took up Banda's nationalistic cause, including the assumption of control over missions originally established by the English colonizers.

It is only in this context that Tembo's rebellion can be fully appreciated. *Abadwa Mwatsopano*, literally meaning "born again," placed a strong emphasis on the present and future, rejecting Banda's nationalistic histories. In the intense process of being born again, the youth were effectively detached from history and culture. In a sense, the past no longer existed. What time did exist was present and future time, the latter leading to the Second Coming of Jesus. Not only was the novitiate disembedded from history, but also from family, kin, and community. As a young people's movement, it sought to break the traditional age-grade hierarchy of authority, with the elders firmly on top. The sheer emotionality of the central element of worship—speaking in tongues—served to create new boundaries around the individual, at once setting him off from the wider world while encompassing him in tight community of those of similar experience. As one of the 10 poorest countries in the world, Malawi offers little hope for young people to obtain an education, find jobs, or be able to pay for health services. Townships are crowded and strife ridden. *Abadwa Mwatsopano* offers a protective barrier against this hopeless world.

Tembo's refusal to accept an arranged marriage with the daughter of a government official was thus a profoundly political act, because he was also rejecting the entire structure of culture and history so carefully erected over decades by the government in its quest for legitimacy and national unity.

THE ADAPTIVE VALUE OF DEVIANT RELIGION IN PERU

Although religion is often conceived of as conservative or reactionary—even revitalization movements often hearken back to some idealized traditional past—it can also have a strongly adaptive function, helping to restructure society during periods of rapid change. In some cases, this function seems primary, because the religion may neither legitimize the dominant power nor resist that power. Such was the case with the Handsome Lake Religion of the Seneca, mentioned above. Seventh-Day Adventism is a fundamentalist denomination of Christianity that in the United States tends to be highly conservative (its main difference from other fundamentalist groups is that it holds Saturday, not Sunday, to be the sabbath). However, when transposed to the mountains of Peru, it became an important mechanism for adapting to radically new conditions.

The Aymara Indians living in the community of Soqa, in the Lake Titicaca region of Peru, were first missionized by Seventh-Day Adventists around 1915. At that time, most Aymara followed their traditional earth-mother religion. (They had adopted from Catholicism a few saints and the Virgin Mary, who had been added to the indigenous pantheon, and a fiesta system that consisted largely of dancing and getting drunk for a few days every year.) The Aymara were economically self-sufficient, monolingual, and cut off from any but the most cursory market relations with the exploitive *mestizo* class. The Seventh-Day Adventists, after many years of utter failure, established a mission in a small village and began to offer their religion as a package deal: health, education, and Jesus—in that order. Contrary to the usual theory, it was not the cultural deviants, but the more intellectually oriented—often community leaders—who were willing to try the package, which in practice meant abstinence from alcohol, some degree of modern medical aid, and sufficient education to read the Spanish-language Bible and hymnal. To the north of Lake Titicaca, where literacy threatened the hacienda system, there were many murders and burnings of Adventist churches, but the worst that happened to the freeholding Adventists near the lake was that they were once beaten and dragged off to jail. Generally, persecution consisted of Adventist baiting, such as capturing them at fiesta time and forcibly pouring liquor down their throats until they were drunk. Although persecution was relatively mild, it was constant; the small group was ostracized and their formal leaders lost all authority. The situation remained as such for almost four decades.

The political system at that time was based on the *ayllu* (discussed in chapter 2). Over the centuries, many *ayllus* had become so loosely structured that they were held together largely by means of numerous and proliferating fiestas throughout the year. These fiestas provided both leadership, through sponsors, and an excuse to come together as a unified social and political group. However, in the early 1950s, as population began to overgrow the carrying capacity of the land for subsistence farming, the fiesta system with its enormous outlays by sponsors became too expensive to be maintained. In 1955, with a federal government engineer as a guide, young progressives replaced the *ayllu* system with a community-based political structure, complete with mayor, vice mayor, and lieutenants. This radical transformation, considered and decided by democratic means, accomplished two important things for the handful of Seventh-Day Adventists on the island. First, because the mayor was directly responsible to the provincial governor and the vice mayor was directly responsible to the commandant of the regional army post, formal lines of communication were established between Soqa and the *mestizo* world. Second, the end of the *ayllu,* which had been held together by the Catholic fiesta system, meant the secularization of local government for the first time in centuries. The Seventh-Day Adventists, who had been persecuted and ostracized for three generations, had also been educating themselves all that time. They were the only ones in the community who could read and write Spanish, and because they had fought for their right to practice their religion in the halls of government as far away as Lima, they were experienced in dealing with the national bureaucracy. Naturally, the Adventists quickly stepped into both formal and informal positions of power in the new Soqa government. Their unique abilities allowed them to act as culture brokers during this time of transition from a subsistence-agriculture economy to a money economy. As a result, the long-despised Adventists held a monopoly of political power in numerous communities throughout the Peruvian *altiplano.* Because Adventist schools tend to be superior to public schools, the power derived from education might well be retained for many years to come (Lewellen 1978, 1979).

The Aymara study shows how a "deviant" religion, such as Protestantism in a traditional Catholic society, can provide the pool of variability necessary for adaptive change.

SUGGESTED READINGS

Aigbe, Sunday A. *Theory of Social Involvement: A Case Study in the Anthropology of Religion, State, and Society* (New York: University Press of
America, 1993). Examines the relationship between Pentecostal Christianity and the state in Nigeria. The emphasis is on how religion and
state adapt through both conflict and symbiosis to the demands of creating democracy and nationhood.

Aronoff, Myron J. *Religion and Politics: Political Anthropology*, Vol. 3 (New
Brunswick, N.J.: Transaction Books, 1984). A slim collection of five
articles on religion in modern state societies, four of which are on the
Middle East. The fifth article is a historical examination of the Bible in
U.S. political tradition. Unfortunately, two introductory overview essays,
one by editor Aronoff and one by sociologist Irving Herskovits, are very
brief and offer little that is new.

Kertzer, David. *Ritual, Politics, and Power* (New Haven, Conn.: Yale University
Press, 1988). For Kertzer, Political Man responds better to gut-level symbolism than to rational arguments and objective facts. Ritual is the glue
that holds states and societies together, and the author offers a detailed
and highly readable examination of political ritual from the Aztecs to
the United States. The focus is on secular ritual, but it quickly becomes
evident that it is not that easy to distinguish the secular from the sacred.

Packard, Randall M. *Chiefship and Cosmology: An Historical Study of Political
Competition* (Bloomington: Indiana University Press, 1981). In contrast
to Middleton's synchronic analysis, this study of the interrelation between politics and religion among the Bashu of Zaire is very much of
the process school. The author not only shows the ritual functions of
chiefship today, but also traces the historical adaptations that have taken
place over the last century and a half.

Wallace, Anthony F. C. *The Death and Rebirth of the Seneca* (New York: Vintage, 1972). A detailed history of the Handsome Lake Movement of the
Iroquois, a revitalization movement based on the visions of a Seneca
prophet. Wallace goes deeply into the reservation culture of the period
and into the dynamics of the religion's dissemination and growth.

Werbner, Richard, ed. *Memory and the Postcolony: African Anthropology and
the Critique of Power* (London: Zed, 1998). Of these eight postcolonial
studies of politics in southern Africa, the last three focus on various
Pentecostal movements, revealing both legitimizing and resistance aspects. The focus of the book is on the ways in which memory is constructed and used.

British structural-functionalists often ignored the colonial context of the African societies they studied. Here, a native king is flogged by native colonial soldiers. Courtesy of the Library of Congress.

Chapter 5

STRUCTURE AND PROCESS

"Structure may go to the wall," wrote F. G. Bailey in 1968, "but people survive." This could have been the rally cry for an entire generation of political anthropologists who, during the 1950s and 1960s, guided the transition from the study of norms, values, and atemporal social structures to an emphasis on competition, conflict, history, and change. The paradigm so self-consciously and often vehemently repudiated was the structural-functionalism of A. R. Radcliffe-Brown, which had dominated British anthropology for more than 20 years. Because the new political anthropology is, to a great degree, a reaction to this theoretical orientation, it is worthwhile to take a critical look at it.

STRUCTURAL-FUNCTIONALISM

If one were to reduce the structural-functionalist position to only four words or phrases, they might be *synchronic, teleological, Africa,* and *closed system.* The term "synchronic" is defined by Webster as "concerned with the complex of events existing in a limited time period and ignoring historical antecedent." This would be the definition favored by the critics of structural-functionalism, who constantly complained that societies were ripped out of their historical contexts and treated as though they were static over long periods. In reality, however, the early political anthropologists did not so much portray their societies as excessively stable or unchanging (although this might be implied from their method of analysis), but rather as outside of time, in the same way that a still photograph captures an instant without denying temporal processes. In addition, just as a still photograph may suggest a great deal of movement as well as a past and a future, the structural-functionalists allowed for all sorts of tensions and conflicts within their frame of reference.

In a sense, then, these researchers can be compared with intelligence personnel who analyze aerial photographs—they tried to look at society from above, as a whole, and to map the interconnections between the various subsystems of the society, including kinship, marriage, religion, politics, and so forth. The society itself was considered not only outside of time, but also isolated in space. Although a tribe or chiefdom might be contained within a nation state, it was viewed as a thing unto itself, relatively independent of its wider social environment; that is, as a closed system with its own culture, its own values, and its own mechanisms of adjustment.

The question immediately arises: adjustment to what purpose? The structural-functionalists had a ready answer: adjustment to the equilibrium of the whole. Far from being static, institutions within the society were constantly changing shape as smaller groups formed and reformed, alliances were made, and feuds and wars were fought—but all of these were interpreted as contributions to the integrity of the whole. Thus, any particular institution was analyzed with regard to the way in which it functioned to aid the survival of the larger system. In this sense, structural-functionalist causality was the reverse of Aristotelian causality; effects were not pushed from behind, so to speak, but pulled from in front. One would not explain a religious ritual in terms of its historical development but rather in terms of its purpose or function, which was ultimately the maintenance of societal equilibrium. In short, institutions and activities were analyzed teleologically; that is, in terms of a goal toward which they were directed. It was recognized, of course, that the people themselves would offer completely different reasons for their behavior; but these manifest functions, although certainly important and often recorded in great detail, were not analytically significant. The anthropologist was much more interested in the latent functions, of which individuals were unaware, and these could only be determined by looking at the whole system, just as the liver can only be understood in relation to the survival of the body.

One reason that this paradigm could be sustained for so long was that virtually all fieldwork was done in the part of Africa that was under British colonial rule, where cultures remained separated by language barriers, distinctive cultural patterns, and the paternalistic prejudices of the ruling class of British administrators. Also, there was a tendency to seek out for fieldwork the more typical villages—those that were most traditional—and to use them to represent the entire language group. This naturally had the effect of minimizing culture contact.

All of these elements are either implicit or explicit in E. E. Evans-Pritchard's classic *The Nuer* (1940a). The basic goal of the book, including a chapter on the political system, was to show how a society of 200,000 people could maintain equilibrium despite almost constant feuding and an utter lack of any kind of centralized government. Radcliffe-Brown's explanation, based on the concept of complementary opposition (discussed in chapter 3), demonstrates how the equilibrium of the whole can be maintained, not just in spite of conflicting parts, but actually as a result of them.

It is no accident that the demise of structural-functionalism coincided almost exactly with the demise of British colonialism after World War II. The synchronic approach required a fairly clear still photograph, and the image tended to blur when the action got too chaotic or when too many different groups crowded into the frame. The repudiation of structural-functionalism began blandly enough, but quickly turned to revolution, with all of the vehemence radical change seems to require. Most of the criticisms now seem rather obvious: societies are not in equilibrium, teleological arguments are not scientific, no society is isolated from its social surroundings, societies are not homogenous, and colonial Africa is not the world. Structural-functionalism and British anthropology as a whole were accused of having been servants of colonialism. Perhaps the most telling criticism was simply that the theory had become routinized and was threatening to degenerate into a simplistic game in which one could point out, with a semblance of great profundity, that a religious ritual brought many people together and thus maintained social equilibrium.

All these objections are justified—process does indeed stand triumphant over equilibrium. However, it is possible to look back from the vantage of victory and discern in the defeated enemy certain admirable qualities that were not visible during the smoke of battle. In retrospect, a book like *The Nuer* seems an enduringly brilliant and perceptive piece of analysis. The idealized portraits painted by the structural-functionalists of entire societies are very close to pictures of what is now being called political culture—that set of values and interactions common to a traditional society. In this respect, structural-functionalism seems close to the symbolist school of political anthropology, which views culture, including politics, as involving powerful sets of unconscious symbols. These symbols form a setting in which political action takes place; what has been added is the emphasis on the ways in which symbols are used and manipulated by individual actors. Even in the midst of the repudiation of structural-functionalism, one of the pioneers of the new process school, F. G. Bailey (1960: 240), felt it necessary to caution his colleagues, "I cannot emphasize too strongly that without the fixed points which are provided by a static structural analysis, we have no means of describing the change that is taking place."

The idea of latent functions was taken over, virtually intact, by ecological anthropologists, who view societies as unconsciously adjusting to maintain ecological balance. Teleology, once considered one of the most taboo words in science, was incorporated into both biology and physics and moved, via general systems theory, into the social sciences, in which goal direction was viewed as a prime force for both individuals and groups. Also from general systems theory comes the concept of boundaries, the defining qualities of a social system that block or filter inputs from outside the system. Within these boundaries, constant adjustments are taking place to maintain the system, but the boundaries themselves may be stable for long periods of time. Thus *for a relatively closed system* the picture one gets from applying the concepts of general systems theory are not very different from that of the structural-functionalists. Although the superiority of a process approach cannot be denied—if only because its scope is so much wider and its analytical tools are so much more diverse—there is indeed in society something that is continuous, something that forms the backdrop for change. This is what the structural-functionalists were able to describe with such perception.

THE PROCESS APPROACH

It is easy, in retrospect, to impose too much coherence on the reaction against structural-functionalism, to suppose that these writers had some philosophical view in common and were all moving in the same direction. Actually, their explorations could hardly have been more varied. Turner's *Schism and Continuity in an African Society* (1957) and Edmund Leach's *Political Systems of Highland Burma* (1954) represent opposite poles, one focusing on a few individuals in one small village, the other on ethnic populations interacting within a modern nation state. Perhaps the only thing these two seminal works have in common is that both seem to cling to the old paradigm with one hand, while feeling their way toward a new paradigm with the other. In fact, the field situation itself—whether uniform in population or of great ethnic diversity, whether tribal or state, in conflict or at peace—was much more significant in determining the line of analysis than was any common theoretical point of view.

It is a curious fact of political anthropology that its major position papers are often contained in relatively brief introductions to anthologies. In 1940, the Introduction to *African Political Systems* (edited by Fortes and Evans-Pritchard) provided the stimulus and theoretical basis for the first generation of political anthropologists. In 1966, three writers who were in the forefront of the reaction against structural-functionalism—Marc Swartz, Victor Turner, and Arthur Tuden—modified the foundation concepts for a generation of process theorists in their Introduction to *Political Anthropology*.

For these authors, the study of politics "is the study of the *processes* involved in determining and implementing public goals and in the differential achievement and use of power by the members of the group concerned with these goals" (Swartz, Turner, and Tuden 1966: 7). There are several key words in this tight definition. The emphasis on process is obvious, but the political anthropologist is only concerned with public processes. This provides an escape from overgeneralized views of politics or power that seem to include almost any relation of power, even at the level of the family; but still it leaves enough flexibility to include neighborhood or nation. The concept of goals has taken a marked shift from the orientation of the synchronic analysts, who were interested mainly in the latent functions that led to the goal of equilibrium or survival. The process theorists were much more interested in the consciously held goals of the group, whether they were lower taxes, better roads, or leadership in war. The ability to make and enforce such decisions constitutes power. Political anthropology thus consists mainly in the study of the competition for power, and the way in which group goals are implemented by those possessing power.

Three broad trends emerged. First, process became the key word of political anthropology as societies were studied in their historical, or at least temporal, context; thus, the emphasis was shifted from equilibrium to change. Second, a significant group of researchers narrowed their focus to a sharp concentration on the activities of individuals vying for power within very limited political settings. Third, another group of researchers broadened the perspective to include the national system, with a strong emphasis on the adaptive changes that traditional cultures must make as they are incorporated politically into the modern industrial state; sometimes the state government itself is the subject of analysis. These three theoretical perspectives are summarized in Table 5.1.

Table 5.1
Three Theoretical Perspectives in Political Anthropology

| | Structural-Functionalism | The Process Approach | |
		Process Theory	Action Theory
Goals	To show how particular institutions serve to maintain the equilibrium of the whole society	To define the processes involved in political competitions and in implementing public goals	To describe individual strategies for gaining and maintaining power
Unit of Analysis	A society, tribe, social group, etc., usually treated as an ideal whole; this group was considered for analytical purposes as a closed system insofar as little regard was paid to the wider environment	The "political field," a flexible and relative concept referring to any area in which political interaction takes place; may involve a part of society or extend beyond social or ethnic boundaries	The "political arena," an area in which individual actors or small groups vie for political power. Political arenas may be, or be comprised all or in part of, factions, patron-client relations, parties, elites, and other informal parapolitical groups
Analytic Approach to Time	Synchronic: society is viewed as though outside of time, in ideal present	Diachronic, or "in time": analysis may focus on actual history or on ideal processes of change through time	Diachronic, but often focused on the actions of individuals within the duration of the anthropologist's fieldwork
Attitude toward Change	In some writings, there was simply no interest expressed in change; society was treated in a purely structural fashion; in other writings, change (in the sense of adaptive adjustments of the parts) was emphasized, but the whole was seen to be in equilibrium	Conflict, tension, and change are viewed as the normal condition of society	Change within a political arena is virtually constant, though there may be a relative stability of the wider system
Key Terms	Structure, function, equilibrium, integration	Process, competition, conflict, power, legitimacy, support	Strategy, manipulation, decision making, roles, goals, games, rules
Examples	African Political Systems, ed. Fortes and Evans-Pritchard The Nuer, by Evans-Pritchard	Political Systems of Highland Burma, by Leach (transitional) Political Anthropology, ed. Swartz, Turner, and Tuden	Schism and Continuity in an African Society, by Turner Lugbara Religion, by Middleton "Political Anthropology: Manipulative Strategies," by Vincent, in Annual Review of Anthropology 1978

Field and Arena

The unit of study was formerly a specifiable group, even if that group was not always well defined. Anthropologists examined political structures within a village, a lineage, a clan, a tribe, and sometimes even a culture (usually meaning a particular language group). Unfortunately, politics does not confine itself so neatly to such social units, and even if we were able to discover the locus of political behavior within a society, it may not stay put. For example, if we were to examine a medium-sized American town over time, we would find that most people were both apathetic and ignorant about the day-to-day running of the government. Local elections would create factions, but these might encompass only a minority of the citizens. Hot issues, such as busing to attain racial balance in the schools or a threatened police strike, might involve almost the entire community. Periodically, the people would be drawn into state-wide elections and statewide political problems, and every four years, many of the people would become involved in national politics along with local politicians trying to get a grip on the encumbered coattails of one or another presidential candidate.

This recognition—that political structures overlap but do not coincide with other social structures and that they tend to wax and wane over time—led to the concept of the political field. The structural-functionalists seemed to conceptualize politics as a one-set stage play; there might be hints of a wider world, but the action was confined within a coherent and specifiable environment. Process theorists tend to view politics more in the sense of a passion play: there is an ongoing coherence of plot, and the same actors and groups may participate continuously, but the action shifts from area to area over time. This would be the political field, a fluid area of dynamic tension in which political decision making and competition takes place. To return to our passion-play analogy, much of the action would involve broad scope and grandeur, but periodically the drama would narrow to a sharp focus on two or a few actors. Although these actors might be essential to the story line, their behavior could only be understood in relation to the wider setting. In this case, out of the whole field we would have chosen to concentrate our attention on one small arena.

Actually, the concepts of political field and political arena remain ill defined. Some writers use the terms interchangeably; others have very specific meanings in mind. F. G. Bailey (1969), for example, considers a political field as one in which the rival groups do *not* share agreed-on rules for regulating their conflict; he sees an arena as an area in which the same rules are accepted by the various competitors. Pragmatically, the very relativism of the two concepts is their primary virtue. A political field is nothing less, or more, than the wider area of political activity defined by a particular researcher, whereas an arena is an area within the field on which the researcher wants to concentrate at a particular moment. Although these concepts are quite relative, they need not be arbitrary; different field workers in the same society might choose to concentrate on different levels of political interaction, but they would probably have little trouble agreeing (to the extent that anthropologists agree on anything) on the boundaries of the various levels. The concepts of field and arena both allow and insist that the researcher precisely define that aspect of the social system that has been separated out as the unit of analysis.

Power

A Maori shaman cures meningitis through an infusion of *mana,* an invisible force into the body of his patient. A Cree Indian chief plans a wedding. A United States president unleashes a bombing of unprecedented scope on an impoverished Asian country. A Lugbara sorcerer invokes ghosts to inflict sickness upon a neighbor. An Aztec priest tears the living heart from a human sacrifice.

What these disparate actions have in common is that they all exemplify the use of power. In the first case, the shaman's power is impersonal and supernatural. The United States's war with Afghanistan was a case of the direct application of massive force by an advanced technological society. Among the egalitarian Cree Indians, planning a wedding is one of the few areas in which the chief is permitted to exercise authority and demonstrate his leadership. For the Lugbara, actual sorcery, as well as making accusations of sorcery and witchcraft, is a common means of manipulating public opinion to gain political support. Finally, for the Aztec, the priest became the servant of the enormous power of religious tradition.

Any concept that must encompass such a range of situations can hardly be defined in too narrow a fashion. (Postmodern concepts of power are examined in chapter 10.) For the process theorists, power does not come from physical force alone. During the Iranian revolution, the Shah had direct access to the best modern weaponry that the state's enormous oil riches could buy, as well as to an efficient police apparatus skilled in murder and torture; yet the real power belonged to the Ayatollah Khomeini, a fundamentalist Islamic holy man with neither weapons nor troops. Even in the United States, the President, who as Commander in

Chief of the Armed Forces commands great world power, may lose that power simply because his right to hold office has come into question, as the Watergate incident so aptly illustrated. This is not to say that power cannot exist independently of public support. The right to rule in many governments has been based on control of armies, secret police, and death squads. Any definition of power must include both that which relies on force and that which does not, that which derives from the individual and that which derives from a system or an office.

Ronald Cohen (1970: 31) defines power as "an ability to influence the behavior of others and/or gain influence over the control of valued actions." This is broad enough to include the gamut of our examples, but requires further distinction between private power (e.g., power exercised by a domineering father over his family) and public power, which is exercised in the political arena. It is the latter that is of interest to the political anthropologist.

Power may be independent or dependent (Adams 1973). Independent power is a relation of dominance based on the direct capabilities of an individual, such as special knowledge, skills, or personal charisma. Many North American and Oceanic societies conceive of power as an objective force inherent in individuals. Everyone possesses some of this force, but real power relationships come into being when one individual is recognized to have more of the kind that is needed for group decision making. At the band and tribal levels of political development such personal qualities will be the primary means by which one person gains influence over the group, an influence that is usually limited to arbitrating disputes or setting an example. In more centralized societies, independent power may become objectified and formalized, attaching to a particular office, no matter who holds that office; also, it may give rise to extremes of political domination, as is seen in the elaborate ritual and taboos surrounding the divine Inca, the ancient Hawaiian chiefs, or even the emperor of Japan. Although these examples may be foreign to American democratic values, in reality everyone is constantly assessing the power of those with whom they come into contact and adjusting their behavior accordingly, either through simple deference or through obedience to elaborate social rituals. Dependent power comes into existence when an individual with independent power—either by nature of personality, office, or both—lends another person the right to make decisions. This can be achieved in three ways: (1) an individual can grant decision-making powers to another, (2) a group holding power can allocate such rights to individuals, or (3) a group or individual can delegate such rights to a number of other people.

Another way to look at the concept of power is to separate that which is based solely or largely on force and coercion from that which is based on group consensus. Force alone is certainly effective in the short run as a means of political control, but if it is the only basis for the people's assent to be governed, the society will be extremely rigid. Talcott Parsons once compared force in a political system to gold in a monetary system: it is effective as long as it forms a basis for other systems, but day-to-day transactions require a lesser coin if the system is not to become so rigid that it cannot adapt to new conditions (Swartz, Turner, and Tuden 1966). The Cuban revolution of the late 1950s is a case in point. The Batista regime was so corrupt and brutal that it alienated the majority of people, including many from the upper and middle classes who would later oppose Fidel Castro as well. Because wealth was centered in a small elite and there were few methods for redressing popular grievances without threatening the system as a whole, Batista's main basis of support came from the Army. It is doubtful that Castro won the revolution in any military sense, because his own army never consisted of more than 2,000 men and he never succeeded in controlling a single province. However, the Batista regime had become so ingrown, so self-serving, and so alienated from the populace that it virtually collapsed under the weight of its own corruption. When Batista took his money and ran, the old system lacked resilience enough to form a new government; Castro, with the only major organized force in the country, simply stepped into the power vacuum.

A government may maintain itself through force: Stalin, Idi Amin, Trujillo, Papa Doc Duvalier, Pol Pot, the British in India and Africa—twentieth-century examples are, unfortunately, legion. If such a government is to have the flexibility to adapt to entirely new conditions, however, it must also possess consensual power that derives from the assent of the people. In state societies, such assent is not given to the wise and just alone; children, idiots, sadists, and lunatics may well be the beneficiaries of popular assent as long as they take office through established means of succession, such as being born into a kingship. Consensual power may, in fact, derive more from a grudging acquiescence to tradition than from respect—much less love—for those in positions of domination.

In states, consensual power is virtually always conjoined to centralized control of the use of physical force; thus, it may be difficult to tell whether one is consenting out of respect for the system or out of fear of being thrown in jail. Would I pay my full income tax if the government did not impose physical or economic sanctions? Perhaps not. Would I voluntarily pay some part of my salary to support roads, schools, welfare, police and fire protection, and other benefits of government even in the absence of sanctions? I like to think that I would. I would be hard pressed, however, to specify just how many of my tax dollars are calculated to keep me out of jail each year and how many go for support of a system that seems to provide me with certain benefits. In other words, within a state society, consensual power and power by force are so intertwined that there may be something artificial in separating them for analysis. However, the distinction provides a useful basis for evaluating governments both objectively and morally. Objectively, a government that possesses very little in the way of consensual power is too rigid to make the necessary adjustments to serve all of its people; morally, such a government would have little justification for continued existence.

In uncentralized, egalitarian societies, leaders do not usually have access to physical coercion, but must depend entirely on consensual power. This may mean little more than setting an example. In *The Feast,* one of Napoleon Chagnon's many films on the Yanomamo Indians of Venezuela, a village headman is shown alone on his knees scraping the ground with a machete in order to shame his neighbors into helping him clean up the village compound. Similarly, during my fieldwork among the Aymara of Peru, the community mayor had to work for three days, virtually alone, on roofing a public building before others slowly began to join the labor; by the fifth day, almost the entire community was involved.

In these examples, the benefits of following the leader were immediately obvious, but in many cases, a leader must get people to do something they do not want to do in the absence of foreseeable benefits. This may be especially true of a community leader working with a national government. The Aymara mayor mentioned above was, on another occasion, faced with the problem of implementing a census and questionnaire for the Peruvian Ministry of Education. The people were fearful that this information would be used to tax them or to cooperativize their privately held lands, and they knew the federal government could do nothing to punish them if they refused. The fact that they finally did assent to the questionnaire (and provided surprisingly accurate responses) suggests that they believed their mayor would use this cooperation in a long-term strategy to gain benefits—such as roads, schools, food aid, and a clinic from the government. It is this lack of specificity about the reasons for performing an action that sharply differentiates consensual power from power based on threat and differentiates legitimacy from coercion.

Legitimacy

Consensual power has the advantage of being free from specific sanctions and specific rewards, and it can therefore be employed in a wide variety of situations. People perform public duties because they trust either their leaders, or the system the leaders represent, to bring about general benefits over the long run. In the United States, it is probably true that no individual finds every president to his liking, and many may vehemently disagree with the policies of one president or another; but few would object to a president's right to hold office. In other words, a president's legitimacy depends not on the continuing support of the people (indeed, polls show that at some point a majority of the people might despise a given president), but on the legal process by which that person came into office. The president draws power from the Constitution, over two hundred years of history, and the belief of the American people (a belief into which they have been socialized since birth) that this particular form of government is better than the alternatives.

We might compare the situation in the United States with that of Bolivia, which at last count had undergone over 150 coups in as many years. A major reason for the instability of Bolivian governments, and for their periodic dependence on the most brutal repression to maintain power, is that there is very little basis in Bolivian society for the legitimacy of any government. In the absence of kingly succession, or any evident divine guidance, one government is about as good as another, and none can claim much right to rule. In such situations, if there is economic collapse or social unrest under democratic rule, it might be democracy itself and not a particular leader or political party that is called into question, and there might be widespread calls for a return to military dictatorship.

The legitimacy of power derives from the group's political culture—that is, the people's expectations about the nature of power and how it should be attained. For a Polynesian big man, legitimacy may be obtained by giving the largest pig feasts; for a British king, by being born to the proper lineage; for a prime minister, by having the controlling votes of the parliament; and for a nineteenth-century Cheyenne "chief," by being brave in battle in youth and wise in age. There are cases in which legitimacy does not derive from tradition at all, but is earned in a novel manner. A dictator who comes to power through rebellion or a coup might gain legitimacy by providing benefits to his people.

Legitimacy may, moreover, have very little to do with how power is actually used. Hitler was a legitimate ruler (he became dictator through a legal loophole in the enlightened Weimar constitution); so was Stalin. Masses of people may be sustained in subjection and poverty for literally hundreds of years under legitimate governments—witness ancient Egypt and Rome, or the despotic dynasties of China. As is learned again and again from European history, a king's arbitrariness and incompetence may not deter a devoted following if his claim to the throne is legitimate. On the other hand, dictators who have no legal or traditional claim to power will almost invariably try to legitimize their positions through orchestrating demonstrations of support, staging fraudulent elections, rewriting the constitution, or creating a parliament of sycophants.

Support

Legitimacy and coercion are opposite kinds of *support*, a term that has been defined by Swartz, Turner, and Tuden (1966: 10) as "anything that contributes to the formulation and/or implementation of political ends." If we consider that warfare, police arrests and intimidation, labor strikes, public speaking, voting, and simple persuasion are all encompassed in this definition, we can see that there is a continuum of supports that run the gamut from legitimacy to forceful coercion. Because support can be lost as well as gained, a government would be well advised to seek out and employ as many forms of support as possible. In analyzing a political group, one will find different supports operating in different areas and various political competitors trying to manipulate the various sources of support in their favor.

Support may be either direct or indirect. Even considering the anachronistic complexities of the electoral college, when I vote for a president in the United States, I am providing direct support. In England, however, one votes not for a prime minister but only for a representative of a certain party, so support for a given person as prime minister is once removed, or indirect. Similarly, an African village headman may try to sway his people directly by speaking out against an opponent, or he may do so indirectly by initiating a rumor that his opponent has been indulging in witchcraft.

Process, political field, power, legitimacy, coercion, and *support* are some of the primary conceptual tools that the post-structural-functionalists find useful to analyze political systems. Although these tools do not comprise a coherent philosophical school of thought, they do provide the means for analyzing a wide range of political systems.

SUGGESTED READINGS

Eisenstadt, S. N. 1990. "Functional Analysis in Anthropology and Sociology: An Interpretive Essay," *Annual Review of Anthropology* 19: 243–60. The author, a major figure in political sociology, outlines the major arguments against "classical" functionalism, and then offers a re-evaluation to bring functionalism into the 1990s. The article—which includes an extensive bibliography—reveals that functional analysis is still alive, although in a more sophisticated form than in the heyday of structural-functionalism.

Evans-Pritchard, E. E. *The Nuer* (Oxford, U.K.: Oxford University Press, 1940). The author sets out to discover how an African pastoral group that is totally lacking in government not only maintains continuity and cohesion but also rapidly forms a united military force when necessary. His analysis is hotly argued even to this day—perhaps the highest form of compliment for one of the foundational works of political anthropology.

Fortes, M., and E. E. Evans-Pritchard, eds. *African Political Systems* (Oxford, U.K.: Oxford University Press, 1940). This is the book that started it all. The eight ethnographic studies, all by big men of British anthropology, represent the high standards of fieldwork already attained during the 1930s. Special mention should be made of Max Gluckman's contribution on the Zulu, which already reveals the seeds of his later rebellion against structural-functionalism, and Evans-Pritchard's highly compressed summary of Nuer political organization.

Gluckman, Max. *Custom and Conflict in Africa* (New York: Barnes and Noble, 1956). The titles of the chapters—"The Peace in the Feud," "The Frailty in Authority," "The License in Ritual"—give a good idea of the author's fondness for paradox. Gluckman, founder of the Manchester School of social anthropology, believed that constant tension and conflict created a rough equilibrium. Although some writings from this period might now be relegated to the status of historical curiosities, Gluckman remains a jolly good read.

Swartz, Marc J., Victor Turner, and Arthur Tuden, eds. *Political Anthropology* (Chicago: Aldine, 1966). The introduction to this book provides an incipient philosophy and model for the process approach, and the book as a whole is a virtual manifesto against structural-functionalism. The articles are too diverse to fit neatly into the categories provided by the editors, but many are of high quality. Of special mention: Ralph Nicholas's "Segmentary Factional Political Systems"; Ronald Cohen's "Power, Authority, and Personal Success in Islam and Bornu"; and John Middleton's "The Resolution of Conflict among the Lugbara of Uganda."

Chapter 6

THE INDIVIDUAL IN THE POLITICAL ARENA: ACTION THEORY AND GAME THEORY

Two quite different lines of inquiry are implicit in the process approach. On the one hand, the breakdown of the domination of structural-functionalism freed anthropologists to widen the scope of their study of relatively uniform tribal societies to include complex nation-states. On the other hand, researchers could also shift their focus from the broad structural view of whole systems to the actions of individuals or small groups operating within those systems. The latter orientation came to be called action theory, a term derived from German sociologist Max Weber and applied to political anthropology by Abner Cohen (1974: 40–13).

As is true with so many theories, action theory was developed ex post facto by seeking out the common denominator of a wide variety of studies by authors who probably had little conception that they were part of a coherent new orientation. That common denominator was the focus on individuals and their manipulative strategies to gain and maintain power. The individual involved in this process might be a named person who was described with as much depth of characterization as one would find in a good novel, or he might be an abstraction: Political Man. In contrast to his close cousin, Economic Man, Political Man does not maximize wealth or profit, but rather power. Place two or more of these beings in the same arena (which is redundant, because it is their presence that in fact creates a political arena) and we have the personae for a *social drama* or, if one prefers, for a *game* in which various moves are restricted by rules and in which there can be but one winner at a time.

Chiefs among the Kwakiutl of the Northwest Coast of America maintained their power through hereditary titles, crests, and ceremonial privileges. Purchase of an expensive copper shield brought great prestige. Courtesy of the Library of Congress.

In this microcosmic setting, the crucial concepts include goal orientation, manipulative strategies, maneuvering, and decision making. However, individuals can never act alone in politics; they must seek followers, make alliances, and interact with other individuals in positions of either dominance or subordination. It is therefore impossible for anyone who studies politics to ignore groups. Action theorists tend to look at groups from the point of view of individuals and to emphasize groups—such as factions, cliques, and elites—that can best be understood in terms of face-to-face interactions.

THE SOCIAL DRAMA

One of the earliest studies to develop this orientation was Victor Turner's *Schism and Continuity in an African Society* (1957). Although in the line of Max Gluckman's Manchester School of anthropological theory, this work has several aspects that are unique. Instead of examining the whole group of the Ndembu of northern Rhodesia, Turner focuses on individuals as they pass through a series of crises (in Turner's terminology, social dramas). Each of these dramas is analyzed as the culmination of a long period of building tensions in which new power alignments and shifts of allegiance have been taking place.

For Turner, "the widest community of Ndembu is . . . a community of suffering"; and indeed his central antagonist, Sandombu, is a true tragic hero. In the first of a complex series of social dramas involving this man, who has ambitions to be headman of Mukanza village, Sandombu twice insults the village headman, Kahali, as a challenge to his authority. This results in a fierce dispute between them, each threatening the other with sorcery. Sandombu leaves for another village where a notorious sorcerer is supposed to live. A short time later, the insulted headman falls sick and dies. Sandombu is allowed to return to Mukanza, but there is sufficient suspicion to prevent him from replacing the headman, and a man from another lineage is chosen.

This train of events is deceptively simple. Sandombu's insult to Kahali was a breach of one of the deepest principles of Ndembu social organization—the authority of the elder generation over the younger. Furthermore, Sandombu was Kahali's sister's son, and succession from older to younger within the same lineage was looked on with disfavor. There were other reasons to put a check on Sandombu's ambitions. He was sterile and his sister was barren. This, in itself a sign of sorcery, had important implications; because the Ndembu are matrilineal and a leader must draw his strength from his kinsmen through the female line, the sister's lack of children would narrow Sandombu's basis of support. Also, his indiscriminate generosity—a function of his ambition—had brought in strangers who were threatening to the conservative villagers. Finally, rivals for headmanship had an obvious vested interest in accusing Sandombu of sorcery. The result was that the village's three most powerful lineages united in opposition to Sandombu.

For Turner, the norms and structures that had so interested the generation of the 1940s have become the social field, the background before which the real action takes place. Lineage systems, marriage rules, values, and behavioral norms are not unalterable realities, but rather are social idealizations subject to constant manipulation. For example, the norm regarding succession within the lineage was applied to Sandombu but not to Kosanda, who later succeeded his mother's brother as headman. Accusations of sorcery were used to justify the public consensus that Sandombu should not be headman; they were only secondarily the basis for such consensus. Thus norms and rules were not abjectly followed but were emphasized or de-emphasized according to a complex set of criteria.

Such an approach rests on certain underlying assumptions about the nature of society. Society is viewed as a field of forces in dynamic tension in which centrifugal and centripetal tendencies constantly pull against each other. When the tension between fission and cohesiveness becomes acute, a crisis develops, climaxing in the re-establishment of a temporary and unstable equilibrium. There is seldom a complete resolution of tensions; rather, the result is a readjustment of forces that lends more strength to one side and depletes the strength of the other. Along with Marc Swartz and Arthur Tuden (1966), Turner has elaborated this process into a diachronic model of political phase development in which a period of mobilization of political capital is followed by an encounter or showdown. The latter involves some sort of breach of the peace in which one party in the conflict attempts to openly challenge the other. This leads to a crisis—"a momentous juncture or turning point in the relations between components of a political field"—which in turn brings about counteracting tendencies as the social group marshals peacemaking forces to avoid complete cleavage of the two sides. Deployment of adjustive or redressive mechanisms may involve informal arbitration, legal machinery, or public ritual. Finally, there will be a restoration of the peace as the two parties either readjust to a new set of asymmetric power relations or schism entirely.

Although Turner's book was transitional and still grounded in the structural-functionalism of the 1940s (his stated goal was "to isolate the cardinal factors underlying Ndembu residential structure"), many of the ideas that would later coalesce as action theory were already evident. In Sandombu, Political Man is seen as a real-life individual, manipulating cultural rules, making choices, and developing strategies—in short, making goal-oriented decisions.

A major reason for focusing on individuals rather than on groups is that in the individual a number of different systems meet. A group may act out a single role at a particular time, but the individual always embodies conflicting roles, at once father and son, leader and follower, warrior and peacemaker. The individual thus expresses the contradictions that may be invisible in studies of groups.

GAME THEORY

An interesting and influential variation of action theory is the non-mathematical game theory developed by F. G. Bailey in *Stratagems and Spoils* (1969). Because this is one of the more comprehensive anthropological political analyses, it is worth reviewing in some detail. Bailey started this book after he became fascinated by the revelations emerging from the television interrogations of Mafia informer Joseph Valachi, which exposed not only a rational structure underlying organized crime but also a set of rules of the game by which mobsters fought and murdered one another in ongoing power struggles. Processes of leadership succession seemed to be nearly identical to those described by Frederick Barth (1959) in his game-theory analysis of the Swat Pathans of Pakistan. It seemed that "the edge of anarchy is fenced off with rules"; that no matter how amorphous a political system may be, political combat is regulated by a code of which the participants may or may not be consciously aware.

Each culture develops its own set of these rules of political manipulation. It is therefore possible to view politics as a competitive game with agreed-on rules and, equally important, an agreed-on goal. In a real sense, politics is this set of rules, for a struggle in which each party could make up rules along the way would simply be a fight. There are two types of political game rules: normative rules, which are publicly professed, usually vague (honesty, sportsmanship,and so forth), and according to which actions may be judged ethically right or wrong; and pragmatic rules, which have to do with the actual winning of the game, as opposed to public display. Bailey focuses on the latter, because the real question, as he sees it, is not whether an action is publicly approved, but whether it is effective. Competition takes place within a political field, which may be defined as a society or segment of society in which two or more rival political structures exist, but in which there is an absence of an agreed on set of rules between these structures. Within the political field are arenas in which teams that accept such rules attempt to build support for themselves and to undermine their opponents through subversion. Competition may not be confined to an arena but may move from one arena to another within the wider political field. Sometimes competitive groups within an arena might unite temporarily against an outside threat.

There are five major elements of political structure when it is viewed as a game. First, there must be prizes or goals, which are culturally defined and must be sufficiently valued by the participants to make competition meaningful. Second are the personnel involved in the conflict: this includes the entire concerned political community, the political elite (those entitled to compete), and the political teams involved in competition. The third element is leadership, which includes the individuals supported by a group of followers on the one hand, and those individuals who actually make decisions and settle disputes, and who may be quite different from the overt leadership on the other. Fourth is the competition itself, which is of two types: confrontation, or a move within the political arena that announces to an opponent one's strength in resources and one's possible intentions; and encounter, in which both contestants publicly agree to test their strength against each other. Finally, there are judges, who define the rules to be followed when one or another of the opponents breaks the rules.

Although Bailey emphasizes rules as essential to the game of politics, he notes that outright cheating or playing one set of rules against another are also part of the game. In the Watergate scandal that brought down President Richard Nixon, pragmatic and normative rules came into conflict. Spying on opponents has long been part of American party politics, and might even be considered legitimate within the pragmatic rules, but such behavior must be kept out of sight. When the attempted bugging of the Democratic headquarters surfaced, a Pandora's box of purely pragmatic actions emerged with it—an enemies list, dirty tricks played on Democratic candidates, tampering with evidence, and a cover-up conspiracy. None of this should have been particularly surprising to American voters, who as a group are fairly well imbued with a healthy cynicism toward politics. Perhaps even more damaging than the actual crimes was the revelation in the Watergate tapes of the appallingly petty and downright sleazy manner in which the most powerful men on earth were conducting business. With Nixon's resignation and the criminal conviction of his aides, normative values temporarily triumphed over pragmatic politics, even creating the temporary illusion that a government could be conducted by normative rules. Jimmy Carter ran for election on the basis of his high morality, and he even promised that he would never lie to the public. He lasted only four years.

Political Teams

Broadly speaking, there are two types of political teams: contract and moral. A contract team is one that is united, not by conscience, but by the profit or potential profit to be derived from following a certain leader. A relatively loose form of contract team is the transactional team, which is based largely on interchanges of a material nature—money, food, clothing, contracts, and licenses—so that the bond between leaders and followers is based strictly on perceived material benefit. In big man systems, such as those found in Polynesia, the leader must buy loyalty through loans and feasting. In a labor union, the leader's power may depend on his subordinates' perceptions that he can gain them more pay and health benefits than can his competitors within the movement. Because a leader's position may be based on face-to-face transactions with individual followers, and a leader would be well advised to avoid sharing his power for fear of creating a rival, such teams are extremely limited in size. The bureaucratic team, another form of contract team, avoids some of these difficulties. Here, leadership is allocated to a number of different functionaries, each with a specialized place in the hierarchy of power, so that the core leader can avoid any direct challenge. Such a group also has the advantage of being able to expand indefinitely, because it does not depend on personal interactions with one individual.

In contrast to teams in which loyalties depend on personal benefits, a *moral team* is united by a shared ethic: religious belief, nationalism, or a utopian political ideology. A leader in such a team pays the price of being rigidly confined within the normative values of the group, but a certain sense of security may also be derived from the knowledge that his followers will not shift to one who can offer better material benefits. The leader of a moral team may claim a monopoly on certain mystical attributes, such as access to the gods, which will effectively cut off opposition. For example, among the traditional Lugbara of Uganda, only the elders could use the power of the ancestor spirits, which prevented the younger generation from seriously challenging the elders' authority.

Whatever the type of team, a leader must fulfill certain functions: decision making, recruitment and maintenance of the group, and interaction with the world outside the team. Day-to-day decision making will follow the lines of normative or pragmatic rules, or a combination of both, so that real leadership is called for only in conditions of uncertainty.

In making decisions, the leader must always calculate the political expense, especially when normative rules cannot be routinely applied. The safest strategy in such cases is for the leader to make the decision that requires the smallest social adjustment possible. The least expensive decision will be consensual; that is, the leader gains prior consent and simply announces the decision of the group. However, attaining such consensus can be a long, difficult, and divisive process and might even suggest weakness in the leader. The most politically expensive form of decision making is simple command. The leader who knows the game would, of course, seek that middle ground in which he could assert power while maintaining maximum support.

Political Encapsulation

Over the long run, teams that regularly compete for power must be more or less equal in strength. Periodically, however, politics in one arena will spill over into another, larger arena in which one team will find itself encapsulated by a much larger political structure; neither the normative nor the pragmatic rules of either group will apply to the other. Three types of relations are possible in such cases. First, the larger structure may maintain only the most nominal relations with the smaller, especially if the cultures of the two groups are markedly different and the smaller group maintains a significant degree of power within its limited domain. During the colonial period in India, for example, there were large areas on the borders of China and Burma that were ignored by the British overlords except for paramilitary tours of inspection to maintain an illusion of control (however, British normative values were so offended by the practices of human sacrifice and infanticide among these people that they ultimately fought a 20-year war to subdue them). A second alternative is predatory encapsulation. At its most primitive, this is simply a national form of the gangster protection racket: as long as the weaker group pays its tribute, it will be left alone. A more sophisticated version is the indirect rule elevated to an art by the colonial British in Africa. Finally, the smaller group may be incorporated into the larger group through either radical change or abolition of the indigenous political, economic, and social structures. This has been tried periodically with the American Indians through processes of forced assimilation and detribalization, but it has failed because the values of the dominant and the subordinate groups have differed too radically for such incorporation to take place.

Whatever the process of encapsulation, middlemen will assume an important political role in mediating between the two structures. The success of a middleman depends on his ability to deceive, because a compromise will usually be possible only if each side is misrepresented to the other. As a result, these middlemen will be despised by both sides. This is evident, for example, in the use of the term *cholo* (which has a derogatory connotation) for an intermediary class of Indians who are between the peasants and the *mestizos* in highland Peru and Bolivia. *Cholos* are Indians who have left the land for jobs in trucking, contraband, and small-market sales, and who prefer to speak Spanish and dress in *mestizo*-style clothes. Although distrusted by the peasants—who consider them exploitive—and despised by the *mestizos, cholos* fulfill an important function in bridging two radically different cultures during a period of rapid acculturation.

The problem facing any encapsulated political structure is one of survival—how to maintain itself with a minimum of change within its changed environment. A moral team, especially one based on a religious ideology, might assume the fanatic's stance and vow to fight to the last man, woman, and child. Unfortunately, the more powerful group may be thoroughly unimpressed, in which case the encapsulated group will find itself forced to change. Bailey isolates three types of political change. *Repetitive change* is quite radical change that can take place within a wider equilibrium. All groups, for example, must face the problems of losing a leader, periodic war, famine, or flood. In such cases, normative rules and pragmatic rules, such as rules of succession, will be sufficient to bring the society back to normal. Whereas with repetitive change, there is no cumulative element—small changes do not necessarily add up to a fundamental change of structure—in *adaptive change* there can be no return to the original equilibrium. In this case, normative rules can be maintained, but the pragmatic rules will have to change to account for new conditions. When Plains Indian tribes were forced onto reservations, they were able to maintain most of their original culture and political values, even though their political situation had shifted from one of autonomy to one of abject dependence. In cases of *radical change*, both normative and pragmatic rules are irrevocably altered—as seen, for example, in the independence of the British colonies after World War II or the collapse of the Soviet Union.

FACTIONS

One of the direct outgrowths of the process approach in the late 1950s was an increasing focus on the role of temporary political conflict groups or factions. As long as equilibrium was considered the goal of social organization, factions were viewed as maladaptive. From the point of view of process theory, however, it was evident that in certain circumstances factions could be more adaptive than could conventional politics in organizing and channeling political conflict, especially during periods of rapid social change. Factionalism could even comprise the permanent politics of a group. Edwin Winkler (1970: 333) proclaimed the concept of faction to be "perhaps the most distinctively anthropological approach to the study of inputs to a political system." It was factionalism, in Winkler's view, that had refocused anthropology from its structural obsessions to a concern with how structural principles are manipulated. Naturally such enthusiasm required dampening. Janet Bujra (1973: 132) protested that factions and factionalism "are fashionable concepts enjoying a vogue which outstrips their present clarity of usage." In any case, faction seems firmly established in the anthropologist's lexicon and thus must ultimately face the same barrage of criticism as do terms such as tribe or segmentary lineage.

In contrast to ongoing corporate groups with fixed structural properties—such as political parties, lineages, clans, or secret societies—factions tend to be informal, spontaneous, leader-follower groups organized for a particular purpose and disbanding when that purpose is accomplished or defeated. They are primarily conflict groups organized in opposition to one or more other groups; thus, by definition, there can never be only one faction in a specific political arena. Because a faction leader draws support from any and all available sources, his following may cross-cut normal party, class, or caste lines, with the result that there is often a lack of ideological focus.

Within this broad definition, a number of different types of factions may be delineated. Common-parlance factionalism refers to temporary conflicts within formal political groups; for instance, within the Republican party before a national convention. In contrast, pervasive factionalism develops when external pressures cause the breakdown of normal political mechanisms. In such circumstances, unorganized and temporary factions may arise with little provocation (Siegal and Beals 1970). The phrase "segmentary factional political system" has been applied to groups in which factions constitute the dominant mode of political organization. Although cohesive, the potter caste in Govindapur village,

India, is not large enough to act as an effective political unit. It therefore serves its own interests by regularly aligning with one or another of the factions of the dominant caste. As with pervasive factionalism, this type is usually found in systems undergoing rapid change, in which rules of political conflict have become ambiguous (Nicholas 1965, 1966). On the other hand, types of political systems that are relatively stable may have factionalism as a virtually institutionalized form of decision making. This would be true, for example, of the traditional Ndembu or of modern Japanese government with its myriad fluctuating political parties.

Because factions are born and nourished in conflict, they cannot reach a point of even relative equilibrium and still maintain their status as factions. There are four possibilities: first, a faction may so decisively defeat its rival that it becomes legitimized and begins to organize itself as a formal group, while the defeated faction disappears altogether. Second, in states in which there is only one legitimate political party, as in communist China, factionalism may simply serve the functions of party politics. A third possibility is that factions within an arena may continue over time with neither side winning a victory, so that conflict itself becomes increasingly ritualized and gamelike. Finally, factions may be institutionalized as political parties (Bujra 1973).

POLITICAL SYMBOLISM

For Abner Cohen (1974) man is fundamentally two dimensional: he is both Man-the-Symbolist and Man-the-Political-Being, and these two functions are in constant and inseparable interaction. Power is no less than what is expressed in any relation of domination and subordination, and is therefore an aspect of *all* social relationships. To think of power in terms of physical force or coercion is to miss entirely the subtlety with which it is usually manifested, for in day-to-day transactions power is "objectified, developed, maintained, expressed or camouflaged" by means of symbolism. All symbolism—or virtually all—has a political component.

Directly political communication, no matter how eloquent, may not be particularly effective. A blatantly political speech is incapable of further elaboration or manipulation and may actually be divisive; the funeral of a statesman, on the other hand, resonates with unimpeachable and deeply felt meaning—a reaffirmation of cultural values, ideas of continuity and rebirth, and much more. Politics is thus most powerfully manifested in overtly nonpolitical institutions such as kinship, marriage and other rites of passage, ethnicity, and various group ceremonies.

If symbolism is virtually synonymous with culture, and if all symbolism is political, one might suspect that Cohen (1979: 81) has postulated that "political anthropology is nothing other than social anthropology brought up to a high degree of abstraction." This direct quote from Cohen is one for which he admits to having been widely criticized. Symbolism and politics would seem to be such wide-ranging concepts that they lose meaning, almost as though one were to resort to God as a primary element in scientific explanation. If this were truly so, Cohen would rate no more attention from his colleagues than so-called scientific creationists rate from evolutionary biologists. Fortunately, however, Cohen is quite capable of bringing these abstractions down to earth, defining them precisely, and demonstrating their application in specific incidents, as he has done in some insightful political ethnographies.

All symbolism is *bivocal:* it serves both existential and political ends. It is existential in the sense that it integrates the individual personality while relating that individual to his group. A painful puberty initiation ritual involving circumcision, for example, will be a powerful personal experience in which the child feels that he is in some way transformed, that his old self has been obliterated and a new, more adaptive self has been reborn in its place. At the same time, the ritual will be an opportunity for a lineage to come together to reaffirm its unity, for the mythology of origin to be reiterated, for decisions to be made, for leaders to present themselves, and for males to reaffirm their moral and physical domination over females, elders over young, and wise over merely strong. Although symbolism is largely unconscious and is virtually constant in every person's life, its political component is most clearly manifested in the compressed dramas of ritual and ceremony. A study of these within any particular group will reveal the location of power as well as how it is manipulated.

In *The Politics of Elite Culture* (1981), Cohen applied these general concepts to politics in a small African nation. Sierra Leone was then a nation state of about 2.5 million people, of which something less than 2 percent—nearly all of whom lived in the capital, Freetown—were Creoles who viewed themselves as the descendants of slaves emancipated by the British. They were not an ethnic group, a tribal group, or a class (many non-Creoles shared the same economic status), and their relation to slave ancestors was partly mythical, because their kinship system was sufficiently open that many had been incorporated who could make no claims to special ancestry. They possessed virtually no executive power in the state, lacked any access to physical force, and had only the most negligible role as businessmen or producers of tangible goods.

The Creoles were not only a closely-knit, ongoing group, however; they also controlled enormous political power within Sierra Leone. To understand how they accomplished this, Cohen examined the manner in which symbolism was used to create the mystique of eliteness and to legitimize that mystique outside their own ranks so that others would accept their claim to power.

Elitism is a way of life. People outside the group can be trained, through schooling or apprenticeship, in the technical and administrative skills necessary for government, but one can join the elite only through undergoing a long period of socialization. Elitism derives not from wealth or specific social functions, but from a vast and complex body of symbols including manners, styles of dress, accent, recreational activities, rituals, ceremonies, and a host of other traits. Skills and abilities that can be taught are conscious, whereas the great body of symbols that form true elitism are, by and large, unconscious.

Such symbols must serve a dual purpose: they must be at once particularistic, serving to unite the group and maintain its unique identity, and universalistic, legitimizing it as an agency of power to the great majority of outsiders.

The continuing existence of the Creoles as a separate group was constantly threatened. Most Creole wealth rested on property ownership in and around Freetown, and rising property values created a strong temptation to sell to outsiders. In addition, a former power base in the civil service was eroded as educated provincials competed for these positions. Although Creoles comprised 64 percent of all professionals—dominating the judiciary, medicine, teaching, and the clergy—they had already lost the niche they once held in business. To counter these challenges, the once loosely knit Creole elite had to create more formalized institutions and more intensive means of communication, and to increasingly emphasize ceremony and ritual.

Women always played a primary role in maintaining Creole separateness, mainly through the socialization of children in group symbols and values, and through the socialization of men in proper decorum. Equally important, women were the center of both family and kin networks (because men were more preoccupied with careers and male clubs) and were thus the pillars of a Grand Cousinhood that formed the underlying structure for the Creoles as a corporate group. This cousinhood involved dense networks of overlapping families, uniting each individual to many different families through participation in various ceremonials.

For men, Freemasonry provided an important means of group maintenance and a system of interpersonal communication. Although Freemasonry was not limited to Creoles, they comprised the majority of the 17 Masonic Lodges in Freetown, and held most of the upper positions. Frequent ceremonies, often of a costly nature, formalized and cemented group relations, and an enforced system of brotherhood encouraged the amicable settlement of misunderstandings among individuals. Freemasonry thus provided the setting for a group identity among men, and for individual face-to-face interaction.

All of these institutions not only served the particularistic ends of group maintenance, but also universalistic ends oriented toward the wider public. Women were involved in running a variety of associations, societies, clubs, and activities that were either partially or wholly devoted to public welfare. The Freemasons were also involved in public works projects; but more importantly, the Masonic Brotherhood provided a setting for wheeling and dealing and exchange of information among men who were responsible, either directly or indirectly, for national policy decisions. Thus, the same sets of institutions and symbols that united the Creoles into a closed group legitimized them as spokespersons for the public good.

This was true also of the various ceremonies and rituals that emerged from the five cults of the Creoles: the cults of the dead, of the Church, of Freemasonry, of family, and of decorum. Funerals, thanksgiving rituals, Masonic initiations, balls, marriages, and other social events were carefully orchestrated dramas—tightly defined and intensely meaningful actions set apart from the aimless meandering of the normal flow of daily life. Through such drama, private experience, such as marriage or the death of a loved one, was elevated to collective experience. For participants, such dramas were intensely tangible and immediate, but at the same time they connected the individual and group with the timeless motifs of male and female union, victory and defeat, and life and death. At every point, then, the acted symbol united the immediate and the timeless, the individual and the collective, the parochial and the national, the selfish and the giving, and the private and the public.

Although it was Cohen who was most responsible for introducing the term action theory into political anthropology, it is debatable whether his symbolic approach should be so classified. He does not analyze individual or even small-group action, except to provide examples for more general processes, and he is emphatic that individual decision making must not be unduly snatched from its cultural context to give an illusion of more freedom than really exists. On the other hand, it is perhaps Cohen more than any other person who broadened the scope of action theory by clarifying the symbolic field within which individuals act and which provides both the constraints and the raw materials for those striving for power.

SUGGESTED READINGS

Bailey, F. G. *Stratagems and Spoils* (New York: Schocken Books, 1969). Bailey's theory (summarized in the foregoing chapter) provides one of the few systematic models in anthropology for analyzing political systems. One important aspect of the theory is the explicit differentiation between the ideal political system and the real political system.

Barth, Frederick. *Political Leadership among the Swat Pathans* (London: Athalone Press, 1959). "In Swat, persons find their place in the political order through a series of choices." This simple observation and his supporting analysis placed Barth in the forefront of the reaction against purely structural studies that ignored individual decision making. As a result, this book and several journal articles on the Pathans of the Swat Valley in Afghanistan became the basis for Bailey's political game theory.

Cohen, Abner. *Two-Dimensional Man* (Berkeley: University of California Press, 1976). For Cohen, Man-the-Symbolist and Man-the-Politician are complementary and mutually reinforcing. In this work, Cohen presents his theory of the dialectical relationship between power and symbolism. The argument tends to become abstract; thus, it helps to read it in concert with one of Cohen's excellent ethnographic studies, such as *The Politics of Elite Culture* or *Custom and Politics in Urban Africa*.

Cohen, Abner. *The Politics of Elite Culture* (Berkeley: University of California Press, 1981). Cohen is at his best when applying his concepts of power and symbolism to the analysis of a specific group. This book is one of very few studies of a power elite that is based on participant-observation fieldwork. Although the subjects are the Creoles of Sierra Leone, one feels that this could just as well be a study of a United States elite.

Fogelson, Raymond D., and Richard N. Adams, eds. *The Anthropology of Power* (New York: Academic Press, 1977). Power is defined in an extremely broad (and not always political) sense in order to provide a common thread to tie together these 26 ethnographic studies and four theoretical articles. Of the latter, Richard Adams's evolutionary model of power is a significant contribution. One will also find excellent analyses of the concepts of *mana* in the South Pacific, *Wakan* among the Sioux, and shamanism among the Northwest Coast Indians.

Turner, Victor W. *Schism and Continuity in an African Society* (Manchester, U.K.: Manchester University Press, 1957). There are few books in political anthropology that deserve the status of classic; this is one of them. In many ways, this minute examination of power struggles within a single village of the Ndembu of northern Rhodesia is reminiscent of Chinua

Achebe's famous novel *Things Fall Apart;* here also is found the tragic overreacher, barred from the status and power he so desperately desires. In spite of Turner's scholarly presentation, Sandombu comes to life. The methodology is the case study or social drama, in which a few specific events are examined in detail.

Chapter 7

THE POWER OF THE PEOPLE: RESISTANCE AND REBELLION

Power is often portrayed as a top-down imposition by elites on under-classes, a matter of state monopoly of the legitimate control of violence, or the ability of those who control the means of production to force others to work for them. For poststructuralist French philosopher Michel Foucault (see chapter 10), power is a subtler thing, a force suffused through discourse and knowledge, implicit in all human relationships, a manner in which modern institutions surveille, discipline, and control. There is, however, also power at the bottom, and this power can be almost invisibly diffuse or brutally focused. The potential for naked vi-olence must always be a consideration for those who wish to hold the masses at bay. Violence, whether as an undercurrent of threat or as an explosion of killing, is only one of many instruments available to the poor and marginalized. Labor unions, peasant associations, political par-ties, and ethnic and nationalist organizations regularly seek means of exercising power, although often at a high cost and not always, or even usually, with success. Although structural-functionalists perceived such conflict as pathological to equilibrium systems, protest is increasingly viewed as normative.

A dominant theme in political anthropology has been how indigenous peoples have been crushed by state power. In books such as *Assault on Paradise* (Kottak 1983), *Victims of Progress* (Bodley 1982), and *Victims of the Miracle* (Davis 1977), the emphasis has been on the exploitation

Sugar cane production in the West Indies, from *The Graphic* magazine in 1876. Recent anthropological research suggests that workers and peasants do not passively submit to domination, but resist in subtle but effective ways. Courtesy of the Library of Congress.

or destruction of tribal cultures. With the rise of the world-system perspective during the 1970s, the detrimental effects of colonialism became almost de rigueur in any study of native politics. It would be almost unconscionable to speak of the American Indians without mentioning their oppression by European conquerors. The underlying assumption, usually tacit, has been that the underclasses could do no more than submit, or that they alternated between rebellion and passiveness. This is a legitimate perspective in many cases. However, anthropologists increasingly pay attention to the ways in which people fight back, nonviolently or violently, with whatever weapons they have at their disposal.

EVERYDAY RESISTANCE

In the United States during the Civil War, the Confederate army lost nearly a quarter of a million qualified whites to avoidance of conscription and to desertion. Although certainly not the major reason for the South's defeat, this was an important contributing factor (Scott 1985: 30). In Iran, the nonviolent refusal by Muslim fundamentalists of the Westernization programs imposed by the Shah created a climate and structure that helped to bring about the Shah's fall from power (Skalník 1989: 14). Among the Lusi of New Guinea, and in many other societies, revenge suicide was an effective political strategy by women who were otherwise utterly powerless; suicide could mobilize support and direct community action against the woman's oppressor (Counts 1984). Throughout the world, despite attempts by powerful state governments to force assimilation, ethnic groups have been able to maintain and even strengthen their cultural identities (Castile and Kushner 1981).

These are all examples of what political scientist James Scott calls *Weapons of the Weak* (1985).

Although the state claims a monopoly on the legitimate use of force, if power is defined as the ability to affect the decisions and actions of others, then there are many forms of power available to the people at the bottom of the state hierarchy. Some of these forms of power may be individual, as in hiding from military conscription or deserting an army; or they may be well organized, as in Gandhi's or Martin Luther King's nonviolent protests.

Pierre Clastres, in his *Society against the State* (1977), sees this type of power, disseminated among the people, as actually preventing state formation in tribal societies and chieftainships. In nonstate societies in times of war, a strong leader may come to the fore, but in peacetime the very structure of kinship-based systems prevents any single person or elite group from assuming dominance. There is a constant pull back from the temptation of state formation. A Tupinamba chief in Brazil might be unchallenged during times of war, but in peacetime would be carefully supervised by a council of elders. Geronimo spent 30 years trying to become the sole leader of the Apache but failed; as a young man he was given authority to lead a revenge attack on a Mexican garrison, but once that revenge was accomplished, despite his military renown, he had a difficult time getting others to follow him on what was perceived as a personal quest. The Apache would allow no man to lord it over them. As Clastres puts it, "the history of peoples without history is the history of their struggle against the State" (p. 186).

However, once the state is there—and virtually all indigenous peoples today live in imposed states that they had little or no part in forming— new strategies for cultural survival and individual autonomy must be developed. Peter Skalník (1989: 9–11) lists some of these strategies. If a group has a valuable resource at their disposal—as did the eighteenth-century Cree Indians, who had furs—they can force a reciprocity on the conquering power, demanding gifts and special treatment. Another tactic is to collaborate with the state and actually use the state's own policies against it—as did the Malaysian *negris,* who accepted British-imposed party politics and then created pro-*negri* parties that prevented the co-lonial power from carrying out its policies. If an indigenous group is powerful enough, or far enough from the centers of state power, it may be left alone and the people may go about their business as though they were not even part of a state. A fairly drastic strategy is to avoid the state by moving away from the sources of oppression; the Old Believers in revolutionary Russia moved to China, then to Brazil, then to the United States, and finally to Canada in search of freedom from perse-cution. People might wait a generation or two; once state pressures for assimilation have waned, they can return to traditional ways, often with a vengeance, as many Blackfoot Indians did when they resumed the once-banned Sun Dance religion. The power of people against the state may be on a much more massive scale. In his international best-seller *The Other Path* (see chapter 9), Hernando De Soto (1989) shows how the Peruvian economy became dominated by an informal and illegal economy of squatter housing, gypsy transportation, and black-market exchange.

EVERYDAY RESISTANCE IN MALAYSIA

The phrase "peasant resistance" is more likely to conjure up images of violent and bloody uprisings—such as the Tupac Amaru II rebellion in Peru or the Chinese revolution—than villagers sitting around the local bar gossiping about a stingy landlord. However, according to James C. Scott in his book *Weapons of the Weak* (1985), it is this latter form of protest that is the most common and, perhaps, the most successful, given the failure rate of revolutions and the repression that inevitably follows such failure. Such resistance is an ongoing, everyday process through which the peasantry struggles against exploitation by pilfering, lying, foot dragging, slander, minor sabotage, and arson. Resistance may be more or less organized, but it is not linked to any wider political movements or ideologies. This runs counter to the more commonly held view of peasants as alternating between mindless eruptions of violence and passive acceptance of their fate; peasants have never really been quiescent, but their protest may take place, almost unnoticed, day in and day out.

Malaysia has been one of the Third World's more successful examples of export-led economic development, with rapid increases in gross national product and in per capita income. As is normal in such processes, progress was paid for at the cost of a growing maldistribution of wealth and income. Between 1960 and 1970, the incomes of the rural poor declined, while the rest of the people were moving ahead. In the next decade, the poor showed a modest recovery of about 2.4 percent a year, but because their incomes were starting at such a low base level, the real increase was almost negligible. By the early 1980s, 44 percent of the rural population lived below Malaysia's already low official poverty line. There was no suggestion of significant restructuring of property relations to solve the problem of the poor; rather, the government turned to the soft options of providing roads, schools, clinics, piped water, electricity, mosques, community halls, and resettlement schemes.

Sedaka, a community of 70 families, was affected by a massive irrigation project that opened the area to green revolution inputs, resulting in the double-cropping of rice, in which only one crop a year had been possible before. Although this did not lead to a significantly greater concentration of land, as was the case in Latin America and India, those who already had large landholdings were in the best position to take advantage of the innovations. Only the well off were able to obtain government aid and loans, which never needed to be repaid if one belonged to the Farmer's Association and the dominant political party. Wealth and power increasingly accrued to the already wealthy and powerful.

Traditional rice growing is very labor intensive. The four stages—land preparation, transplanting, reaping and threshing—must be done by hand. The landless and land poor relied heavily or entirely on wages provided by paddy work. However, tractors and combines took over most of this labor. Because of the increased value of the land, tenants without the capital to invest in green revolution technology were displaced, and rents on land rose considerably. The predictable result was that the rich got richer while the poor suffered the dual loss of access to the means of production and of lost work and income. The poor were also faced with surrendering what little status and dignity they previously had, as they became more dependent on loans and charity from the rich.

In this rapid process of agricultural capitalism, a new ideological system consonant with the new political economy had not yet emerged among the wealthy or the poor. To be sure, the earlier system had been exploitive, but it was based on a bond of mutual dependence between the landowners and their tenants and workers. Now—except for the transplanting process, which was still done by hand, mainly by women— there was little need for human labor, and often it would be more profitable for tenants to relinquish their claims on the land. In other words, the poor were no longer needed by the wealthy. However, the wealthy had to continue living in a community where everyone knew everyone else; they had to not only maximize profits, but also try to gain and retain status and leadership in a setting in which they no longer had structural claims on the larger part of the population.

The situation was potentially explosive. Early on it almost did explode: combines were sabotaged and even burnt, and there was a brief, and ultimately futile, attempt at a boycott by women transplanters. However, there existed many constraints against this type of direct confrontation, not the least of which was the atmosphere of routine repression that pervaded Malaysia. An Internal Security Act provided for preventative arrest and proscribed some types of protest. There had been large-scale police roundups following demonstrations. More locally, and more subtly, violent confrontation was prevented by the complex and overlapping class structure and by webs of kinship, friendship, and patronage that tied together all segments of the community. Also, the green revolution changes emerged over a period of decades, so there was no single point at which resistance would have been naturally mobilized. Finally, the problem was not one of direct exploitation, which would have made it easier to find a common enemy—a common target of protest—but rather that the poor were simply removed from the productive process.

To understand how the class struggle took place, we must look at it through the eyes of the participants and within the particular ideological context. Scott (1985) defines class resistance as any act by the poor intended to advance its own claims or to mitigate claims by a superordinate class. Such resistance is designed to prevent competition among the poor for jobs, land, and loans. It carefully avoids direct confrontation with the rich and is always couched in a language of deference and conformity (although seldom cringing, because the poor person's claim to status is also at stake).

The poor could humiliate the rich through malicious gossip, inventing derogatory nicknames, or by boycotting a feast or only showing up for a brief time. The refusal of loans or of charity, a prime value of Islam, would be the occasion for accusations (never made to the offender himself) of stinginess, arrogance, or conceit. This led to a euphemizing of relations between rich and poor, in which direct transactions were nearly always hiding something, virtually always inauthentic. The wealthy man universally known among the poor as Haji Broom, because he "swept up" all the land in his path, was never called such to his face. An employee who thought himself underpaid would thank his employer but quickly spread his complaint among family and friends. When asking for a loan or for charity, the poor always used a verb that suggested that what they sought was their moral right.

There were more concrete forms of resistance, of course. When threshing, one could fill up the sacks faster—important in piecework—if each bundle was not beaten enough to get all the rice out; this forced the owner to observe the process every minute. When working in waterlogged fields, not amenable to combines, one could always threaten to walk off the job if the wages were too low. There was constant grumbling and negotiating for higher wages and endless complaints that the paddy in which one was working was too deep in water or that the grain was immature. More to the point, thievery from the wealthy was normative, despite the smallness of the community. Fruit from trees, gunnysacks of rice, chickens, water cans, bicycles, water buffalo, and even motorcycles were stolen. Resistance might also be expressed by killing the livestock of the rich after claiming that they were getting into crops or storage facilities.

Routine resistance was maintained by an imposed mutuality or sanctioned solidarity among the poor. There was an unspoken agreement not to undercut each other in demands for wages or to offer higher rents for land. Competition was prevented among the poor by sanctions such as gossip, character assassination, ostracism, the threat of being excluded from information networks about jobs and credit, and the subtle threat of violence.

Scott's analysis is contrary to Marx's attribution of peasant quiescence to mystification or false consciousness, emerging from the elites' domination of the symbolic, as well as physical, means of production. Marx believed that elite control of the media and other means of communication brainwashed the exploited into assuming elite values. Looked at from the point of view of the actors themselves, this is not true; the rich and poor see the world very differently. The poor view themselves as being pushed down by the rich. The rich perceive themselves as being generous and kind, doing what they can for the poor while still earning a living. There is, to be sure, a moral context of village life, which is a common set of expectations about class relations and about individual behavior. This moral context, however, is used by the poor to intimidate the rich, just as much as it is used by the rich to legitimize their power.

Far from being brainwashed, the peasants of Sedaka were aware of the limitations of their power, which was precisely why they resorted to routine resistance rather than revolution. There was no use attacking modern capitalism, which was the real cause of their plight. Basic structures are notoriously difficult to change. Individual capitalists, however, could be attacked, although only behind a facade of deference and conformity.

SPHERES OF POLITICS

One reason that the British were so successful for so long in their colonial project was that they implicitly understood the importance of keeping spheres of politics separate, allowing the colonized people a political space within which traditional ideas of hierarchy and legitimacy could be practiced. The technique was to leave intact existing local systems as long as such systems were not seen as threatening, adding a layer of administration at the top while leaving a broad political space for the local headmen, chiefs, rajahs, princes, or sheiks. Colonizers— such as Belgium or Spain, which attempted a more total domination— found themselves fighting endless wars and paying the exorbitant cost of power by force alone.

This is not a strategy open to the masters alone; local peoples have often found that they could create a separate sphere of power for themselves with or without the approval of the official government. When the Indian Reorganization Act of 1934 required U.S. tribes to adopt constitutions and democratic governments at odds with the elder-based consensus politics of tradition, many tribes created such formal governments merely as window dressing, voting in people with no leadership abilities or political followings, while at the same time maintaining informal governments that actually exercised power. While traveling with Sandinista political organizers in the peasant highlands of Nicaragua in 1981, I noticed that at democratic meetings the real leaders were observing from the back row, subtly passing signals about who was to be nominated for each official position; it was clear that they would continue their informal leadership once the organizers had left. This ability of people to stake out spheres of limited control within broader formal structures of power has been undertheorized by political anthropologists.

Parallel Politics in Micronesia

The politics of the island of Ponape in Micronesia, as described by Glenn Petersen (1989), reveals how two noncompetitive political systems can exist side by side, and how the assertion of traditional values can moderate colonial influences. Ponape, like the other islands of Micronesia, experienced a long history of foreign rule. After a half-century of off-and-on contact, the island became a colony of Spain in 1886, followed by various degrees of subjugation by the Germans, Japanese, and finally Americans. During World War II, the islands were occupied by the United States and after the war became part of the U.S. Trust Territory of the Pacific Islands. Micronesia remained a trusteeship of the United States from 1947 until 1986, when it assumed free-association status with the United States.

During the long period of external rule, the official political structure imposed on Ponape represented centuries of historical development in Europe and the United States, and bore little relation to the indigenous political culture of the island. Although U.S. rule was not particularly heavy-handed, it did tend to be autocratic because it was based on the absolute authority of the state and on a hierarchy of power similar to the hierarchy of municipal/state/federal authority in the United States. The imposed government of Micronesia consisted of a wide array of appointed and elected individuals and groups—governor, executives, a state legislature with elected representatives, legislative committees, courts, departments, agencies—each with its arena of power and each under the control of a higher officialdom. In addition there was a constitution, charters, and legal codes, all based on abstract principles of government and law.

The traditional Ponapean chieftainship system also recognized hierarchy, but only in close conjunction with a contrary trend toward individual autonomy. Chiefs, who assumed their positions through ranked lineages, could not rest on their inherited statuses, but had to continually maintain their positions through a ceaseless round of feasting in which great quantities of food were redistributed to the community. At a feast, a chief was seated on a raised platform. He presented gifts to other chiefs according to their rank, which they in turn distributed among kin, friends, and followers. Because the yams, kava, pigs, and community service that bestowed status were not in scarce supply, authority did not inhere in the control of such resources but rather in the ability to produce and distribute them. Chieftainship was earned and maintained through social skills, resourcefulness, and hard work.

The ritual predominance of the chiefs did not translate into a predominance of power. The five paramount chiefs, representing the five municipalities, supposedly ruled through the section chiefs, but in reality there was little ruling to be done. Most aspects of life were thoroughly routinized. Special projects were organized by section chiefs, who could demand community participation, but if the project was too onerous, the section chief would simply be ignored. Most chiefly decision making revolved around organizing and supplying rituals and celebrations, but even then the threat of ostracism or ridicule by the community was a stronger sanction than was chiefly commands. A generous chief could expect cooperation, but only within limits. Although social and political hierarchy was firmly embedded in the culture, it was hierarchy without coercive power. In a sense, the locus of authority was the community itself.

How was this traditional system maintained in a colonial situation, when the colonial concept of hierarchy and power was so totally different? The traditional system survived mainly because it was confined to the sphere of community decision making, ritual, ceremony, and status, with which the imposed electoral/bureaucratic system did not involve itself. The chiefs did not make decisions or try to enforce compliance with regard to modernization: schools, roads, public health, and export agriculture. In other words, there were two spheres of politics, each with its own hierarchy: a traditional sphere of face-to-face politics based in personal relations, and a colonial sphere of impersonal, legalistic politics based on abstract principles.

The two spheres were not entirely distinct. Many Ponapean natives achieved office within the bureaucracy and identified with the imported values. Although they might consider the old ways illogical and inefficient, they remained a part of that culture. Similarly, the people themselves had no trouble functioning within the European political culture when that was practical.

COOPTING THE CONQUERER

Cooptation is one of the most irresistible of political tools. Instead of fighting the opposition, the government absorbs it. The Inca would bring local leaders of conquered communities to the capital, Cuzco, teach them the Quechua language, train them in administration, and send them back home with new official titles and even more power than they had before. Almost all colonial powers depended on some form of cooptation, elevating local chiefs and giving them special privileges.

Cooptation, however, is not just a tool of the powerful. After 1000 A.D., the Toltec expanded into the Yucatan, conquering the Mayan city of Chichen Itza, but the conquerors were gradually absorbed; it is Maya, not Toltec, that is spoken in the region today. In the following example of Nicaragua, cooptation is seen moving both ways: first the revolutionary Sandinista government attempted to absorb people down to the neighborhood level through a process of populist corporatism, but ultimately the organizations that were taken over or formed by the state changed function, excluding the state and assuming only the interests of the local people.

Local-Level Power in Nicaragua

Corporatism is a model of the state in which the government functions through a limited number of monopolistic interest groups that are recognized and sometimes created by the state itself. It is based on the idea that individuals gain their rights, their identities, and their privileges through group membership. Corporatism is often contrasted with *pluralism,* with its emphasis on the individual voter and its articulation of power via innumerable competing interest groups, such as unions, political parties, and lobbies. Corporate groups do not operate in such a laissez-faire political environment. There is only one interest group in each major occupational, vocational, or social category: factory workers, large-scale agriculturalists, or cattle ranchers. Each organization speaks for all of its members and, ideally, the government makes policy affecting that group only after close consultation with its leadership.

Although corporatism was widely proclaimed at the turn of the century as *the* system of the future, the two most notorious corporatist examples in Europe—fascist Italy and Nazi Germany—did not exactly inspire emulation. However, the corporatist model, imported from Spain and Portugal, firmly took root in Latin America, where it was distinctly elitist, providing the wealthy sectors of society and sometimes urban labor with inputs into government while excluding the masses of poor. Two countries made significant, if ultimately unsuccessful, attempts to use the corporatist model to integrate the poor: Peru under the Velasco regime (1968–1976) and Nicaragua under the Sandinista National Liberation Front (FMLN).

The Sandinistas, who ran Nicaragua from the ousting of the Somoza dictatorship in 1979 until their electoral defeat in 1990, were self-proclaimed Marxists, although the state they actually created borrowed heavily from Iberic-Latin corporatism. Mass organizations, some pre-existing from the previous era of the dictatorship of Anastasio Somoza and others having evolved out of the violent revolutionary struggle, were integrated into the government from the outset. The original colegislative body, the Council of State, included six officially recognized corporatist groups, such as the Rural Workers Association, the National Union of Farmers and Ranchers, and AMNLAE, a women's organization. The largest of these groups, and thus the one to be awarded the most seats on the council, was an umbrella organization comprised of 15,000 Sandinista Defense Committees (CDS) with nearly 600,000 members.

Unlike other governing political parties in Latin America, the Sandinistas drew their support from the underclasses. Thus, the CDSs were seen as "the primary and elemental connection between our people and the revolution." The groups were hierarchically ordered by block, neighborhood (barrio), zone, region, and nation. At each level, leaders were chosen by vote, with block members in voting neighborhood leaders, neighborhood representatives voting in zonal leaders, and so on. The task of the CDSs was to oversee virtually every aspect of neighborhood life. In a study of the San Benito CDS in the town of León, between March and December 1984 alone, the organization was involved in 3 censuses, 15 mass demonstrations, 2 vaccination campaigns, 3 military recruitment campaigns, 3 voluntary work brigades, plus registration and election campaigns. This was in addition to regular meetings and routine "revolutionary vigilance," which involved nightly patrols to reduce crime and keep an eye out for saboteurs and spies. In addition, the FSLN attempted, without much success, to merge the informal and formal sectors of the economy by establishing a network of retail organizations that sold goods at state-established prices, which were often considerably lower than peasants could receive by selling on the open market (Ekern 1998).

Built into the system were opportunities for corruption, especially given the low levels of training and education of the leaders. Licenses to run local government-subsidized food stores were handled by the CDSs, as were guaranty cards, distributed to each family to ensure access to low-cost staples such as sugar and rice. Licenses and guaranty cards could be withheld for political or personal reasons or could be illegally sold. As early as 1982, one of the top Sandinista commanders sent a letter to all CDS coordinators condemning such abuses. However, the lack of regularly scheduled elections made it difficult to get rid of bad leaders.

Nevertheless, a study of five such organizations in Estelí (Lewellen 1989b) suggested that problems of corruption were not as severe as often believed. The real problems—the problems that led to the dissolution of the CDSs—had more to do with the structure of the system itself than with corruption. Although ostensibly conceived as the representatives of the masses to the government, the CDSs quickly became the representatives of the government to the masses. Instead of demands flowing up, demands flowed down, so that local members found themselves constantly involved in doing unpaid work for the government and in implementing government policy that they had little part in deciding. This was especially true as the U.S.-supported contra invasion increased in intensity. Between 1983 and 1987, national defense became virtually the entire focus of activity, to the detriment of projects of purely local value. This could be justified as long as the country was under attack. However, the contras were effectively defeated on the battlefield in 1987 when the bulk of fighters were driven out of Nicaragua (bloody harassment incursions run across the border from Honduras continued for three more years). With the cooling down of the war, people wanted more autonomy and more focus on local needs, but the existing CDS structure would not permit it.

The people fought back in a very simple manner: they stopped participating. It is doubtful that there was ever any significant organized opposition at the grassroots level. Rather, interest flagged as people were unable to see the results of their efforts on their own lives. In cases in which government depends on voluntary compliance, refusal to participate can be an extremely powerful weapon. This was not the only weapon, of course. Because the organizations were democratic, voting and complaining were equally employed. In one meeting of CDS coordinators in Estelí, 15 minutes were spent discussing local achievements and four hours were spent complaining about failures.

The result was that the local CDSs were officially dissolved, starting in 1988 (notably two years before the elections that ousted the Sandinistas). They did not disappear, however, at least not most of them. Instead, they gradually became Communal Movements, often changing function before changing title, which were not tied to the Sandinista party and which had no obligations to any higher body, including the government. Their tasks were entirely local—health, roads, sewage, education, electricity, water, and care of orphans and war widows. In many communities, the reorganization was welcomed by a resurgence of participation. Because they were no longer associated with a particular political party, many of the Communal Movements continued after the Sandinista electoral defeat in 1990.

The CDS experiment revealed three structural contradictions of any corporatist attempt to integrate the masses into the political processes. First, is what might be called the contradiction between *verticality and horizontality*. The state, which represents a broad alliance of interests, will constantly attempt to impose a structure of top-down control, whereas the people themselves want autonomy. A second, closely related conflict, is that of *national interest versus local interest*. Organizing military conscription, local militia training, handling rationing, and store licensing can be onerous for people who lack such basics as electricity and running water. People may identify with national interests in a crisis or for a brief time, but ultimately local needs will prevail. Finally, there is a conflict between *elite leadership and popular leadership*. Although the CDSs were supposedly open to everyone, in reality the leadership came from members of the FSLN. This led to much nonparticipation by those who were unsympathetic to the Sandinistas. It is notable that these conflicts were ultimately resolved in favor of the neighborhoods, not the state.

Despite their many problems, the CDSs were a necessary precursor to the Communal Movements. It is doubtful that local-level organizations would have been formed on such a scale without initial direct government involvement.

VIOLENCE: WHEN EVERYDAY RESISTANCE FAILS

For structural-functionalists, violence is seen as a disruption in equilibrium systems, a pathological state demanding a restoration of normality. However, for many societies, violence is normal, a part of the social structure and self-definition of a people; groups such as the Yanomamo are virtually always in a state of war. Different societies perceive violence so differently that it "cannot be regarded as a thing-in-itself, as an ideal-typical act, an inherently meaningful sociological condition or category of behavior, which is directly investigable; it cannot be defined as abnormal or pathological, or as any one thing at all" (Rapport and

Overing 2000: 382). At the level of the common man living in state societies, violence may often be perceived as the last or the only means of addressing abuses of power. Violence is usually represented in outbursts with defined beginnings and endings, as in riots or state-to-state warfare. However, violence may also be a long-term strategy of either those holding power or those resisting power, as has been evident in the Israeli-Palestinian conflict and in the Protestant-Catholic conflict in Northern Ireland (Schroeder and Schmidt 2001: 14–15). Historically, wars, insurrections, riots, and political killings have been so numerous as to achieve a degree of statistical normalcy. On a global or continental basis, each era seems to emphasize certain types of violence and not others; peasant rebellions, so prolific in the past, are becoming rare as peasants multiply their subsistence strategies and assume other means of protest such as street demonstrations and unionization (Edelman 1999). Cross-border wars for the purpose of expanding territory are fewer today than at any time in the past. On the other hand, terrorism, drug-related violence, and ethnic conflict are on the rise, often taking the form of virtually demilitarized low-level wars utilizing handguns, machetes, or suicide bombs. Much of this is what Richard Robbins (2002: 311–36) terms "antisystemic protest"; that is, protest against the globalization of capitalism, which increases inequalities in both power and wealth and threatens to marginalize large sectors of Third World states.

Within the United States, violence has been an integral part of history since the earliest permanent settlement at Jamestown. Much of this violence has been racial or ethnic, as is revealed in the following analysis of a little-known uprising in Texas.

The *Plan de San Diego* Insurrection

On May 18, 1912, in the town of San Diego, Texas, Charles Gravis and three other men armed with rifles waited in a Buick touring car outside of the Duval County Courthouse. Don Pedro Eznal, a local rancher and political leader of Mexican Americans in the region emerged and was immediately confronted by Gravis. When two of Eznal's friends saw what was happening and ran to help, shots rang out and all three Mexican Americans lay dead in the street. The Anglo killers were quickly arrested, but the trial was moved to a more hospitable environment near the Louisiana border where all were acquitted two years later. The situation seethed for another four years, until 1918 when a Mexican American separatist insurrection raged across southern Texas, leaving scores dead.

As analyzed by anthropologist Candelario Sàenz (1999), whose grand-parents had been intimately involved in the conflict, the *Plan de San Diego* rebellion had its roots in the last decades of the nineteenth century. By the 1880s, Duval County was the center of a prosperous wool in-dustry, largely of Mexican Americans. The Wool Tariff Act of 1867 had been designed to protect wool production in the East, but it was much more successful in encouraging sheep ranching in south Texas, where land was widely available, labor was cheap, and profits were high for ranchers and merchants who were protected from competition across the border. A "structure of peace" ensured that there was little of the ethnic conflict that was endemic over much of the region, often resulting in an American version of ethnic cleansing. Although the wealthier Mexican Americans might claim authority among their own people, formal power was in the hands of a small minority of Anglo Protestants. In 1888, a united faction of Catholic Anglos and Mexican Americans made a suc-cessful challenge at the polls, but the results were thrown out on fraud-ulent grounds. A rough equilibrium was established in which the Mexican American community was allotted its sphere of informal poli-tics, while Anglos maintained their hold on formal offices. This did not mean that Mexican Americans were quiescent, but rather that their power was directed elsewhere. In 1891, Catarino Garza led a revolutionary force of 600, recruited from the San Diego area, against the Mexican dictator Profirio Diaz. The ragtag army routed the Texas Rangers sent to stop them, and the revolution only collapsed when the Third U.S. Cavalry was called in to defeat Garza's forces.

Around the turn of the century, the wool industry began to decline. Reductions in tariffs brought wool by steamship from Australia, New Zealand, and Argentina. As foreign competition weakened the economic power of Mexican American ranchers, they became sufficiently vulner-able that they could be attacked. In 1908, the wool market collapsed completely. The courthouse shootout was the opening barrage in what would briefly become all-out war. Realistically perceiving the murders as an attempt to completely disenfranchise the Mexican American com-munity, the ranchers and wool merchants were not about to give in to their complete political subjection.

On February 1, 1918, the Texas *Brownville Herald* reported that a document called the *Plan de San Diego* had been found in the possession of a young Mexican American. The document, which turned out to be authentic, called for a violent revolution to begin on February 20. A wide region of the Southwest would renounce theUnited States and de-clare its independence. Non-Anglos—Mexicans, African Americans, Indians, and Japanese—would be incorporated into the new nation, but all Anglos over the age of sixteen would be killed. The slogan, "Equality and Fraternity," and the insurrection's red flag bespoke of communist and anarchist influences and led early historians to assume that Mexican Americans, who were considered illiterate and stupid, could not have written the document; it must have been composed by Europeans. In reality, it was written in a bar in San Diego by a group that conspired there on a regular basis.

The target date came and went without incident. By summer, however, the insurrection was flaming across southern Texas. Ranches were attacked, railroad bridges were blown up, and trains were attacked. Retaliation by Anglo posses and by the Texas Rangers was even bloodier than the revolt. Mexican Americans were shot on sight. Protestants also turned their wrath against Anglo Catholics. When Federal troops were finally brought in, it was more to protect the Mexican American community than to subdue it.

Sàenz's personalized ethnohistory has a familiar ring today when ethnic violence and counterviolence has become almost normative throughout much of the world. Like so much contemporary conflict, "this violence was played out against the rhythms of global capitalism. When the ethnic minority was prosperous due to its wool production, marry them; when the bottom had dropped out of wool, and prosperity was gone, kill them" (Sàenz 1999: 104).

RECONCEPTUALIZING POWER

These examples suggest a need for a reconceptualization of the notion of power. They reveal that power belongs not only to the chiefs or to the state or to those that control official discourses, but also inheres in the general populace. Even within the most authoritative of polities, people will find niches of autonomy and control, or they will create them. As James Scott (1985: 36) puts it, "Just as millions of anthozoan polyps create, willy-nilly, a coral reef, so do thousands upon thousands of individual acts of insubordination and evasion create a political or economic barrier reef of their own."

We should be wary of romanticizing this power of the people, whether subtle or violent. Violent rebellions and the everyday resistances of the kind described by Scott seldom are capable of bringing about the structural changes that would provide formal power to the underclasses. Now and then a violent "people's revolution" will be successful, but even then it will probably result in merely a different type of oppression. The large majority of uprisings fail and end like the Mexican American insurrection in Texas, with little changed and the oppressed even worse off than before. Nevertheless there is real power there, often hidden or temporarily quiescent, which it behooves officeholders to acknowledge and to fear.

SUGGESTED READINGS

Castile, George Pierre, and Gilbert Kushner, eds. *Persistent Peoples: Cultural Enclaves in Perspective* (Tucson: University of Arizona, 1981). Thirteen articles dealing with cultural enclavement, emphasizing the "continuity of common identity in resistance to absorption by a dominant surrounding culture." The studies, mostly from the Americas, range from blacks and Mormons in the United States to Mayans and Pimas of Mexico. A variety of strategies are analyzed, from outright opposition to the state to collaboration and fusion.

Cheater, Angela, ed. *The Anthropology of Power: Empowerment and Disempowerment in Changing Structures* (London: Routledge, 1999). A number of the 14 articles in this anthology deal with the empowerment of subordinated people. Although the editor assumes a postmodern definition of "power" based on the works of French philosopher Michel Foucault, the articles represent a wide spectrum in theories of power.

Edelman, Marc. *Peasants against Globalization: Rural Social Movements in Costa Rica* (Stanford, Calif.: Stanford University Press, 1999). The magic of the marketplace so touted by ideologues of global neoliberal capitalism is here revealed to have a devastating impact on Costa Rica's peasants. They have fought back against increased global competition and International Monetary Fund-mandated cuts in social programs with marches, riots, roadblocks, and occupations. Although peasants are often portrayed as illiterate and fatalistic, Edelman reveals their sophisticated knowledge of the world, their skillful manipulation of the media, and their effective organization.

Ekern, Stener. *Street Power: Culture and Politics in a Nicaraguan Neighborhood* (Bergen, Norway: Norse, 1998). Ekern did his fieldwork in 1984 when the proxy war by the United States against Nicaragua was in full force. He shows in detail how the Sandinista Defense Committees functioned in one community in the town of León, revealing its impact on the daily lives of its members. The book also gives a close-up view of the highly individualistic political culture of Nicaragua.

Scott, James C. *Weapons of the Weak: Everyday Forms of Peasant Resistance* (New Haven, Conn.: Yale, 1985). Scott, a political scientist who spent two years of ethnographic fieldwork in Malaysia, provides a minutely detailed examination of how the introduction of green revolution cropping has exacerbated class conflict in one small community. His focus is on the perceptions of the different actors in the struggle, and the tactics that peasants use to fight back.

Schmidt, Bettina E., and Ingo W. Schröder, eds. *Anthropology of Violence and Conflict* (London: Routledge, 2001). The analysis of violence and war has become a subdiscipline in itself within anthropology that has already produced a large number of ethnographic studies. The editors' Introduction and nine articles in this book provide a good introductory overview to the subject.

Skalník, Peter, ed. *Outwitting the State: Political Anthropology,* Vol. 7 (New Brunswick, N.J.: Transaction Publishers, 1989). From the title, one would expect a focus on tactics and strategies for getting around state power, but the eight ethnographic selections in this book do not so much exemplify outwitting the state as learning to live with it while maintaining cultural identity. The examples represent a wide variety of cultures, from the James Bay Cree to the Russian Old Believers. Skalník provides an introductory overview of the material and a classification of outwitting tactics.

Indira Gandhi was prime minister of India from 1966 to 1977. Women have often attained such positions of power, but this does not necessarily translate into an increase in the status or power of women in general. Courtesy of the Library of Congress.

Chapter 8

GENDER AND POWER

Although it is commonly accepted that what has come to be known as feminist anthropology or the anthropology of gender has passed through a number of stages, the specification of these is dependent on how detailed one wishes to be, and what aspects are emphasized. Very broadly, one might distinguish three overlapping phases in a distinctly anthropological view of women with regard to power and politics. The first "revolutionary" phase, which began in the early 1960s, is marked by the belated recognition of a pronounced male bias in ethnographic writing and anthropological theory. Interest in kinship and marriage ensured that women would be represented, but usually as passive and powerless adjuncts to husbands and fathers. The woman's voice was muted, both in the sense that there were few in-depth studies that focused on the woman's point of view and in the sense that there lacked a specific feminist theoretical viewpoint within anthropology. Much of the concern of this early phase was with rooting out male bias. Another arena of interest was the biological determinants of behavior as they might apply to the sexes; it was essential to show the degree to which gender was culturally constructed. The focus of this research was women, and the effect was to bring the ethnography of women into the mainstream.

In the second phase, interest in biological determinants faded, and the focus turned from women to gender. The anthropology of gender had two connotations absent from the anthropology of women. "Gender" was by definition cultural, distinguishing it from "sex" (although it would later be argued that sex, too, was socially constructed, because people have very different views and expectations about the physical body). Gender was also, by definition, relational—that is, it always involved the interaction between males and females. The focus was on women's subordination: was such subordination universal? If so, why? If not, why not? It quickly became evident that "subordination" was an extremely complex idea, and much analysis attempted to sort out its various aspects. The question of male domination was a natural for Marxist theorists who produced some historical ethnographies that revealed the interconnection between such domination and evolving economic systems (Moore 1998: 1–11).

The third phase is a fusion of three separate but related theoretical orientations: postmodernism, postcolonial theory, and globalization. A core theme of postmodernism is the rejection of grand theory, or meta-narratives—including such quintessentially Western orientations as Marxist cultural materialism. As a result, studies began to be more tightly focused and less interested in cross-cultural generalizations. They have also become more intuitive, self-referential, and cognitive in the sense of focusing on subjectivity and the way in which the world is experienced. From colonial/postcolonial theory came a renewed interest in the effects of history, especially the often-subtle consequences of Western hegemony, and a tendency to give a greater voice to the subaltern subject. Finally, the impact of globalization, especially the virtually unchallenged economics of neoliberalism as propounded by the International Monetary Fund (IMF) and the World Bank, has been explored in relation to its differential effects on males and females.

THE SUBORDINATION OF WOMEN

Until the 1970s, the universal political subordination of women was one of the accepted fundamentals of cultural anthropology. E. E. Evans-Pritchard (1965: 54) observed that "in almost every conceivable variety of social institutions, in all of them, regardless of social structure, men are in the ascendancy. . . . " Robin Fox (1967: 31) includes male domination as one of only four "basic principles" of kinship (along with female gestation, male impregnation, and incest avoidance). In an overview of "cultural universals," Donald Brown (1991: 91n) categorically asserts the "universal dominance of men in the public-political arena."

There remains a popular myth of primeval matriarchy. This view is a survival of a nineteenth-century belief, most exhaustively articulated by

J. J. Bachofen in 1861 in *Das Mutterrecht,* that women's invention of agriculture gave rise to a cult of the Mother Goddess and a long period of female domination. Drawing on classical studies, rather than cross-cultural investigation, Bachofen set women's rule as the very cornerstone of civilization, the first emergence from savage anarchy. Unfortunately, no evidence for a period of matriarchy—or even for *a* matriarchy—has emerged from the ethnographic or archeological records (Webster 1975).

From the perspective of evolutionary biology, female subordination may be postulated as an inevitable result of two million years of evolution of Man the Hunter. Women were too busy birthin' babies and keeping the home fires burning in the old cave to have much to do with anything as momentous as the survival of the fittest. The end result of all that evolving was a demure and passive female forever barred from politics by her physical inferiority and lack of testosterone. At best, women could gain authority in the domestic sphere, although the public sphere remained off limits.

Although the universality of male domination remains controversial, even among feminists, it is certainly true that a form of academic male domination prevailed in anthropology at least through the 1950s. Paradoxically, some of the most influential researchers of the first generation of professional anthropologists in the United States were women: Margaret Mead and Ruth Benedict, among others, were successful in turning the question of gender from biology to socialization and in establishing cultural relativism as a major tenet of anthropology. However, for decades women virtually disappeared from both ethnographies and from theory, where they were usually treated, if they were treated at all, as appurtenances to males. A major problem that revisionist researchers have encountered in searching the ethnographic record is the relative paucity of detailed information on women. The same omission is found in textbooks. As Sandra Morgen (1989: 10) observes, "Dominant anthropological understandings of gender are revealed not only by where anthropology textbooks and theory do discuss women and/or gender, but also by where those discussions are significantly absent. Two of the most striking examples of this absence are in our teaching of human evolution and of stratification, power and political economy."

The emergence of feminist scholarship over the last 40 years has challenged many of anthropology's fundamental assumptions while helping to fill out the record with new ethnographic data. Only a portion of this material is overtly "political"; that is, having to do specifically with group decision making and leadership. However, in a wider sense, most of it is political, because a dominant thrust of feminist scholarship has been *power*, especially the relative power of the sexes. Is male domination really universal? If so, what are its causes? If not, how did it evolve culturally? What are the specific contexts that encourage or discourage gender differences in status and power? Is male domination really a meaningful concept?

As in any revolution in thinking, the questioning of anthropological assumptions about gender has intermixed both scholarship and ideology. Whether one believes that gender inequality is a universal or what one believes are the causes of male domination will have profound implications for how one perceives the world and how one recommends changing society. Although there is hardly any point on which all feminist anthropologists agree, one important implication is clear: gender can no longer be ignored; it must be considered as "an analytical category—which, like race, ethnicity, class or caste, tends to be crucial in the construction of both group identity and structures of power in society. . . . " (Morgen 1989: 8).

Man the Hunter versus Woman the Gatherer

Until the 1980s, the standard theory for the evolution of homo sapiens placed the emphasis on cooperative hunting of big game. The advantages of freeing the hands for the use of tools in killing and butchering resulted in bipedalism, which led to greater efficiency in hunting and an increased dependence on animal protein. In a complex feedback process, selection for new skills generated larger brains, which in turn brought about more cooperatively and complexly organized hunts. Larger brains meant longer periods of immaturity for children; women were saddled with protracted child care, which effectively prevented them from hunting or traveling extensive distances. Thus dependent, women were required to remain at "home base," foraging a bit and taking care of children, while men elaborated their tool kits and evolved incipient civilization out of hunting strategy.

Frances Dahlberg (1981: 1) refers to this traditional Man-the-Hunter schema as a "just-so story," not that different from other myths that explain the origins of language, tool use, and civilization. Women are represented as passive. The selective pressure of evolution is almost entirely on the male.

Offering an alternative perspective, Sally Slocum (1975) points out that hominid evolution is based on a relatively small amount of data, leaving gaping holes in the evidence to be filled in with hidden, and often unconscious, assumptions that cannot help but be influenced by the male-dominated culture from which such ideas emerge. For example, the earliest tools, no more than barely worked rocks, have been assumed to be "hand axes" when they could just as well have been used as aids in women's gathering and in preparation of plant foods. Cooperative hunting of large game, which is claimed to be the initial kick in human evolution, could only have occurred *after* brain size had begun to increase. On the other hand, the postulated pair bonding of one man taking care of one woman could only have taken place after the hunting adaptation was already well established. Initially, an increase in child dependency would have led to a pair bond between mother and offspring, not man and woman.

An alternative schema would give Woman the Gatherer at least equal weight in evolution with Man the Hunter. Natural selection obviously operated on both sexes. The lengthening of infant dependency would have placed a premium on a mother's skills in finding food for herself and her young. Far from being dependent on their male consorts, women may have supplied the bulk of the food for their families, as they have done in many hunting-gathering societies of recent times. Gathering is hardly a simple process; it involves finding and identifying edible plants, a knowledge of seasonal variation, a good sense of geography and weather, the development of containers for carrying food (and babies at the same time), and the invention of tools and techniques for food preparation. Longer gestation and more difficult births would also require greater social skills and communication *among women* that would select for larger brains. Women, far from being the passive recipients of evolution, were certainly as active as men.

Another version of the Man-the-Hunter concept comes from sociobiology, where it is acknowledged that both women and men were instrumental in evolution, but that natural selection led to different evolutionary strategies for each sex, resulting in male dominance. The "selfish gene" school theorizes that from an evolutionary point of view, all organisms, including humans, are basically containers for genes, and that there is an innate drive to spread one's own genetic program as widely as possible. The best male strategy is to have as many partners as possible, leading to aggression and competition. Women, on the other hand, have a larger genetic investment in their own offspring, so there would be a greater tendency toward long-term relationships and cooperation (Draper 1985). This argument is buttressed by studies of higher primates. Some species of baboons show marked sex role differentiation and strong dominance hierarchies, and many others, such as gorillas and orangutans, also reveal significant sexual dimorphism.

Feminists, however, point out that, once again, male biases are evident. In chimpanzees—humans' closest evolutionary relatives—there is little sexual dimorphism, and males compete for females not by aggression and dominance but through sociability, mutual grooming, and sharing food. Even among baboons, the most notoriously hierarchical of primate species, environment may have more to do with behavior than with instinct. Among some forest-living baboons, the "political" decisions on troop movements are made by older females, and, although males posture and threaten when confronted by a predator, they are also the first to find safety in the trees if the threat persists, leaving females encumbered with infants to fend for themselves (Dahlberg 1981; Leibowitz 1975). In short, the sociobiological argument often rests on which species one chooses to compare to humans.

Theorists have not yet settled on any particular evolutionary model, but it is already evident that the role of women must be considered equally to that of men, and that this consideration devastates traditional notions of Man the Hunter as the primary force in human evolution. Similarly, the consideration of the female role in evolution makes theories of male dominance based on Darwinian notions questionable at best.

Biological Differences in Gender

Differences in gender are indisputable, although the existence of innate *behavioral* differences remains hotly controversial. There have been two basic perspectives: (1) the culturalogical school, which views the entire explanation in the socialization of children into role behavior proper to their cultures; and (2) the "prepared learning" school, which assumes a biologically based propensity to learn and to perpetuate role behaviors peculiar to each sex (Draper 1985).

Psychobiological evidence comes from four sources: studies of cross-cultural uniformities, observations of infant behavior, comparisons with higher primates, and descriptions of physiological characteristics. A cross-cultural study revealed that young boys are consistently more aggressive than are young girls, although in only 20 percent of the sample were boys actually socialized for aggressiveness. Also, observations of children raised together in Israeli Kibbutzim, where, supposedly, socialization was the same for both sexes, revealed that boys were more aggressive and competitive and girls were more "integrative" (affectionate, willing to share, cooperative, and so forth). Research on infant behavior, ostensibly prior to socialization (including in orphanages, where little socialization took place), revealed a similar pattern. Throughout mammalia, including the primates, males are normally more aggressive, although there are exceptions, as noted above. The muscular strength of women is 55 to 65 percent that of men. Males seem to have higher energy potentials and females, lower metabolic rates. Early brain differentiation suggests diverse behavioral potentials by sex. Androgyny in girls (prenatal exposure to male hormones) leads to "tomboy" behavior. Finally, the association of the male hormone testosterone with aggressiveness is well known (Parker and Parker 1979). More recent neuropsychological studies of hormonal effects on brain development reveal different male and female patterns: the "lifelong effects of early exposure to sex hormones are characterized as 'organizational' because they appear to alter brain function permanently during a critical period in prenatal or early postnatal development" (Kimura 2002: 33).

Some subtle biological differences are now well established, although laboratory studies tend to focus on such measurable things as differential spatial and linguistic abilities that appear to have little to do with political behavior or issues of dominance and subordination. Many claims for biological differences continue to be disputed. It has been pointed out, for example, that sexual socialization of infants really begins at birth, often in very subtle ways. "Intersex" children—who lack an enzyme for converting testosterone and therefore growing up with "ambiguous" genitalia—after puberty easily assumed the male identities for which they were socialized. The study that found that prenatal androgyny led to tomboy behavior in girls has been challenged, and there are biologists who strongly contest evidence of prenatal brain differentiation between the sexes. Even muscular strength and endurance is strongly affected by environment; differences in performance levels in sports are narrowing rapidly as women receive training and encouragement similar to that of male athletes (Lott 1987).

Even if there are prepatterned behavioral differences between the sexes—males being more "agonistic" (aggressive, exploratory, hierarchical, and competitive) and females more socially "integrative" and "nurturent" (Parker and Parker 1979)—all behavior in humans is filtered through culture. If such propensities do exist, the degree to which they will be manifested, assuming they are manifested at all, will be determined by culture and individual psychology. The wide variety of sex role behaviors among societies and within any particular society testifies to the extent of human malleability, no matter what innate predispositions there may be.

The problem comes not from admitting possible behavioral differences derived from biologically based propensities, but rather from the logical

(or illogical) jump to male domination. There is little in these hypothe-
sized innate differences to suggest gender stratification or the superiority
of one sex over another (in fact, males respond worse to stress than do
females, are more vulnerable to physical and psychological illness
throughout their lives, and have a lower life expectancy). The assumption
that physical strength alone or higher testosterone leads to dominance
fails to account for the fact that almost nowhere does strength or raw
aggression imply leadership; leaders in many societies are selected for
sociability, sharing, and their intuitive understanding of others, all traits
that are supposedly feminine. Also, if stratification or male dominance
were biologically based, one would expect it to be universal, but, as will
be seen, there appear to be egalitarian societies at both the foraging and
horticultural levels.

The debate over the biological bases of sexual stratification was ar-
dently fought throughout the 1970s; presently it is pretty much a dead
issue outside of sociobiology. Feminist anthropologists have gone on to
more complex, and more fruitful, questions.

WOMEN AND POWER: THE CROSS-CULTURAL EVIDENCE

Although no matriarchies exist, the range of female statuses among
prestate cultures is extensive. The three societies described below are
more representative of the extremes than of the norm, but they do reveal
how variable sexual stratification can be.

The Iroquois

Among the Iroquois, a confederacy of five culturally related "tribes"
in the northeastern United States, women had higher status and more
power than in just about any group known. This might seem odd, because
the Iroquois were extremely warlike, exactly the type of group one might
associate with a "male supremacist complex." However, a number of
factors contributed to the power of women.

The Iroquois were mainly observed in the eighteenth and nineteenth
centuries; thus, their society had already undergone considerable change
due to contact with Europeans. Individual men or groups of men were
away much of the time, often for a year or more, on extensive hunting
or trapping trips, trading, or involved in warfare. Thus, in the local village units it was the women who maintained continuity. Women provided
most of the subsistence, through shifting cultivation of corn, beans, and

squashes, in addition to many wild foods. The society was both matrilineal and matrilocal. Matrons arranged marriages. When a man married,
he moved into his wife's longhouse, a large structure of bark and wood
with many compartments connected by a central aisle. Each family in
the lineage occupied a compartment, sharing a fire with several other
families. Matrons presided over the lineage longhouses, so that a man
had no power in the house in which he lived, and had to tread lightly
lest he offend his wife's female kin, who could expel him if they were
so inclined. Hereditary transmission of titles, rights, and property were
all in the female line. It was the women who had the power of life and
death over prisoners.

However, according to Judith Brown (1975), it was neither women's
contribution to subsistence nor matriliny that gave women their power;
rather it was women's command of the economic organization of the
tribe. Women not only controlled distribution of plant foods, both domestic and wild, but also handled the distribution of animal foods from
the men's hunts. It was the women who preserved the meat and the
matrons who distributed it. Women thus had the power to provision
hunts, councils, and war parties. Apparently, they could, in some cases,
hinder or prevent a war by withholding supplies.

As a result, women, although lacking official political offices, had
great informal political power. The highest ruling body of the League
was a Council of Elders. Hereditary eligibility for office passed through
the women. Iroquois matrons could raise or depose the ruling elders,
could attend the High Council, and could influence council decisions.
They had occasional power over the conduct of warfare and the nego-
tiation of treaties. When a chief died, the women held a meeting to select
a new candidate; if the clan chiefs vetoed the selection, the women would
meet again. Women also sent representatives to the public councils.

Although the Iroquois can by no means be considered a matriarchy
because men held all formal offices, the power of women was firmly
institutionalized. It should also be noted that such power was not confined to the "domestic" sphere, but was equally evident in the public
arena.

The Chipewyan

Almost at the opposite pole from the Iroquois were the Chipewyan of
northcentral Canada. According to Henry S. Sharp (1981), women were
severely "devalued" in this society; reputedly they were treated worse
than in any other North American tribe.

Historically, about 90 percent of the Chipewyan diet was from flesh, mainly caribou, but also moose, musk ox, small game, and fish. After contact with Europeans in 1715, they became increasingly involved in the fur trade, and by the end of the nineteenth century had adopted repeating rifles.

The low status of women would seem to be related to a strong division of labor and to the insignificant contribution of women to the food supply. Men obtained virtually all of the food. Women, however, did contribute significantly to subsistence, because they had the job of processing the food, mainly the long, arduous task of drying meat and fish. As in most foraging societies, some sort of sharing was necessary for survival, but this was not automatic. In difficult times, preserved meat and fish had to be "borrowed," but such borrowing was antithetical to the masculine ethic. Thus, women were relegated this job, although borrowing bestowed no status.

Women might have low status and be treated accordingly, but they were at the same time perceived to be possessors of great power. Such power, however, was of a negative sort. The roles of male and female were surrounded with complex symbolism. Men gained power through hunting, whereas women were potentially polluting, capable of destroying the efficacy of men's magical materials. A menstruating woman, for example, could destroy the magic of a sled dog harness by stepping over it. "To be female is to be power," observes Sharp (1981: 227), "to be male is to acquire power. Men *may* have power but women *are* power just by being women." This symbolic power did not, however, translate into the ability to make group decisions or to lead.

The Agta

The mountain Agta of northeastern Luzon in the Philippines is the only known culture in which women routinely hunted large game.

Centuries ago, all Agta may have been dependent on hunting, fishing, and gathering, although today the language group includes a great variety of lifestyles, including horticulture, farming, trading, and wage labor. The mountain Agta, who were least in contact with outsiders, ate animal protein almost daily. Wild pig, deer (both considered large game), and monkeys were commonly hunted with bow and arrow and machetes. Some forest plant food was also gathered, although the Agta preferred to trade for corn, cassava, and sweet potatoes.

There was a sexual division of labor, but it was modest. Both women and men participated in virtually all subsistence activities. In at least two

Agta groups, women were active hunters who hunted frequently, sometimes with other men or women, but often alone. Women made their
own arrows (although blacksmithing points was an exclusively male activity). Girls started hunting shortly after puberty and continued as long
as they wished.

The anthropological belief that women never hunt big game is based
on an ostensible incompatibility with childbearing and with nurturing
infants. How was this solved among the Agta? Older siblings, grand-
parents, or other relatives might care for young children. Sometimes the
father would take care of the children. Women did not hunt in late preg-
nancy and the first few months of nursing, but, despite the small size of
the settlements, there were usually sufficient women available to hunt.
Women were also more frequently, and more aggressively, involved in
trade, mainly of dried meat.

No formal or institutional authority existed, and group decisions were
based on consensus, which included, of course, the women. The Agta
would appear to be at least close to a truly egalitarian culture (Griffin
and Griffin 1981).

Agta culture thus challenges a number of assumptions about women's
roles—not only the old truism about Man the Hunter, but also the new
emphasis on Woman the Gatherer. It may be that female big-game hunting is unique to the Agta, but not necessarily; it is also possible that
male-dominated anthropology has missed other cases in which women
regularly hunted big game. Agta hunting does throw into question the
assumption that childbirth and child care are a universal constraint on
the range of women's activities.

WHAT DOES THE "STATUS OF WOMEN" MEAN?

Universal male dominance and the lowly status of women have been
assumed with little regard for what is meant by "dominance" or "status."
These concepts have many dimensions. Status may, among other things,
mean either deferential treatment or actual power over resources and
decision making (Brown 1975). Thus, upper-class women in the romantic
traditions of feudal Europe and Victorian England were given the highest
status—idealized and placed on pedestals—but they had no real power.
Status can refer to the rewards that society offers certain people, to prestige, to power over others, to authority without coercive power, to official
office, to control of resources, or to one's freedom or autonomy, and
each of these has many permutations. Also, status is not an isolated thing,

but is embedded in the many subsystems of a society, so that there may be separate statuses for the spheres of kinship, subsistence, politics, economics, religion, ideology, and so forth. Status in religion may not carry over into the economic sphere. Status may be fluid, changing throughout one's life and often changing from one situation to another. Indeed, the attempt by anthropologists to assess status—especially some universal concept of status—may be ethnocentric, devoid of meaning within the society to which it is applied.

This multivariate approach was validated by an extensive cross-cultural study by Martin King Whyte (1978), who examined 93 preindustrial cultures, using 52 variables associated with gender status, such as sex of political leaders, division of domestic work, and physical punishment of the spouse. He concludes that "One can no longer assume that there is such a thing as *the* status of women cross-culturally. Nor can one search for *the best* indicator of the status of women, or for *the key* variable that affects the status of women. Instead, one has to start with a very different assumption: that there is no coherent concept of the status of women that can be identified cross-culturally" (p. 170). In other words, status is not a universal, but can be understood only within specific contexts—not merely particular societies but particular subsystems within those societies.

Whyte's findings on male dominance were similar. There was considerable variation in dominance both between and within societies, ranging from absolute male supremacy to broad equality between sexes. Although no matriarchies were found, there were spheres of activity within which women had power over men.

Women's Power and the Distribution of Resources

Such studies have added to the complexity of the issue, but they have not stopped researchers from defining particular types of status—such as social prestige or power in group decision making—and seeking key variables that would explain cross-cultural differences.

Male dominance is often related to the division of labor by sex. Cross-cultural studies reveal that women are commonly assigned such tasks as food and fuel gathering, grain grinding, water carrying, food preservation, cooking, pottery making, weaving, basket manufacture, dairy production, and laundering—in other words, activities that can be performed near the home and involve monotonous operations that can be interrupted and resumed. Men are more likely to engage in activities that require travel, danger, and sometimes sudden bursts of energy, such as hunting large game, warfare, lumbering, trapping, mining, herding, fishing, and long-distance trade. Such division of labor seems to be more closely related to the demands of motherhood than to size, strength, or innate propensities. Tasks that are dangerous or remove women for long periods from home may be perceived as incommensurate with the demands of childbearing and child care (Coontz and Henderson 1986: 115; Dahlberg 1981: 13; Schlegel 1977: 35).

These are only statistical probabilities, however, not universals. There is virtually no job that is not performed by women somewhere. Foragers such as the !Kung and Mbuti pygmies seemed little restricted by childbearing in their extensive travels. As noted previously, Agta women regularly hunted big game. Among the nineteenth-century Plains Ojibway and in the African kingdom of Dahomey, women were warriors. Often women were assigned the heaviest jobs, such as clearing jungle or carrying water and firewood. Among Northern California Indians, most of the shamans were women.

In any case, there is no intrinsic reason to value one set of jobs over another, and as Karen Sacks (1979: 89) points out, there is something ethnocentric about the assumption that all cultures rank economic activities—an assumption that is most common in capitalist inegalitarian societies. The division of labor by sex may become a basis of sexual stratification, but it cannot be the sole explanation.

It has been argued that it is not the division of labor that determines the status of women, but rather women's contribution to the subsistence of the group. Cross-cultural studies, including different levels of social complexity, reveal that women contribute on the average about 30 to 45 percent of the food (Dahlberg 1981: 14–15). However, this can vary from women providing virtually none of the food (as among some Eskimos) to upward of 70 percent (the !Kung). Unfortunately, the "common sense" view that degree of contribution to subsistence determines status is wrong; cross-cultural comparison reveals no such pattern (Whyte 1979: 169).

Ernestine Friedl (1975, [1978] 1990) hypothesizes that power does not rest on the contribution to subsistence per se, but rather on the exchange of goods outside of the family. It is control of public exchange, not control of domestic production, that is the key, because such exchange creates the obligations and alliances that are at the center of political relations. The greater men's monopoly is on the distribution of scarce resources, the greater their dominance is over women.

This is most evident in less-complex societies. In hunting-gathering groups, plant foods are distributed only within the family, whereas animal protein is shared with the entire band. Usually, only men hunt big game; therefore, the range should extend from egalitarianism among groups in which there is little hunting to extreme male dominance among groups in which hunting is the primary means of subsistence. Among those groups in which both women and men hunt and gather communally, such as the Washo Indians of North America, women and men are roughly equal. In groups in which women and men each collect their own plant food, but men supply some meat, such as the Hazda of Tanzania, there will be a slightly greater tendency toward male dominance. The subordination of women will be even more pronounced if there is a sharp division of labor by sex, with females gathering and men hunting, as among the Tiwi of Australia. Finally, in societies such as the Inuit in which men supply virtually the entire food supply through hunting, women will have a very low status.

When this theory is applied to industrial society, it is obvious that jobs that do not give women control over productive resources do not garner power (although, it should be noted, this is also true of men's jobs).

Friedl has put her finger on one of many influences on male domination. However, as a universal theory, hers does not work. In his cross-cultural study, Whyte did not find any variable to determine gender status (although, his sample of hunting-gathering societies was relatively small, and he may have slighted African examples in which the correlation between status, economic contribution, and control of property is more clear [Duley and Sinclair 1986]). There are also some rather blatant exceptions to her theory. As was previously mentioned, among the Chipewyan it is the women who distribute the meat, yet male domination is very pronounced. There also may be considerable variation within particular groups; the Eskimo women described by Jean Briggs (1970) do not seem nearly as subservient as Friedl claims for Eskimos in general.

Domestic/Public, Nature/Culture

The belated recognition that "male dominance" is neither a universal nor a singular characteristic, the same for all societies in which it is manifested, has led to a search for the structural and cultural factors that give rise to gender differences. Michelle Rosaldo (1974) noted that men often control the "public domain," where the broader political issues of society are decided, whereas women are confined to a "domestic domain" largely concerned with the interests of their own families.

It is true that in preindustrial societies, women's activities are most often confined within the context of the family or the lineage. This can imply considerable power, however, especially in matrilineal systems in which inheritance of property takes place through the women and women run local lineage affairs. If matrilocality is combined with matrilineality, the man may have little power in the home where he lives with his wife and in-laws, as is the case among the Iroquois. Among the Hopi of the American Southwest, women control the lineage pueblos, so that men must exercise their authority through religion and community councils. From this point of view, "politics," which deals with *public* decision making and the *public* allocation of resources and authority, would belong to the men's sphere. This perspective does not deny women power, but suggests that each gender has its own sphere of power.

This is certainly true in many societies, but the domestic/public dichotomy is by no means universal. Women often do exercise power in the public sphere—for example, queens and female prime ministers (however, it should be noted that the existence of a woman in an official position of power does not necessarily raise the status of all women in that society; more often, formal power by women serves only an elite group or maintains a patriarchy). Also, in societies oriented around kinship, it may be very difficult to distinguish the domestic from the public. Often the family and the lineage are the mechanisms through which public decisions are manifested. In peasant villages, distinctions between public and private may be all but irrelevant, because the real locus of power—where decisions are made about land tenure, taxes, war, and education—is outside of the peasant community altogether (Hammond and Jablow, 1976). The private/public distinction would seem to be most clear-cut in state societies, but even in patrilineal states such as China, women moving from their natal homes at marriage may maintain lineage ties that bind them into a wider political world (Moore 1988). It should also be noted that there is a paucity of information on women's participation in public politics, partially because few researchers have been looking for it and partially because such influence may be less formal and less overt than that of men.

Another dichotomy that has been suggested as useful for explaining male dominance is *nature/culture* (Ortner 1974), which emerged from an approach, influenced by the works of Claude Lévi-Strauss and Clifford Geertz, that views gender as basically a symbolic construction that closely intermeshes with the other symbol systems of a society. From this perspective, females are associated with nature mainly because of their procreativity and, in many societies, their occupation of tilling the earth. They are bound up within such symbol sets as earth, moon, planting, and fecundity. Men, on the other hand, are enmeshed in the symbol sets of culture: sun, language, law, architecture, and politics. Such symbolic definitions would tend to place women in the domestic sphere and men in the public sphere.

There are problems here too, of course. Although many societies do relate women symbolically to nature and men to culture, many do not; some societies relate men to nature and women to culture (in the United States, it is much more common to refer to men as "beasts" or "animals," and to believe that their warfare, hunting, and football emerge from feral instincts). In addition, despite Lévi-Strauss's contention that the culture/nature dichotomy is embedded in the very structure of the human mind, many peoples do not make the distinction at all. It has been argued that distinctions between nature and culture and domestic and public are really Western categories that have been imposed on, rather than derived from, non-Western cultures (Rapport and Overing 2000: 145).

These insights may be valuable in the analysis of some particular cultures, and certainly the idea of the "cultural construction of gender" is a sophisticated approach, replete with possibilities. However, as anthropology has found time and time again, the reduction to simple dichotomies, no matter how extensively they may be elaborated, tends to obscure the enormous intricacy and complexity of human behavior.

Residence Rules, Socialization, and Violence

General explanations of gender stratification that rely on a single variable—whether nature of subsistence, distribution of public goods, or motherhood—have not been particularly successful; there are too many exceptions. Marc Howard Ross (1986) offers a multivariate explanation based on a cross-cultural survey of 90 preindustrial societies. The inevitable problems with any such survey are compounded by the lack of material specifically concerned with female participation and with women's ownership or allocation of resources. It was necessary to code for titled offices and attendance at meetings and also for private conversations, indirect influence, and control over information.

Female power could not be measured along a single dimension but had to be, at the least, broken into two independent categories: (1) female involvement in group decision making, and (2) politically important positions or organizations controlled by women. There was no significant overlap between these two categories; each emerged in different types of societies.

Women's control of organizations and positions of power was most closely correlated with socioeconomic complexity, and seemed to be part of a more general social and economic differentiation. However, such organizations did not necessarily proffer higher status or more power on women.

Women's involvement in group decision making corresponded strongly with the organization of men; patrilineal kinship and other strong fraternal organizations had a negative effect on female status. Postmarital residence was also significant; women who remained within their own communities after marriage had greater power. Early socialization of the male that was warm and affectionate led to little conflict between genders, with a resultant relative equality. Finally, in situations of high internal conflict, women were encouraged to be politically active in negotiations and as peacemakers; in situations in which internal violence was low, there was little stimulus for them to act outside of the domestic sphere (in situations of high external violence, women were relatively excluded from politics).

Such cross-cultural studies suggest that differential female status and power will be explained not by a single universal cause, but by a number of factors working together.

THE HISTORICAL DEVELOPMENT OF GENDER STRATIFICATION

Many researchers have noted that cross-cultural surveys and structural explanations suffer from a common defect: such studies are synchronic. They do not consider the crucial variable of *time*. A group of mainly Marxist-influenced scholars have attempted to correct that deficiency by providing the historical context of gender stratification.

It was not Marx but Frederick Engels ([1891] 1972) who provided the most detailed schema for the cultural evolution of the exploitation of women. According to Engels, matrilineality (or "mother right") emerged out of a period of primitive anarchy and promiscuity. Engels saw this early matrilineality as egalitarian. Property, the basis of all power, was owned communally, so that no one had control over others. With the emergence of private property, men overthrew matrilineality and installed the patriarchal family, introducing differences of wealth both within and between families. Excluded from control of property, women found themselves in a subordinate position. Women produced only for domestic use, freeing men to produce for consumption by the group or for trade. Technology, which was controlled by men, exacerbated these inequalities. Thus, male control of private property resulted in female subordination.

Eleanor Leacock (1981) further developed Engels's ideas. She postulates an egalitarian stage among foraging (hunter-gatherer) societies. Present-day foragers that are not egalitarian, according to Leacock, have been contaminated by centuries of contact with Western stratified society. In early foraging bands, which were highly flexible to take advantage of variations in food supply, there was a direct relation between production and consumption, with no market system to intervene. No one had the power to control or withhold resources. Each individual enjoyed autonomy; each person was responsible for his or her own activities. Group decisions were arrived at by consensus. Domestic/public dichotomies had not yet emerged. There was no necessity for women to be especially responsive to the needs of men, or vice versa.

As long as the public and private spheres were not differentiated, societies remained egalitarian. Thus, some precolonial horticultural societies, as well as foragers, were egalitarian. However, when goods began to be produced for exchange as well as for consumption, new economic ties undermined the ties of the collective household. Control of production was removed from the hands of the producer, leading to exploitation. Women lost control of their own production, which was taken over by men. Because of the constraints imposed by childbearing, a sexual division of labor developed in which women became the small-scale producers and dispensers of services within male-dominated households. Women were effectively pushed out of the public arena altogether. With the rise of capitalism, sexual stratification became even more entrenched, because men, almost exclusively, control the means of production and thus can further exploit women as wage laborers.

The Bari

The Bari, tropical horticulturalists of Colombia and Venezuela, illustrate this process. Despite 400 years of successfully fighting off settlers and missionaries, they retained an internal social organization that was egalitarian; their language even lacks a term for "chief." No one, man or woman, could give orders to anyone else and expect to be obeyed. Lacking a concept of private property, they shared equal access to resources. Group decisions were made via consensus by all—again, men and women—who were affected by the decision. There was a minimal division of labor—cooking, child care, housebuilding, fishing, and planting were done by both sexes—and the work of no individual or group was considered more important than that of others.

All of this changed rapidly after 1964, when the combined pressures of oil explorers, settlers, and missionaries forced a "truce" that enmeshed the Bari in the processes of Western capitalism. To better deal with the Bari, the Colombian government officially recognized a group of "chiefs" or *caciques*—all men, of course. Although traditional Bari had no concept of surplus production, they were brought into the market economy and encouraged to produce manioc and plantains for sale; men came to control the cash produced by these sales, creating a basis for male exploitation of female labor. Wage labor, available only to men, provided the cash for manufactured goods, such as machetes and clothes, thus making women dependent on the men for the new necessities. Collective fishing, a task shared in the past by both men and women, was disrupted because men were away much of the time on wage labor jobs. Fishing thus became the province of a few men with weighted nets and motorboats, excluding women from a primary subsistence activity. Women's forest collecting was minimized by the availability of manufactured foodstuffs, purchased with men's earnings. These, plus many other changes, rapidly moved the culture from egalitarianism to male domination (Buenaventura-Posso and Brown 1980).

Sisters and Wives

Leacock's theory is extremely important in providing a diachronic model for the development of gender inequality. This adds a new, and crucial, dimension to the debates. The theory is also valuable in showing how sexual stratification may be related to class stratification in general, and the important role of colonial contact in introducing inequality among foragers and horticulturalists. However, there are some real problems with this theory. Although there is no evidence of a general matrilineal stage of human cultural evolution, as Engels claimed, neither is there evidence for a general egalitarian stage, as Leacock claims. Many contemporary or recent-past hunter-gatherers are *not* sexually egalitarian, and relatively few horticultural societies might make claim to equal status among the sexes. Leacock's claim that all nonegalitarian foragers were contaminated by contact or that they were misdescribed by biased males is not convincing. Also, male dominance clearly exists in societies that lack private property. Whyte (1978: 165n) cross-culturally tested the relation between private property and female status and found only a weak correlation; ownership or nonownership of private property was not a critical factor.

Karen Sacks (1979) offers a similar, but somewhat more complex schema, based on kinship. In foraging societies with a communal mode of production, there is little distinction between the roles of spouse and sibling in terms of production and ownership. Because property is "owned" by everyone equally, there is no claim of one person or group upon another, and women live their lives among their close kinfolk as well as their own families. However, when the communal mode gives way to the "kin corporate" mode of production—in which ownership is claimed by lineages or clans—"sisters" and "wives" are separated into two distinct productive roles. In patrilineal and patrilocal societies, sisters share in the ownership of their lineage's resources, but are removed from the exploitation of those resources. Wives, on the other hand, working within the confines of their husband's lineage, are producers but not owners. It is the separation of women from ownership of their own production that gives husbands in particular, and males in general, power over them. Class societies, growing out of these kin "patricorporations," put the ownership of production in the hands of male-dominated elites, thus even further demeaning the role of women.

Sacks's model is subject to some of the same criticisms applicable to Leacock's—mainly that there is no evidence for a universal phase of egalitarianism in the evolution of cultures. However, Sacks's emphasis on kinship and on residence after marriage fits well with cross-cultural studies that show a correlation between patrilineality, patrilocality, and the subordination of women. Also, Sacks has pointed out the importance of women's culturally assigned roles—"wife," "sister," and "daughter"— in gender stratification.

Christine Gailey (1987) applies these ideas to a complex historical analysis of the Tongan Islands of Polynesia, arguing that sexual stratification and class stratification parallel one another, but derive from different dynamics. For Gailey, state formation is an ongoing *process*, one that leads to an increasing decline in women's status and authority. Gailey emphasizes that in Tonga, the communal mode of production that preceded the state did not produce egalitarianism. However, the woman's position as "sister" was traditionally more valued than that of "wife," with the result that women remained in a protected position and maintained their importance in production and in the control of resources. Women were also the only creators of wealth, such as carefully crafted mats, bark cloth, and baskets. Two processes of capitalist penetration shifted the society toward increased stratification. First, commodity production and exchange transferred control to men and turned women's labor into a commodity. Second, Christian missionaries aggressively pushed for male domination while providing the moral and supernatural legitimization for such domination.

Such studies reveal that structural analysis alone is not sufficient to account for female subordination. Stratification—whether of status, rank, class, or gender—takes place within history. Feminist writers such as Leacock, Sacks, and Gailey have provided a major first step in delineating the particular factors involved in the evolution of male dominance.

Summing Up

The issue of male political domination and female subordination has been revealed to be far more complex than it originally appeared. This issue is no longer argued as fervently as it once was; most feminist anthropologists have moved on to other questions. If the larger issues have been left unresolved, at least a rough agreement emerged from this extended dialogue:

- The "Man the Hunter" myth of evolution can no longer be supported. Women had as much influence on the processes of physical evolution as did men.

- Whether there are significant biological bases for male and female differences in behavior remains controversial. However, even if there are innate predispositions—men being more "agonistic" and women more "integrative"—they are always filtered through culture and, in any case, they are an unlikely explanation for gender stratification.

- Neither "status" nor "male dominance" can be clearly defined cross-culturally. These concepts mean different things in different societies, and often there may be considerable variation among the subsystems of a single society.

- Even if, for analytic purposes, we hypothesize universal male political dominance, this is empirically questionable. There are many societies that have been sexually egalitarian, such as the mountain Agta, the Mbuti pygmies, the Bari, and the !Kung.

- Women's power must be measured along at least two divergent lines: (1) control of organizations and positions of power, and (2) involvement in group decision making. Each of these correlates with different factors in the society.

- Gender stratification cannot be predicted from division of labor or from women's contribution to subsistence. However, in many cases (but not all), there is a correlation between women's political power and the degree to which women control resources distributed outside the family.

- Postulated dichotomies that place women in the domestic domain and men in the public domain, or associate women with nature and men with culture, may have some value in analyzing particular societies but are *not* valid cross-culturally.

- As would be expected, matrilineality is more closely associated with female equality than is patrilineality. However, the marriage residence rule may be even more important; women who move into their husband's lineage after marriage may have to abandon their protected status as "sisters" to assume, almost entirely, a male-dominated status of "wife."

- Although there is no evidence for egalitarianism as a universal primary stage of political evolution, it does appear that the development of gender stratification is closely related to the emergence of corporate kin groups and the state. In each case, the removal of women from control of their own production appears to be a crucial factor.

POSTMODERNISM AND GLOBALIZATION

Recently, a number of theoretical trends have coalesced within feminist anthropology. Postmodernism (see chapter 10) shifted attention from grand theories and from the search for cross-cultural regularities to an emphasis on cultural difference, on understanding the subjectivity of postcolonial peoples, and on microanalyses of particular groups. The asymmetry of power and status between the sexes, which dominated the first phases of the anthropology of women and gender, became only one issue among many, and not necessarily the principle one. Interest often centered on the activities of women in daily life or on the symbolic aspects of culture (Lampere, Ragoné, and Zavella 1997; Yanagisako and Delaney 1995). From a purely political perspective, perhaps the most significant of the multitude of influences affecting contemporary feminist anthropology has been the increased attention to the role that gender plays in the state (Moore 1988: 128–85) and within the context of globalization.

Survival Politics and Globalization: Market Women in Peru

No single example could epitomize the myriad topics and perspectives that are encompassed in contemporary feminist works on power and policy. However, Linda Seligman's (1998) study of "survival politics" in Peru captures many of the themes of current feminist political studies. The brief ethnography is tightly focused with no attempt to tie the material to some grand theory. Although the context is globalization, specifically the effects of the imposition of IMF-imposed structural adjustments on market women in Cuzco, the ethnographer does not try to universalize the analysis. These women are not basically political, but in crisis circumstances they become active agents of resistance within a system that favors men.

When Alberto Fujimori became president of Peru in 1990, the country was in even worse economic shape than usual. The 1980s was a "lost decade" for most Third World countries as a global recession combined with spiraling debt destroyed the optimistic development goals of the 1960s and 1970s. Peruvian president Alan García refused to pay down the foreign debt of over $23 billion, with the result that loans and investments dried up. In the decade before the Fujimori presidency, real wages dropped by 40 percent and tax revenues fell by 50 percent. In addition to the economic crisis, a civil war between the government and the rebel forces of the Shining Path and Tupac Amaru Revolutionary Movement had, by 1990, resulted in 30,000 deaths. The economic infrastructure was largely destroyed, and inflation was 3,000 percent.

Market women, along with most others in the informal sector of the economy, supported Fujimori as the "man of the people" who would bring some stability to the country. Once in power, he adopted reforms even more severe than the structural adjustments demanded by the IMF and World Bank. Neoliberal economic ideology requires privatization of government-owned industries and utilities, radical reduction of government subsidies, the removal of price controls, and the aggressive collection of taxes. In order to do this while at the same time fighting the civil war, the promised democracy got short shrift; the 1992 *autogolpe* (presidential coup) established Fujimori as a virtual dictator. Nevertheless, from a macroeconomic perspective the policies were a great success, as inflation dropped precipitously, the service on the national debt began to be paid, and foreign investors returned.

From the microeconomic point of view, the picture was not so rosy. Conservative economic policy's proverbial rising tide that is supposed to lift all boats, in reality, left many of the smaller vessels beached or sunk. Peru's vast informal economy suffered the greatest hits. The informal sector, that which is unlicensed and illegitimate in the eyes of the government, is highly differentiated and includes everything from gypsy transportation and shantytown housing to a diverse commercial economy of self-employed traders and small-scale factories. Although vigorous, the informal economy suffers from a lack of formal protections, such as enforceable contracts, insurance, health benefits, and especially job stability. Many "businesses" assume modes of production more in line with rural than city forms: they are oriented around family, kin, or fictive kin and are strongly based on mutual assistance and on informal networks of supply and information.

The women vendors in Cuzco who were the subjects of Seligman's study between 1988 and 1993 were hard hit by the Fujimori reforms. Selling on the street or in markets was the leading occupational sector within the informal economy, and was mostly the province of women. Men participated mainly as transporters and distributors. Vendors included two opposed groups; the *ambulantes* or street vendors and irregular market sellers competed with the *establicidas* who had permanent rented stalls. The latter complained that competition was unfair, because *ambulantes* did not have to pay for stall space nor were they subject to taxation. Successful *establicidas* might aspire to, and sometimes attain, the middle-class status of the mestiza, lifting them out of the lesser categories of Quechua Indian *campesina* or *chola* (an intermediate status between peasant and the fully acculturated Spanish-speaking mestiza). What little power market women had came through a client relationship with local patrons; the women could receive credit, protection, information, and other resources in exchange for their proper votes at election time.

Fujimori's reforms moved the economy from a focus on extractive and utilities industries to industries designed for export. This shift required massive layoffs without corresponding employment opportunities. For Cuzco, an added problem was a near 70 percent decline in tourism. Normally, the informal sector served as a safety valve for the formal sector, in the sense that it provided employment and assisted the formal sector through cheap transportation and inexpensive manufactures. However, the Fujimori shocks led to such a degree of unemployment in the formal sector that many were forced to seek work in the informal economy, exacerbating an already severe glut of labor and microbusiness. At the same time, fighting in the countryside, and the terrible human rights violations that accompanied it, drove people into the cities where they had no choice but to seek jobs. In 1994, according to Peru's own statistics, underemployment and unemployment ran as high as 83 percent!

A crucial result was to heighten tensions among market women as demand for their goods dropped at the same time that there were large inflows of new sellers, especially *ambulantes*. Any class solidarity that might have been attained by market women was destroyed by the increased competition. As the economic pie grew smaller, networks became defensively tighter and more exclusive. The normal prejudice of those with fixed market stalls against *ambulantes* was exacerbated. Political action became increasingly difficult because the need for survival created a fragmentation that clashed with attempts to organize. Much resistance tended to be of the "everyday" variety described by James

Scott in *Weapons of the Weak* (1985): cheating on scales, for example, and sharing information about the movement of police and tax agents.

The greatest potential for organized protest lay with the unions. The more established vendors had the most freedom to politically organize; almost all belonged to the Syndicate of United Markets. A smaller number of those without fixed stalls belonged to the Syndicate of *Ambulante* Vendors. However, the elected representatives of both organizations were primarily men who had little interest in women's issues such as running water, day care for children, or family soup kitchens. Women were viewed as useful primarily in providing bodies in street demonstrations.

As a result, women sometimes organized on their own. Such social movements—informal protest groups—not only allowed women to focus their efforts on those issues that were of greatest importance to them, but also to assume leadership positions that were beyond bounds in the formal unions. Such movements emerged, according to Seligman's analysis, in particular "discursive sites"; that is, tightly restricted areas of meaning, values, assumptions, and self-identity. Within such sites, which might be physically situated in a particular neighborhood or market, women were able to seek out those areas of common interest that permitted them to unite. Such sites might be quite different from and opposed to the areas in which men dominate.

However, more effective mobilization usually required a greater inclusiveness. Actually getting a social movement to the point of street demonstrations demanded that narrower interests give way to broader formulations. The daily work of the women in the market permitted and even encouraged the discovery of commonalities among a plethora of fragmented interests. When movements were oriented around specific interests that cut across divisions of class, culture, and even occupation, they were capable of wide-scale mobilization. For example, when Fujimori announced plans to impose an 18 percent tax on all workers in the informal sector, street demonstrations that helped defeat the proposal were joined by large and small operators alike: wholesalers, retailers, *ambulantes,* and *establicidas*; men and women.

Seligman's study documents at the street level the inequities that accompany global forces in the form of neoliberal economic strictures enforced by the IMF and World Bank. It also shows the capacity, limited as it is, of those affected to challenge the system in a peaceful manner. Ultimately, however, both the loose structure and lack of continuity of market women's political movements and their marginalization within the wider collective interests of the informal economy reduced the power of women to effect significant long-term political change.

THE FEMINIST CONNECTION

Feminist anthropology has maintained a symbiotic relationship with the larger field of political anthropology, both influencing and influenced by theories and subject areas outside of women's specific interests and discourse. Feminism played a major role in the development of postmodern theory, especially in countering universalist and essentialist theories that had relegated women to positions of invisibility or marginality. Feminist research has also become increasingly interdisciplinary, overflowing from anthropology into Culture Studies and Science and Technology Studies. Globalization, which has radically different impacts on each gender, will also continue to provide a fertile ground for feminist analysis.

SUGGESTED READINGS

Dahlberg, Frances, ed. *Woman the Gatherer* (New Haven, Conn.: Yale University Press, 1981). A very accessible collection of readings focusing on women in hunting-gathering societies. The first two articles challenge the "Man the Hunter" version of human evolution, followed by women-focused ethnographies on the Agta, Australian Aborigines, the Mbuti pygmies, and the Chipewyan.

di Leonardo, Micaela, ed. *Gender at the Crossroads of Knowledge: Feminist Anthropology in the Postmodern Era* (Berkeley: University of California Press, 1991). This work brought together many of the top women anthropologists at a major turning point in feminist scholarship, when postmodernism and postcolonial studies were beginning to have a major impact. With a few exceptions, the 12 articles tend to be analytical overviews rather than ethnographies.

Gailey, Christine Ward. *Kinship to Kingship: Gender Hierarchy and State Formation in the Tongan Islands* (Austin: University of Texas Press, 1987). One of the most detailed ethnographic analyses to date of the subordination of women during the processes of state formation. Gailey shows how, over a 300-year period, gender stratification and class stratification developed together, although from different internal dynamics.

Leacock, Eleanor Burke. *Myths of Male Dominance* (New York: Monthly Review Press, 1981). This collection of essays, from over 30 years, is a good introduction to one of the foremost feminist scholars in anthropology. Leacock's theory of the evolution of male dominance is clearly articulated.

Mascia-Lees, Frances E., and Nancy Johnson Black. *Gender and Anthropology* (Prospect Heights, Ill.: Waveland, 2000). A concise and easily understandable overview of the history, theory, and approaches to the anthropological study of gender.

Moore, Henrietta. *Feminism and Anthropology* (Minneapolis: University of Minnesota, 1988). An analytic overview and critique of feminist anthropology through the 1980s. Of particular interest to political anthropologists are the chapters on "Gender and Status" and "Women and the State."

Whyte, Martin King. *The Status of Women in Preindustrial Societies* (Princeton, N.J.: Princeton University Press, 1978). Cross-cultural statistical studies such as this one have gone out of fashion, but Whyte's major conclusions from a sample of 93 cultures should be agreeable to contemporary feminists and postmodernists: "male dominance" and "status" are highly variable concepts that cannot be reduced to Western representations.

An Armenian woman in traditional dress in early twentieth-century Russia. Modern Armenians utilize the Internet to create and maintain a sense of nationalism in diaspora. Courtesy of the Library of Congress.

Chapter 9

THE POLITICS OF IDENTITY: ETHNICITY AND NATIONALISM

As described by Abner Cohen in his classic *Custom and Politics in Urban Africa* (1969a), the Hausa of Nigeria were renowned traders, who had developed a widespread reputation as shrewd businessmen, exploiters, troublemakers, and geniuses at their profession. There was a certain truth in at least the latter accusation, although their genius resided more in their trading network than in individual brilliance. The Hausa were neither pastoralists nor farmers, and therefore had to make up in efficiency for what they lacked in control over the production of the cattle and kola nuts they traded. The forest zone people of the south could not raise their own meat because the tsetse fly killed off cattle within two weeks. The savanna people of the north put a high value on the kola nut but could not grow this food themselves. Trading between these two ecological zones was a tricky business; because cattle died so quickly in the forest and the kola nut was highly perishable, one could not just transfer these goods from one area to another and wait around for the best price. Information on supply and demand had to be obtained before goods were moved. Nor could one depend on either traders or customers having money on hand when the actual transfer was made. The Hausa trading network solved both these technical problems: information on market conditions moved rapidly through the system, and the Hausa had established a virtual monopoly on credit and trust in these business transactions. There was nothing "primitive" or small in such trading: millions of dollars worth of goods were involved, and the wealth and income of the vast majority of the Hausa were directly or indirectly derived from the dual trading of kola nuts and cattle. However, despite their sophisticated knowledge of banking, insurance, and legal documents, the Hausa quite rationally preferred traditional arrangements based on partnerships of trust and reciprocity.

Cohen's study focused on the "retribalization" of the Hausa quarter of Sabo in the city of Ibadan. Only a few decades earlier, Sabo had been little more than a Hausa sector of a largely Yoruba village; but as Ibadan grew into a major city, Hausa influence was reduced. With independence after World War II, the central government of the newly liberated nation simultaneously emphasized party politics and condemned tribalism in an attempt to unify the country. These pressures combined to weaken the effectiveness of the traditional Hausa chiefs, and both outmarriage and the revolt of the young against tribal ways threatened to detribalize the Hausa altogether. The Hausa were neither particularly self-conscious nor defensive about their tribal heritage, but they became increasingly aware that their trading network, and therefore their livelihood, depended on their ethnic cohesiveness.

The Hausa answer to this political and economic challenge was to reemphasize the tribal unit. The major tool in this process was the development of a Moslem religious brotherhood called Tijaniyia. The majority of Hausa had previously, like the Yoruba, been rather casual about their religion. The Tijaniyia practiced a highly puritanical mode of religion, which involved an intense form of community ritual that clearly set them off from the morally inferior non-Hausa. In addition, the Tijaniyia established a religious hierarchy that provided strong ritual leaders to fill the power vacuum left by the declining authority of the traditional chiefs. Through retribalization, Hausa ethnicity was politicized and used as a weapon in the struggle to maintain their monopoly on trade. The forces of modernization thus drove the Hausa to a degree of exclusiveness more radical than at any time in the past.

Abner Cohen's analysis has become a classic of *instrumentalism,* a cost-benefit theory that holds that the primary motivating force of ethnic identity is the establishment and maintenance of privileged economic and political niches. At the time this book was written, it was widely believed that the processes of modernization would lead to cultural homogenization. Cohen was one of the first to thoroughly document what has now become a truism, namely that modernization regularly leads *away* from assimilation. It turns out that "retribalization," which would today be termed ethnogenesis or the solidifying of ethnic identity, is a very common process.

IDENTITY AND POWER

Although identity politics undoubtedly has a long history, its importance has grown over the last few decades as ethnicity and nationalism have emerged as forms of resistance against the forces of globalization and, at the same time, as a means of taking advantage of those forces. On the one hand, sodalities of identity are created to defend themselves against the threat of marginalization within an unequal global hegemony; on the other hand, cheap travel and new media technologies have been employed to unify distant people and to lay claim to universalized values such as human rights and indigenous sovereignty. These identities take many specific forms:

- Amazonian Indians reinforce Brazilian stereotypes of narrow tribal identity by attending televised meetings in traditional garb, while at the same time forming modern pan-Amazonian organizations that emphasize a broad Indian unity. Politically sophisticated Indian leaders regularly attend international conferences in Europe and routinely tape-record or videotape meetings with government officials so that every promise is documented. (Ramos 1998)

- As an independent country, Tibet possessed no unified ethnic or national identity. In 1959, after 10 years of brutal Chinese communist occupation, 80,000 Tibetans followed the Dalai Lama into exile. Today, over 120,000 expatriate Tibetans, living in numerous diaspora communities throughout the world, have formed a self-consciously unified democratic nation in exile and have become a respected voice for human rights in the United Nations and other global institutions. (Mountcastle 1997)

- Thousands of years of African migration, especially the forced transport of slaves to the Americas, the Middle East, and South Asia, left the descendants spread throughout the world with little sense of their African roots. Over the last decades, an increasing intellectual and popular African consciousness has emerged, along with the concept of a black Atlantic composed of multiple cultures united by a common history of subjection, suffering, resistance, and cultural innovation. (Gilroy 1993; Hall 1990)

- When Indonesia became independent, it consisted of a multitude of different tribal groups speaking different languages. However, Islamic religion, the existence of Malay as a *lingua franca,* and a common history of struggle against Dutch colonialism served to unite the people in a rough, and largely situational, Indonesian nationalism. (Watson 1996: 110)

Such variety suggests some of the difficulties in finding general terms and theories that are universally, or even widely, applicable to political identity groups.

Through the 1960s, identity was not a focus of interest of political anthropologists. According to the theoretical perspectives of the time, politics took place within stable bands, tribes, chiefdoms, and states. Individuals assumed their identities from membership in such groups: one was Nuer, Quechua, Dobu, or Norwegian. Each group possessed a particular social organization and sense of values, including notions of political legitimacy, which have been passed on from generation to generation. Thus, in many ways, identity was coterminous with "culture." However, today the very concept of culture—which has always been subject to numerous and contested definitions—is rapidly losing its authority to designate a bounded, politically cohesive group. From the point of critical theory in anthropology, culture was always more a heuristic ascription of the anthropological imagination than anything that might objectively inhere within some collective. The reification of culture as something objective and measurable is giving way to more fluid conceptions of culture as shared meanings that partially bridge the fragmentation and heterogeneity that has resulted from globalization. Neither culture nor individual self-identity may, any longer, be presupposed to be cohesive, but can be compartmentalized, situational, and deterritorialized (Appadurai 1991). Culture, political and otherwise, has been replaced as the primary foci of anthropological studies of power by two overlapping but distinct concepts: ethnicity and nationalism. Another increasingly common anthropological concept of identity is compressed in the term "hybrid."

In the very real sense that no society has been entirely immobile or historically isolated, all cultures and identities are hybrids, intermixtures of multiple confrontations between unequal societies in complex interaction with the demands and constraints of particular ecosystems. Unfortunately, the biological hybridity of plant geneticists provides, at best, an imperfect metaphor for human identity; in the biological sphere, hybridity usually denotes only two parents, often with sterile offspring, whereas the human variation is much more complex. However, hybridity is the term of the day and has assumed a generally agreed-on meaning that encompasses the changeable, multisourced, and constructed nature of identity today. The book that popularized the term, Néstor García Canclini's *Cultural Hybridity* (1995) focuses on only two of its many aspects: traditionalism and modernism. Because this dichotomy has been associated with long-repudiated modernization theory (see chapter 11), it would seem an odd revival; however, García Canclini finds it useful in the analysis of Mexico, where modern and traditional clash and blend in unexpected configurations in everything from politics to the arts. In the past, the traditional was the province of the anthropologist, whereas sociologists studied the modern; hybridity demands that such disciplinary distinctions be put aside. In one sense, cultural traditionalism represents embeddedness within relatively tight structures of family, kin, and community, such as the religious cargo systems found throughout Central America, whereas modernity represents individualism and social fragmentation. Jonathan Friedman (1994: 91–92) also sees modernism "as a continuous process of accumulation of self, in the form of wealth, knowledge, experience." There is no longer any clear linear trajectory that runs from tradition to modern; the movement can go both ways. *Neo-traditionalism* can be a reaction against the atomization and anomie that modernism implies.

Hybridity is more commonly employed in the wider sense of a syncretism or compartmentalization of different culture traits. Often the emphasis may be on language, such as Creole, or on relative power, such as Chicanos within the dominant Anglo society of the United States, rather than on a tradition/modern tension. In many cases, hybridity is not simply the result of acculturation or assimilation but may be actively sought, as when African Americans assume Islamic identities based on North African models. The range of possibilities for such hybrid intermixtures is virtually infinite.

Despite the historically hybrid nature of ethnic and nationalist groups, self-identity is often, if not usually, legitimized by some form of *primordialism*. This is the idea that identity is based on race or on an essential culture or religion that reaches deep into the far recesses of history or even prehistory. Identity is thus replete with affective meaning, bound up in blood, martyrdom, soil, and perhaps an emotionalized sense of language. One is born into the identity, although it may have been forgotten or repressed and needs to be rediscovered by the new generation, as exemplified, at opposite poles, by the Nazi claims to an Aryan heritage and by the negritude ideology of Leopold Senghor. In the former Soviet Union, a state-sponsored primordialist "ethnos theory" attempted to integrate the numerous non-Russian people into the nation-state through a convoluted Marxist evolutionism (Banks 1996).

Almost all anthropologists today reject primordialist notions, viewing group identity in *constructivist* terms. From this point of view, ethnicity and nationalism are created situationally and constantly changing. There are multiple ways in which this occurs. As Immanuel Wallerstein (1974) and Eric Wolf (1982) have shown, all cultures have been substantially changed since the sixteenth century by the spread of colonialism and capitalism. The continued survival of indigenous tribal peoples and peasantries have required constant adaptation. Some of these adaptations may be forced, as when, under colonial domination, subsistence agriculturalists or pastoralists were brought into a tributary mode of production where they were required to transfer much of their labor to export goods for the colonial or imperialist conquerors. Identity may be constructed or reinforced when a group emphasizes in-group unity in order to maintain control of an economic niche. Groups artificially created by foreign powers may assume the classification of the oppressor in order to gain political power; as, for example, in postcolonial times, when the American Indian Movement in the United States assumed a pan-Indian identity that had no roots in indigenous culture. Constructivism, however, can be easily overstated. Speaking specifically of ethnicity, Milton Esman (1994: 14) observes that such identity, is "seldom . . . invented or constructed from whole cloth: a cultural and experiential core must validate identity and make solidarity credible to potential constituents."

Political Adjustment in a Reservation Context: The Mapuche

For perhaps the majority of indigenous peoples, the postcolonial era resulted less in integration than in increased marginality. This was especially true in the United States, Canada, Chile, and to some extent Brazil, which handled their "Indian problems" through the establishment of reservations. In a few cases, such as some Pueblo tribes in the American Southwest, reservations provided the means for maintaining crucial elements of a traditional culture up to the present day. In most cases, however, cultural continuity has been rendered impossible by the destruction of subsistence patterns, resettlement on land too barren to be desired by whites, crude attempts at forced assimilation such as sending children to off-reservation schools for long periods, and state administrative control of the reservation system. The parameters of the politics of marginality can be very narrow, and reservation populations must constantly adjust to the whims of the dominant power. However, such change may be imaginatively adapted to the needs of the people and to traditional versions of political legitimacy. L. C. Faron's (1967) ethnohistoric account of the Mapuche of Chile reveals tribal politics as a constant process of change in response to the varying policies of the Chilean government.

Traditionally, the Mapuche lacked any centralized political authority. The functioning social unit was the kin group, under the limited leadership of an elder called the *lonko*. During more than 300 years of resistance to European invaders, a powerful military organization with strong war chiefs developed. By the mid-1800s, after a period of relatively peaceful defiance, the Mapuche grew increasingly restive as lands maintained through force of arms were eroded by fraudulent legal claims. Taking advantage of Chile's preoccupation with the War of the Pacific against Peru and Bolivia (1879–1883), the Mapuche staged their last major uprising. They were soundly defeated, most of their lands were confiscated, and they were placed on relatively small reservations.

The Chilean government preferred to deal with each reservation through a single chief. This centralization of political authority was alien to the Mapuche, but there was sufficient precedent in the institution of strong military chiefs for a military-like power to be transferred to a peacetime office. Of course, this meant drawing power away from both the *lonkos* and the lesser military leaders. The federal government reinforced this centralization of reservation power by directly providing the chief with three times as much land as anyone else, at a time when land was a scarce and valuable commodity. Moreover, the chief was given limited legal control of all reservation land, and so many government restrictions were funneled through him that he ended up controlling, directly or indirectly, all of the wealth of the community. Anyone wishing to set up a household within the reservation had to seek permission of the chief. This made it extremely difficult to settle disputes, as of old, by moving to another area. There was no choice but to submit to the chief. In addition, the chiefs were given responsibility for mediating Chilean law for the Bureau of Indian Affairs, and for enforcing the customary law of the Mapuche. Such a concept of centralized power depended entirely on the reservation system and on the intrusion of the federal government into native politics.

By the 1950s, the reservation chief's kingly position had become an increasing irritation to the very national government that had created it in the first place. An extremely powerful chief was in a position not only to exploit his people, but also to defend them from outside exploitation. In a deliberate attempt to break the power of these chiefs, the government began to bypass them and deal individually with the Mapuche as Chilean citizens. The predictable result was that the power of the chiefs declined almost as rapidly as it had arisen.

Some of the chief's powers reverted to the *lonkos*, whose authority nevertheless continued to be localized and traditional. With increasing interaction between the Mapuche and their wider social environment, however, and with increasing threats against their land, mediation was as necessary as ever. Although the chief continued to represent the reservation, a new mechanism of culture brokerage developed: the political pressure group. The *Corporación Araucana* formed to fight for maintenance of the reservations and for increased government assistance to the Indians. A smaller opposition group, the *Unión Araucana,* was conceived by the Capuchin missionaries to promote absorption of the Mapuche into Chilean society.

In sum, the Mapuche continuously remade themselves in a reactive and adaptive process, beginning with authority vested in the elders of local kin groups, followed by the rise of war chiefs, the decline of the power of such chiefs, the emergence of strong reservation chiefs, and finally by the shift of authority into the hands of political action groups.

ETHNICITY

Ethnicity is a relatively new concept for anthropology. Prior to the 1950s, general classifications were mainly race, tribe, and peasant. Race got a bad name from the deadly genetic nonsense of the Nazis, and the gap between common parlance "race" and anthropological conceptions became so wide that the two seemed to have nothing to do with each other. The term "tribe," although still commonly used among North American Indians, assumed pejorative connotations of primitivism and colonial subordination, especially in relation to Africa (Zenner 1996: 393). The term " peasant" also has its problems, as more and more people so designated take on multiple jobs, from transnational migratory workers to shopkeepers, in the process losing the attachment to land and much of the folk culture that once defined them (Kearney 1996). The unfortunate result has been that "ethnic" emerged as the all-in-one term for a number of once-separate categories. The term ethnicity, as now employed, is so broad as to be almost meaningless, because no matter how one defines the term, multiple anomalous examples can be found. Early definitions tended to equate ethnicity with culture—thus replacing one highly problematical term with one equally nebulous—but the fit was tenuous at best. As early as 1969, Frederick Barth argued that among the Pathans of Afghanistan, Pakistan, and Northern India, a traditional culture was retained relatively intact when an individual moved from one area or country to another, but ethnicity—the way in which the group was both socially and self-classified—changed radically. Also, ethnicity only exists in relationship to other groups; isolated people would certainly have culture, but would not have ethnicity. Often, as is the case with Palestinians, ethnicity designates a subgroup of a broader culture (in this case Arab).

Another problem with the term ethnicity is that it does not make the modern/traditional distinction that many anthropologists find crucial; the term would apply equally to the Yanomami in Brazil and English expatriates in Argentina. In reality, different levels of modernity create very different kinds of ethnicity. Among the *davits* of India, formerly known as the untouchable caste, ethnicity is ascribed and whatever unity is claimed is defensive. In contrast, in the United States, a certain shallow ethnicity is purely voluntary as highly educated third- or fourth-generation Italians celebrate their heritage in parades and by serving Italian cuisine (it should be noted that the first generation of migrants did not identify themselves as Italian, but as Sicilian, Neopolitan, or Calabrian) (Pieterse 1996: 31–42). Thus, ethnicity would seem to lend itself either to endless subcategories or to an I-knows-it-when-I-sees-it specificity.

Given the range of possibilities, perhaps Stanley Tambiah's (1996: 168) definition is as good as any: ethnicity is "a self-conscious and vocalized identity that substantializes and naturalizes one or more attributes—the usual ones being skin color, language, religion, and territory—and attaches them to collectivities as their innate possession and myth-historical legacy." The crucial components are ideas of inheritance, ancestry and descent, a territory or place of origin, and at least some shared sense of kinship. This definition assumes an emic point of view—that is, the point of view of the people within the group. However, a clear distinction must be kept between the outsiders' perception of a given ethnic group and that of those who make claim to it. Ethnicity usually refers to distinctions that are recognized by both the in-group and outsiders, but these by no means always coincide. For Anglos, African Americans or Indians may be considered ethnic groups based on skin color or on simple cultural misunderstanding, whereas those so designated may define themselves entirely differently. Thus, much ascribed ethnicity may be more in the mind of the beholder than in the minds of those so designated. Even if only the perspective of the in-group is assumed, ethnicity depends to a great deal on what might be called feeling-tone, that is the individual's emotional sense of belonging to the group, which can range from virtually nil to violently intense. In addition, there is a wide range of emphasis on shared history or on territory. Ethnicities may overlap or be situational; Chinese in Malaysia would be "Asian" in the United States.

For political anthropology, the real issue with ethnicity is its relation to politics and power. Edwin Wilmsen (1996: 3) defines "the essence of ethnic existence" as "the differential access to means of production and rights to shares in production returns." Such a definition would not apply very well to the faddish ethnicity of the thoroughly assimilated American Italian, nor would it accord with the numerous viewpoints that find the essence of ethnicity in symbolic meanings (e.g., Appadurai 1991; Friedman 1994). However, such a perspective is valuable in focusing on the very real power differentials among ethnic groups and the importance of ethnicity in making claims to power. Ethnicity, according to this view, not only exists in a field with other such groups, but is also relational in a power sense; the form and content of a particular ethnicity will be determined by its positions of power relative to other contenders and to the dominant power. From Wilmsen's perspective, because ethnicity arises out of power differentials, ethnic politics are, by definition, the politics of marginality; dominant groups are never themselves ethnic. The dominant group, which need not be in the majority, will consider itself the universal or essential group and thus above the categorization of ethnicity. There is, for example, no English ethnicity in Britain nor any White Tribe in the United States (although the question "Is 'Anglo' an ethnicity from the perspective of a Chicano?" must be asked).

If one assumes, as Wilmsen does, that ethnicity is always subordinate to a dominant group, then within the state, ethnicity is marginal by definition. Nevertheless, it is obvious that ethnicity can become an important form of cultural capital; belonging to a certain group bestows advantages that can be utilized in political struggle (Alonso 1994: 382–405). In high minority areas of Southern California, for example, being Chicano or African American can be an important, perhaps even essential, asset in local elections.

Unity and Fragmentation in Israel

Ethnicity and nationalism are often conflated, and can be conjoined in ethnonationalism. However, these two concepts can also be quite distinct, as is illustrated in the case of Israel. As analyzed by Herbert Lewis (1993), Israel started with a relatively high degree of ethnic homogenization, at least in its ideology, and subsequently fractured into multiple ethnicities within an overarching nationalism.

Zionist immigrants began to settle in Palestine in the 1880s, and until about 1950 the large majority was Ashkenazi, from eastern and central Europe. They brought with them Western Enlightenment values of rationality, secular government, democracy, education, and a firm belief in progress. The Jewish Labor Party, which would lead the way to the founding of the state of Israel and remain the dominant political force through the 1960s, was dedicated to such goals, as were multiple other unions, cultural organizations, sports federations, paramilitary groups, and universities. The founding leaders such as David Ben-Gurion, Yitshak Ben-Svi, and Golda Meir, saw themselves not as reproducing some ideal Jewish nation of the past, but rather as repudiating the past. In the 1950s, similar progressive ideas were solidified and articulated throughout much of the world through the modernization theory of development, which held that traditional culture would gradually be absorbed by a forward-looking industrial sector. Ethnicity was not a part of the discourse of the time, but there was a strong belief that as modernization proceeded, tribalisms, nationalisms, peasant folk cultures, and the like would be integrated into a culturally homogenous nation-state.

By vote of the United Nations, the state of Israel came into formal existence on May 14, 1948. Of the estimated fifteen million Jews scattered throughout the world in 1939, most lived in Europe. However, these European populations were severely decimated in the Nazi death camps, and many of those who survived were trapped in refugee camps. Many who desired to come to Israel were not from Europe but from North Africa and Asia—countries such as Iran, Yemen, Morocco, and India. The Law of Return that came into effect in 1950 opened Israel's borders to all of these. This was to be an "ingathering of exiles," an invitation to Jews everywhere to join in the founding of the new nation. The underlying vision was that a new, unified people would emerge out of the cauldron of war, destitution, and struggle from which Israel was born. This new people would leave old cultures behind. As expressed by the first Prime Minister David Ben-Gurion, "Within the state the differences between various kinds of Jews will be obliterated in the course of time, the communities and tribes will sooner or later fuse into one national and cultural identity" (Ben-Gurion, as cited in Lewis 1993: 209).

It did not happen. Through the centuries of the Diaspora, Jewish people had taken on the cultures of the countries in which they settled. Although they lived in separate communities from their Muslim and Christian neighbors, they could not help but to assume many of the culture traits of those around them. The European and American Jews who had established the goals of Israel found themselves confronted by 50 different languages, and by people who had no knowledge of electricity or plumbing, and who practiced polygyny and child marriage.

North Africans and Asians, who by the 1980s made up more than half of the population, were lumped together in the single category of Oriental Jews, although differences among them were vast. European Orthodox Jews were viewed as an equal problem by the more secular founders of the Jewish state. Toward the goal of cultural assimilation, an official government Absorption Department was established, but failed to accomplish much absorbing. Villages and neighborhoods took on distinctly ethnic dispositions: Yemenite, Iraqi, and Kurd. Many continued to speak their own language at home and in their own communities; although they also learned Hebrew, it was often with a characteristically ethnic pronunciation. Synagogues, traditional dance groups, cultural organizations, and even political parties were formed around such differences. This was not just a matter of cultural variety, but also of class and status. Basically, there emerged two Israels, a dominant Euro-American and a subordinate Afro-Asian. The latter often justly complained that they were discriminated against in terms of jobs, land, and political influence. The Western Jews argued that their dominance emerged not from prejudice but from a more active entrepreneurialism, goal orientation, technical expertise, and high valuation of education. Periodically, especially during elections, conflict would grow heated.

By the 1970s, the total failure of the policy of absorption was blatantly evident. At about the same time, new intellectual currents were sweeping the West; modernization theory's goal of cultural homogeneity was giving way to the acceptance of multicultural heterogeneity. The state simply dropped its absorption policy—without a lot of to-do and not much opposition—and adopted a policy of multiculturalism. From now on, Israel would celebrate difference, not try to do away with it. The government has tended to support its many ethnicities through cultural exhibitions, dance groups, lectures, conferences, and publications.

Lewis emphasizes that despite the continuing "two Israels," the ongoing discrimination, ethnic separation of neighborhoods and villages, and periodic conflict, there are also overarching forces of unity. Above all is the consensus on the oneness of the Jewish people and the legitimacy of the state of Israel. Hebrew is a national language that almost all Jews speak no matter what language they might use at home (Arabic is also an official language, but mainly used by the Arab population). Although ethnic endogamy is common, so is intermarriage; almost all citizens agree, at least when polled, that any Jew should be able to marry any other. Finally, there has emerged a sort of pan-Israeli culture for public places—the job, government, the market—that assumes a degree of conformity to a common set of behaviors. Thus, we find a continuing fragmentation of Jewish ethnicities existing within a strong unifying Israeli nationalism.

NATIONALISM

In the twentieth century, millions of people lost their lives violently either in the support of existing nations or in the attempt to establish new ones, and it appears already that the twenty-first century may follow a similar pattern. When nationalism is involved, dying for The Cause can assume the level of moral imperative, the grandeur of martyrdom. This emotional intensity is one factor that may distinguish nationalism from ethnicity, or turn mere ethnicity into ethnonationalism. Since World War II, every successful revolution, from Cuba to Vietnam, has defined itself in national terms (Anderson 1983: 2). In many cases, however, the uniting factor was *not* ethnicity but the establishment of a state or the maintenance of a state against a perceived enemy.

Nationalism, like ethnicity, is notoriously difficult to define. However, it is possible to delineate two relatively distinct forms, although both share many attributes. In *state nationalism* the territorially bounded state assumes a loyalty that transcends that of family, kinship, culture group, or ethnicity. The nation-state was conceived in Europe in the eighteenth century; it was closely linked to the rise of industrial capitalism and founded on the ideals of the French Revolution (Tambiah 1996: 124–27). Such Enlightenment values as secularization of government, citizenship, equality, and jurisdiction over a clearly defined territory were part of the original ideology of nationalism. Although made up of many sectors, the nation-state would encourage the creation of a single dominant language and a supraordinate national culture that would supercede the claims of classes and subcultures. Nationalism today has evolved far from such Enlightenment roots. Many nationalisms are authoritarian and even genocidal against their enemies. Native India was intensely nationalistic during its opposition to British rule, but today contains neither a common language nor a national culture. Whereas in the past, violent ethnonationalisms were tightly focused on a particular territory and were directed at the nation-state that encompassed that territory, the weapon of terrorism seems to be increasingly employed by deterritorialized nationalisms.

The second form, *ethnonationalism,* is often in conflict with the nation-state. All nationalisms share certain characteristics with ethnicity, such as the very selective and perhaps creative construction of history, some emotive sense of group communion and cohesion, and some overarching sense of unity. However, ethnicity is not nationalism, nor is nationalism ethnicity. What brings the two together is the claims of an ethnic group to its own state or, at the minimum, to sovereignty within a state. In Africa, where imposed colonial boundaries grouped together people with radically different languages and cultures, such ethnic claims may be based on real differences as well as demands for ancient territory. In other cases, the ethnic groups may be linguistically, culturally, and physically identical, defined primarily by religion and selective histories, as is found with the Serbs and Croats in the former Yugoslavia and the Catholics and Protestants in Ireland. It would appear that in many cases in which the actual ethnic differences are the least, the feeling-tone of nationalism is at its most intense.

In *Imagined Communities,* Benedict Anderson (1983) traces nationalism from its roots in eighteenth-century European "print capitalism." Prior to this time, there was little sense of national unity beyond a generalized allegiance to the crown. With the emergence of wide-scale printing in the vernacular and of mass literacy, driven by publishers' search for profits through ever-expanding markets, the common people were for the first time able to identify themselves with others they had never seen and would never meet. These groupings were reinforced by the rapid spread of ideologies that divided people according to their languages, cultures, and legitimizing histories—complete with valiant self-sacrificing heroes—and attached them to specific territories.

On a world scale, nationalism seems to go through periods of peaks and valleys. From the late 1700s through the first decades of the following century, American nationalism succeeded in breaking the bonds of European rule. The "official nationalism" that dominated Europe in the middle of the nineteenth century was challenged by multiple reactionary ethnonationalisms. In the first half of the twentieth century, state nationalism was powerfully combined with absolutist ideologies such as communism and fascism. In the late 1950s and early 1960s, a peak of new-state nationalisms accompanied the process of decolonization. A common pattern emerged. The achievement of decolonization was followed by a period of fervent nation building, with coalition governments steadfastly focused on establishing national sovereignty, integrating the new country, and creating a national culture. When the initial promises did not materialize, regional and subregional resistances emerged. Over a generation or two, these resistances would take the form of ethnonationalisms, demanding formal recognition through sovereignty, state homelands, or special rights (Tambiah 1996: 127–31).

Today, globalization seems to be creating a new spate of intense nationalisms. There are many reasons for this. During the Cold War, both the United States and the Soviet Union provided massive military aide to dictators who would support one side or the other; the termination of such aid ended the unity established by pure force, leading to pent-up fragmentation. The collapse of the Soviet Union released not only a multitude of independent nations within its previous borders, but also opened the way for long-simmering ethnic rivalries in the former Eastern European allies. The relinquishment of economic functions once monopolized by the state to global institutions, such as multinational corporations, the World Bank, the International Monetary Fund, and the World Trade Organization, helped to reduce the power of the state to maintain conformity. A multitude of grassroots organization, sometimes supported by or aligned with global nongovernmental organizations, emerged to fill in power vacuums at the local level. Modern communications and cheap long-distance travel have made it possible for deterritorialized diasporas to make and maintain contact. The Internet may become the contemporary equivalent of Anderson's "print capitalism" in its ability to unite people in many different countries. For example, the numerous Web sites on the Armenian genocide of 1915, complete with histories, survivor accounts, and horrific photographs, provide a new sense of outraged national consciousness (Kojiian 2002).

Arjun Appadurai (1996: 158–77) foresees the emergence of a period of *post*nationalism as the nation-state becomes obsolete and other forms of allegiance and identity arise to take its place. Dominant state cultures will be increasingly diluted by the influx of transnational communities with the ability to maintain their cultures of separateness and their connections to a real or putative homeland. De facto multiculturalism will overwhelm the artificial unity of the nation-state. Although Appadurai may exaggerate the demise of the state, there can be little doubt that new forms of transnational nationalism are already arising to challenge old notions of the nation as a territorially bounded entity.

From Arab to Palestinian

The circuitous route by which a relatively small group of Arabs came to construct themselves as a Palestinian nation reveals many of the theory-defying complexities of the politics of identity in the twentieth century. The Palestinian experience is almost the opposite of the Israeli example above, in which an original national unity fragmented into a multiplicity of ethnic groups. In the Palestinian case, a unified nation emerged gradually out of a broad regional ethnic group (the Arabs). Emile Sahliyeh (1993) argues that this process passed through three stages, and it was not until the Intifada (popular uprising) of 1987 that a true sense of ethnic nationhood was firmly established.

In the nineteenth century and early twentieth centuries, the much-conquered area of the Eastern Mediterranean was part of the Ottoman Empire. It was occupied mostly by rural Muslim peasants, but in urban areas there were also sizable groups of Arab Christians and Jews. Under the Ottomans, the basis of unity was Islamic, not Arab. During World War I, the British convinced many Arabs to join them in overthrowing the Ottoman Turks, but Palestinians were not supportive; Britain actively backed Zionism—and Palestinians viewed the Ottomans as a bulwark against the settlement of Jews in the region and the establishment of a Zionist state. Thus, until the collapse of the Ottoman Empire at the end of the war, Palestinians tended to align themselves *against* Arab nationalism.

The Balfour Declaration of 1917, in which the British endorsed a national homeland in Palestine for Jews, and the League of Nations mandate for British administration in 1922 (which had actually begun two years earlier) signaled the end of the old order. Two distinct trends developed in Palestine, neither of them devoted to the goal of the Palestinian state that the British had promised during the war (and later denied promising). First, the more prominent families of the region, many of whom had business and political dealings with the British, wanted a degree of sovereignty within the British mandate. This group tended to be conservative, assuming a low profile toward the British. The second group was younger, more radical, and had few ties to the occupying administration. They demanded unification with Syria—at that time, under Prince Faisal. Syria was seen as protection against further inroads of Zionism. The collapse of the Faisal government in 1920 left Palestinian Arabs bereft of their major supporter and protector. They found themselves powerless either to stop the Zionists or to gain self-determination.

The second phase in the emergence of Palestinian identity began in 1948 when the United Nations formally created the state of Israel. The establishment of Israeli borders and the resulting war dispersed Palestinian Arabs in different directions: those inside Israel, those on the West Bank and in the Gaza strip, those in refugee camps in surrounding Arab states, and those who had taken up residence in many non-Arab nations. Such dispersal disrupted whatever Palestinian nationalism was emerging prior to 1948, and Palestinian Arabs had little choice but to identify themselves not particularly as Palestinian but as Arab, and to take their place within the broad Arab nationalism that was sweeping the Middle East and that, in the 1950s, found its visionary spokesman in Gamal

Abdal Nasser of Egypt. Palestinian interests were subordinated to those of Arab unity, and many Palestinians joined pan-Arab political organizations such as the Ba'ath Party, the Arab Nationalist Movement, and the Moslem Brotherhood.

The dream that the Arabs would unite to defeat Israel and reclaim the region was short lived. The collapse of the United Arab Republic in 1961 followed by the defeat of the Arab armies in the 1967 war with Israel threw the Palestinians back on themselves. They would have to go it alone.

The turn to Palestinian self-definition as a group separate from the Arabs and the growth of Palestinian nationalism took many forms. The inability or refusal of the Arab states to assimilate Palestinian refugees was one more form of isolation, but one that had its value in reinforcing Palestinian identity. Many took advantage of the geographical dispersal to gain education, establish businesses, and bring modernization back home. The mass media, mainly radio and television, provided means for creating a national identity with common goals. Organization now tended to be particularly Palestinian: for example, the General Union of Palestine Students and the General Union of Palestine Women. Militant groups were tightly focused, undiluted by pan-Arabism. Fatah, under Yasir Arafat, began fighting even before the 1976 war. Afterward, both the Popular and Democratic Fronts for the Liberation of Palestine were quickly established. The Palestinian Liberation Organization originated as a support group in the refugee camps, turning to active militancy when it was taken over by Arafat's Fatah commandos in 1969. Throughout the 1970s, there was a determined consolidation of Palestinian nationalism in the West Bank and Gaza, culminating in the first Intifada.

Sahliyeh argues that his analysis refutes two general theoretical perspectives on ethnicity and nationalism. One perspective views ethnicity as deriving from race, distinct national origins, religious beliefs, and above all a common culture. However, this definition does not apply because Palestinians are culturally, racially, and religiously identical to other Arabs. The other point of view holds that, relative to available alternatives, a united sense of peoplehood serves the practical function of providing security, status, power, and economic benefits. In reality, many Palestinians have refused economic assimilation even when it was possible and clearly to their benefit, and have chosen the more difficult course of economic instability and armed struggle. What this brief history also reveals is that identity is something that is constantly in progress, constantly negotiated against external opportunities and constraints. Above all, identity in this case is distinct from culture. Indeed, what seems to set the Palestinians apart from other Arabs is *not* culture, religion, or language, but a sense of territory and a shared history of crisis.

What's in a Word? The Threat of an Indian "Nation" in Brazil

Identity politics can be so divisive that words themselves are potentially explosive. For example, Loring Danforth (1995) scrutinizes the volatile term "Macedonian" in the southern Balkans and Greece. The term has three different meanings. In general discourse, it refers simply to people who claim a Macedonian identity, in contrast to, say Serbian or Greek. Within Greece, it has a regional meaning, referring to Greeks from Macedonia. Finally, in northern Greece it takes on a more specifically ethnonationalist meaning referring to an indigenous people of Macedonia. These apparently subtle differences have enormous political ramifications. Greece has an ideology of homogeneity and thus refuses to officially recognize the existence of Macedonians within its border and has virulently opposed the independent Republic of Macedonia that was established on Greece's northern border in the 1990s. Both sides in the conflict have developed elaborate histories dating back to Alexander the Great to support their positions.

In Brazil, it is the term "nation," especially when applied to the Indian population, that threatens the state. Unlike in some parts of Latin America, both the terms and concepts "Indian" and "indigenous" are legitimate and accepted (although they tend to go in and out of fashion). Indians have, in fact, captured the imagination of the Brazilian people far out of proportion to their relatively small numbers, rendering them a fascinating exoticism. The indigenous population numbers an estimated 236,000 to 300,000 and is comprised of over two hundred separate groups and 170 languages. Altogether they account for no more than 0.2 percent of Brazil's 160 million people.

Alcida Rita Ramos's (1998: 168–94) analysis of the attempts by indigenous people to move from a relatively benign ethnicity to a politically charged nationalism reveals the power that a single word can assume. It is only recently that the multitude of Indian tribal groups have sought a common voice. In 1972, a militant branch of the Brazilian National Conference of Bishops created the Indigenist Missionary Council (CIMI), based on the democratic and empowering principles of the theology of liberation. This was already well into the period of repressive, often brutal military rule that extended from 1964 until 1988. The Church, and especially the left-leaning theology-of-liberation faction within it, was already distrusted by the extreme right-wing dictatorship. The conservative national daily newspaper *O Estado de São Paulo* ran a weeklong series viciously attacking CIMI. The series was based on a document supposedly from The World Council of Christian Churches (no relation to the World Council of Churches) that revealed an insidious foreigner's plot to challenge Brazil's sovereignty over Indian lands, divide Brazil along ethnic lines, and turn the exploitation of the country's mineral wealth over to an indigenous population manipulated by foreign interests. It turned out that the document was forged and that no World Council of Christian Churches exists, but the articles succeeded in bringing the issue of national sovereignty out into the open while avoiding the political incorrectness of seeming baldly anti-Indian.

Two years after its founding, the CIMI began organized a series of "indigenous assemblies," which funded transport, food, and lodging to representatives of many linguistic and tribal groups. Although quite different culturally, the Indians recognized commonalities in their interactions with the Brazilian "Whiteman": destruction of forests; diminishing land bases; polluted rivers; intrusive roads; settlers; and, all too often, brutality and killing. The holistic composition of the organization was sufficiently unwieldy that ultimately more than a hundred groups broke off from it, ranging from regional and interest-oriented pan-Indian groups to very local organizations. Just as the Church had been the impetus for CIMI, many of these larger groupings were influenced by outsiders, such as missionaries, journalists, and especially anthropologists, and tended toward vertical and hierarchical structures. Smaller, more focused groups were often the indigenous reaction to outsider influence, and reflected more accurately the many different cultures.

Although CIMI routinely referred to its component groups as indigenous "nations," it was only in 1980, with the founding of the Union of Indian Nations, that the term took on a more incendiary tone. Why not simply stick with the term "ethnic"? Ramos (1998: 184–85) answers:

> Because, I dare say, the concept of ethnic group has neither the political strength nor the ideological wallop that nations does. Ethnic groups are regarded as social excrescences that history forced upon the country and that must be leveled out and diluted into mainstream nationality. . . . As a politically insipid term, ethnic has been relegated to the realm of culture. And as a rule culture is regarded as politically innocuous.

If the term "nation" in the title of a major pan-Indian organization was especially potent, it was because it butted against the dominant philosophy upon which Brazil had been founded, a philosophy of homogenization and unity. From its independence from Portugal in 1822, the country had been founded on the "liberal"—in the nineteenth-century sense—ideal of the vertical state in which there was no room for subgroups. "From this perspective social diversity was not regarded as an enemy to be physically wiped out (as in Argentina), but rather as an immaturity to be outgrown" (Ramos 1998: 181). The ideal state was a "collective individual," a single mind and body—a far cry from the United States idea of a "collection of individuals." The Indian claim to nationhood, rather than mere ethnicity, was perceived as a barb aimed at the very heart of the nation-state.

Ramos agrees that the use of "nation" is inflammatory without really designating a definable group. Lacking any real indigenous unity of culture, history, or language, nationalism becomes a divisive political rhetoric that is ultimately impotent.

> Pulled from its historical and multivocal context, the term Indian nation loses the implication both of state organization and of nationalism, for it is a concept that does not refer to nation-state, patriotism, national pride, or imagined communities. . . . In short, it is a nation without a nation. (p. 190)

SUGGESTED READINGS

Anderson, Benedict. *Imagined Communities: Reflections on the Origin and Spread of Nationalism.* Rev. ed (London: Verso, 1983). The nation, according to Anderson, is an imagined community in the sense that its members will never meet the vast majority of those who comprise the group. Already something of a classic, this study of the origins of nationalism in "print capitalism" has been enormously influential in the analysis of identity politics.

Appadurai, Arjun. *Modernity at Large: Cultural Dimensions of Globalization* (Minneapolis: University of Minnesota Press, 1996). This collection of essays by the foremost anthropological theorist of transnational identity emphasizes the declining power of the state and the importance of media in creating ethnicity and nationalism.

Danforth, Loring M. *The Macedonian Conflict: Ethnic Nationalism in a Transnational World* (Princeton, N.J.: Princeton University Press, 1995). Through analyzing the politically heated conflicts over the meaning of the term "Macedonian," especially between Greece and the Republic of Macedonia itself, Danforth describes a process of nationalist identity in the making.

Esman, Milton J. *Ethnic Politics* (Ithaca, N.Y.: Cornell University Press, 1994). Although the author is not an anthropologist, this interdisciplinary perspective will be of great interest to political anthropologists. After developing a detailed framework of analysis, Esman focuses on a number of ethnic movements and conflicts, ranging from Malaysia to Canada Quebec.

García Canclini, Néstor. *Cultural Hybridity: Strategies for Entering and Leaving Modernity* (Minneapolis: University of Minnesota Press, 1995). This book, which popularized the term "hybridity" in the social sciences, is tightly focused on the modern/traditional conflict in establishing overlapping identities in modern Mexico.

Ramos, Alcida Rita. *Indigenism: Ethnic Politics in Brazil* (Madison: University of Wisconsin Press, 1998). Indigenous peoples, mostly in the Amazon region, comprise only 0.2 percent of the population of Brazil, but they have assumed a role in popular consciousness out of all proportion to their numbers. The author, who has spent more than 30 years working with Brazil's Indians, explores their many attempts to maintain their lands and sovereignty through multiple political strategies.

Toland, Judith D, ed. *Ethnicity and the State: Political and Legal Anthropology Series*, Vol. 9 (New Brunswick, N.J.: Transaction, 1993). The editors' introduction provides a good overview of anthropological approaches to ethnicity. The nine articles range from a historical study of Indians in Ecuador in the nineteenth century to contemporary research on the Batak of Indonesia.

Wilmsen, Edwin N., and Patrick McAllister, eds. *The Politics of Difference: Ethnic Premises in a World of Power* (Chicago: University of Chicago Press, 1996). The nine articles, mainly by European anthropologists, tend toward general theory and regional overviews. The editors' Introduction and Jan Nederveen Pieterse's "Varieties of Ethnic Politics and Ethnicity Discourse" are especially valuable for anyone wanting a brief overview of the anthropological perspective on ethnicity.

Postmodern ethnologist Michael Taussig powerfully evokes the horror of colonial oppression of Latin American Indians in *Shamanism, Colonialism, and the Wild Man.* Courtesy of the Library of Congress.

Chapter 10

MODERNISM, POSTMODERNISM, AND THE EMERGING SYNTHESIS

After a long, bitter, and successful struggle against the last remnants of structural-functionalism, the process theorists and individual-oriented political ethnographers of the 1960s and early 1970s might well have believed that they could look forward to a well-deserved day in the sun. This was not to be the case. What could not have been foreseen back when process and structure-function must have appeared to be polar opposites was that both winners and losers would be found to share a common fatal flaw, namely, the Enlightenment idea that they were objectively describing society. Interest soon shifted away from the promising inchoate paradigms to a debate over the very nature of anthropology itself.

The three decades at the end of the twentieth century were a period of extreme ferment within anthropology. During what came to be known—with some understatement—as a "crisis of representation," a furious free-for-all raged between materialist and idealist, scientist and antiscientist, modernist and postmodernist. The "representation" that was in crisis had to do with the authority of the anthropologist to portray cultures in any objective way and to make generalizations. The ripple effects of this self-questioning, sometimes bordering on self-flagellation, encompassed a dethroning of anthropological big men such as Boas and Malinowski, the reinterpretation of the history of anthropology as a colonialist project, the questioning of traditional fieldwork methods, and even a Cartesian doubting of reality itself.

What came to be known as postmodernism was a fragmented synthesis of a multitude of influences, dating at least to the 1950s but possibly back to Frederick Nietzsche ([1883] 1976, [1887] 1989) and beyond. It was Nietzsche who, in the late nineteenth century, proclaimed not only the death of God but also of all the grand theories of his time, who repudiated the dehumanization of science and reason, who demanded a return to subjectivity, who catalogued the myriad ways that men eagerly embraced their own domination, and who understood that power was much more subtle and malicious than simply a matter of who has the guns. It was also Nietzsche who expressed it all in the mocking polemical tones of the prophet Zarathustra. However, if Nietzsche is the very model of the postmodern major theorist, it is only in retrospect: the more visible and direct influences, at least for anthropology, were a number of diffuse trends emerging from literary studies, French philosophy, and the new discipline of culture studies. Postmodernism seems to have started in the field of architecture (Rapport and Overing 2000: 294), but is most associated with such philosophers of society and language as Jean-François Lyotard (1984), Jean Baudrillard (2000), and Michel Foucault (2001, 1972, 1980). In the United States, four overlapping trends more or less coalesced into a broad and indefinable postmodernism: interpretive anthropology, critical theory, poststructuralism, and postmodernism proper (see Table 10.1).

A key element of postmodern conceptions of power is that it is not based solely on force. One of the major influences on this line of interpretation is Antonio Gramsci (1971), a Marxist activist who spent his most productive intellectual life in prison during the Mussolini regime of the 1930s. His writings tend to be tightly focused on Italian history, but have a much wider application. Gramsci broke with the orthodox Marxist emphasis on materialism, stressing the important role of "superstructure"—that is, ideology and culture. His primary influence on political anthropology is his concept of "hegemony," a term that has become increasingly ubiquitous and diffuse, meaning virtually any kind of domination (economic hegemony, cultural hegemony, Western hegemony, and so forth). Gramsci was somewhat more specific, although his multiple scattered mentions of the term can be confusing. Basically, hegemony is "the 'spontaneous' consent given by the great masses of the population to the general direction imposed on social life by the dominant fundamental group. . . . " (1971: 12). In practice, this is a matter of both force and consent, which balance each other recipro-

Table 10.1
"Postmodernism" in Anthropology as a Convergence of Four Theoretical Trends

	Defining Attributes	Key Terms	Major Work
Interpretive Anthropology	• Method of "thick description" requires intensive empirical fieldwork; rejects possibility of scientific objectivity; all interpretation is situated • Ethnography as literary text • Analyzes symbolic systems to understand cultures as experienced • Seeks to express point of view of "others" rather than of researcher	Thick description Text Paradigm (cultural) Systems of meaning	Geertz, *The Interpretation of Cultures*, especially, "Deep Play: Notes on a Balinese Cockfight."
Critical Anthropology	• Anthropological representations reveal more about ethnographer than people studied • Lack of reflexivity leads to false sense of objectivity • Anthropology situated in colonialism, postcolonialism	Reflexivity Crisis of representation Situated knowledge	Clifford and Marcus, *Writing Culture: The Poetics and Politics of Ethnography*
Postmodernism	• Contrasts Enlightenment modernism (progress through rationalism, technology, science) to postmodernity • Against all "grand theory" and "metanarratives" including science, which has become a privileged narrative • Subjectivity, impressionism emphasized over false objectivity • Rejects distinction of high and low culture • "Reality" is socially constructed; knowledge is relative	Hermeneutics Deconstruction Fragmentation Discontinuity Hybridity	Jameson, *Postmodernism, or the Cultural Logic of Late Capitalism*
Poststructuralism	• Studies discourse of historical time periods and institutions • Focus on epistemology and language • Rejects Lévi-Strauss' structuralism's universal claims • Emphasis on power as inherent in all discourse	Discourse Power/knowledge Gaze	Escobar, *Encountering Development*

Source: Lewellen 2002: 38.

cally—force against opposing groups who must be eliminated, or rendered ineffective, and consent for allies or those who can be converted to allies. This gives a special role to intellectuals and to the popular media, which use their moral and persuasive leadership to bring about "not only a unison of economic and political aims, but also intellectual and moral unity" (p. 181) among both dominating and dominated classes. The ruling class may need to make narrow economic concessions (e.g., toward labor legislation or welfare benefits), but it does so without surrendering any of its power base in the ownership of the means of production. Often Gramsci's idea of hegemony is wrongly considered as monolithic and undisputed structure of power; actually, he strongly emphasized that hegemony is fragile, always contested by alternative ideologies, and thus in need of constant reaffirmation and renewal (Alonso 1994: 381). Gramsci was mainly explaining the legitimacy of the state in modern Italian history—more specifically the legitimacy of the populist corporatism of fascism—but his theory better fits the ability of democracies to rule by consent, even in the face of the most blatant inequities.

THE FRENCH CONNECTION: BOURDIEU AND FOUCAULT

Of the multitude of French philosophers who influenced American anthropology, the greatest impact on political anthropology has come from Pierre Bourdieu and Michel Foucault. In many ways, these two authors are quite different: Bourdieu, a field anthropologist turned sociologist, is, in some ways, the consummate social scientist, insisting on precise empirical verification and supporting his hypotheses with intricate diagrams and reams of painstakingly collected statistics. Foucault is more than merely suspicious of social science pretenses at objectification; he views the social sciences as fulfilling a repressive disciplinary function. On the other hand, both men have very similar concerns about how power is invisibly manifested in ostensibly benign institutions and suffused through nonpolitical aspects of culture, such as fine art (Bourdieu) and sexuality (Foucault). With Gramsci, both men posit important power functions for intellectuals. In addition, both repudiate materialism, favoring symbolic interpretations; both firmly reject positivism in the social sciences on the ground that no value-neutral objectivism is possible; both seek to overcome the dichotomy between objective and subjective; and both reject "grand theory" while, at the same time, creating theories that are hardly less than grand themselves.

Bourdieu and Foucault are scholars of enormous productivity and labyrinthine complexity, so it is impossible to briefly condense their theories without ignoring the subtleties of argument or resorting to distorting simplifications. However, only certain aspects of their works have been incorporated within anthropology, sometimes becoming so normative that their sources are often lost (e.g., Bourdieu's "cultural capital" and Foucault's "discourse"). I have made no attempt at a broad summary, but instead have settled on outlining the more significant influences on political anthropology.

Pierre Bourdieu

The young Pierre Bourdieu served in the Army in Algeria during the War of Algerian Independence, staying on after the conflict to carry out intensive fieldwork in the Arab community of Kabylia. Although he would gradually identify himself more as a sociologist than an anthropologist, throughout his career he continued to refer back to his ethnographic work, devoting half of his pivotal *The Logic of Practice* ([1980] 1990b) to applying his developed theories to an intense structural analysis of Kabyle society. His more sociological work, notably *Distinction: A Social Critique of the Judgment of Taste* ([1979] 1990a), combines such sociological techniques as survey research and statistical analysis within an analysis of class and culture. By 1998, his reputation earned him a cover story in a popular French news weekly as "the most powerful intellectual in France" (Lane 2001: 1), rendering him the status of celebrity-intellectual shared by existentialism's Jean Paul Sartre and post-structuralism's Jacques Derrida and Michel Foucault. Bourdieu, however, is more difficult to situate, because he has resisted attempts to place him within past or existing paradigms. Although sharing postmodernism's rejection of Enlightenment objectivism, he also firmly rejects what he perceives as postmodernist attacks on science and scientific method. Strongly opposing both "the vacuous and resounding abstractions of theoreticism and . . . the falsely rigorous observations of positivism" (Bourdieu and Wacquant 1992: 27–28), Bourdieu has sought to unite objective and subjective, macro and micro, agency and structure in a single unified sociological system. Although that system is quite complex, it can be summarized within a few central concepts: cultural capital, habitus, and field.

For Bourdieu, the crucial question faced by the social sciences is one of power: How do hierarchical social systems maintain and reproduce themselves over time? Obviously, in modern democratic societies, social status is not maintained by force, nor is it—a la Marx—essentially a matter of economics, of who owns the means of production. Indeed, teachers, artists, writers, and other intellectuals are often represented in the status hierarchy at much higher levels than might be predicted by their incomes or political power. The answer lies partially in that *all* cultural symbols and practices embody social distinction and thus help to determine the hierarchies of power.

Crucial to this analysis is that culture itself is a form of capital, just as are money and property. Cultural capital is manifested in several different ways. It can be a largely unconscious set of predispositions that emerge from socialization into a particular class: ways of speaking and writing; a general awareness of how society works; preferences for certain types of art, music, and literature; and even posture and stride. Cultural capital can also be objectified in published books, in the possession of scientific instruments that require specialized knowledge, or in paintings that one has produced. Finally, cultural capital includes such things as graduate degrees or licenses to practice medicine that have been achieved within an educational credentials market. Side by side with such cultural capital is social capital: kin relations, circles of friends, and influential old-boy networks. Cultural capital, like economic capital, is a limited and often-scarce resource. One inherits a certain amount of it from one's parents, but much has to be attained and maintained through intense competition throughout life.

Those with the most and most valued cultural capital at once reflect the norms of society and establish those norms. It is they who have the capacity to impose a taken-for-granted worldview on the rest of society. For the middle classes and underclasses this worldview—an unquestioned acceptance of hierarchies of power and of inequalities—is close to what Marx refers to as "false consciousness," but it does not necessarily emerge from nor is it reproduced among the wealthy alone. This is why Bourdieu puts such an emphasis on intellectuals; in France he finds in writers, artists, musicians, and philosophers the means of creating and legitimizing power.

The social conditionings implicit in such legitimization are embraced within the individual's *habitus*. Bourdieu (1990b: 53) defines this term, rather confusingly, as:

systems of durable, transposable dispositions, structured structures predisposed to function as structuring structures, that is, as principles which generate and organize practices and representations that can be objectively adapted to their outcomes without presupposing a conscious aim at ends or an express mastery of the operations necessary to attain them.

In other words, habitus is Bourdieu's solution to the perennial problem of structure versus agency: how does society determine or at least circumscribe individual behavior when individuals are ostensibly free to act of their own accord? Why does the behavior of individuals follow statistically predictable patterns?

For Bourdieu, social reality is objective and subjective, simultaneously in-here and out-there. Habitus is the largely unconscious internalization of the objective norms and rules of society that suggest how we might act within any given situation. It is not determinative, because norms and rules are not rigid; indeed, it may be conflictive; contested; and, within limits, malleable. In fact, in situations in which action is highly regulated, as in a prison or the military, habitus may play little or no role because decision making is minimized. Most human action does not result from consciously selecting among all possible alternatives, but is, rather, the result of mental habit. Given any situation, habitus will provide a framework that will direct action within a very limited number of improvisations. Although habitus has, with some accuracy, been compared to Noam Chomsky's concept of the deep structure of language, there is nothing innate about it; it always derives from class-specific socialization and emerges as a largely unconscious strategy that is directed toward one's own self-interest. Habitus is thus in opposition to rational-actor theories that assume that strategies consciously emerge from an analysis of available information and the range of possible actions. Although habitus has similarities to some anthropological conceptions of culture, there are also some major differences. For example, it contains little of the thick description of Clifford Geertz (1973), in which layer upon layer of symbolic meaning can be peeled away in a sort of cultural psychoanalysis. Habitus is culture as practice, not as symbolism in the sense of imagery.

Habitus is manifested within *fields* of competitive struggle. There are as many of these fields as there are forms of capital: economic capital is the valued resource within the economic field; artistic capital, within the field of art; scientific capital, within the scientific field. Within these competitions, those already established in positions of power will utilize conservative strategies, whereas challengers will employ subversive strategies. Despite these differences, there is general agreement about the ends of the competition and what resources are most valued. As with a series of poker games played on different tables, each field will have its own agreement on the nature of the particular game, the stakes, and the rules. However, there is a major difference from poker: in playing these power games, strategy is based on prereflective rules embedded in the individual's habitus rather than a rational assessment of probabilities. Indeed, there are strong limits to objective knowledge, because it is difficult or impossible to think outside of one's own habitus.

It is through these struggles and through the unconscious assimilation of society's existing rules that hierarchies of power are maintained and reproduced from generation to generation. Thus, for Bourdieu, habitus ties together the macro (the objective social structure) and the micro (individual action) into a seamless unity. Bourdieu thus rejects postmodern subjectivism on the grounds that there really is an objective social structure, describable through systematic data collection and observation, and independent of any specific individual. However, this social structure exists at the individual level through the habitus, guiding action at a nonreflective, largely responsive level, so that the very process of decision making is never really free and never completely based on objective analysis.

This suggests a contradiction, one of which Bourdieu is acutely aware: if we can never get completely outside our given habitus, how can any real sociology be possible? If no knowledge can stand outside of social influence, how can we presume to analyze the society that circumscribes the way that we think? Obviously, we cannot construct such knowledge from the classifications, everyday representations, and individual self-understanding of the people within the society, for their understanding only reflects the surface. The answer is that "reflexive sociology" requires an awareness of the nature of habitus and of the constraints of culture. The sociologist must make himself cognizant of his position within the society that he is describing. Methods that are both systematic and rigorously self-critical must be developed to get below the surface (Bourdieu 1990a, 1990b; Bourdieu and Wacquant 1992; Lane 2000; Swartz 1997).

Michel Foucault

Michel Foucault opens his book *Discipline and Punish* (1977) with an agonizingly detailed account of a public torture that took place on March 2, 1757, in the plaza in front of the main door of the Church of Paris. Over a period of hours, the accused's flesh was torn with red-hot pincers and upon the wounds was poured "molten lead, boiling oil, burning resin, wax and sulphur melted together," and then his limbs were pulled off by six horses. Finally, his still living body was thrown on a fire. The crime that justified such grisly spectacle was an attempted assassination of the king of France, within who resided the power of the state. Public torture was thus a form of ritual that symbolically reaffirmed and restored threatened sovereignty. In the preindustrial economy of France, society was based on a personal relationship between the sovereign and his subjects. Within the theater of pain, spectators were not mere observers, but were active participants in the re-establishment of order.

Although the killing of a regicide was accomplished with exceptional imagination, torture was a routine and expected part of the judicial process—systematic, codified, and strictly regulated. Within a system that recognized degrees of guilt according to the evidence, confession was considered the most important form of evidence, and torture was a legitimate means of gaining it. The imposition of pain and death by the state was the primary means of punishment.

Jump ahead 80 years—the period of the French Revolution. Foucault quotes from the rules governing a prisoner's day. Gone is any deliberate attempt to inflict pain. Rather, what we see is dreary regimentation, based on the belief that the prisoner can be redeemed through control of his most minute behavior. Incarceration becomes the primary means not so much of punishment but of transformation. Public execution continues, but without the torture, and its meaning has radically changed. State killing is no longer an affirmation of the power of the king over his subjects, but has become a morality play in which the public is instructed in proper behavior.

This does not mean that the state has become more benign or less repressive, but only that a new political economy has brought about an alteration in the way that power functions. For Foucault, this was a crucial transitional period, when the mechanisms of power assumed a "capillary form of existence . . . where power reaches into the very grain of individuals, touches their bodies and inserts itself into their actions and attitudes, their discourses, learning processes and everyday lives. The eighteenth century invented, so to speak, a synaptic regime of power, a regime of its exercise *within* the social body, rather than *from above it*" (Foucault 1980: 39). In the world of feudalism, serfs could be easily regulated from above, but industrial capitalism required that the individual regulate himself. This would be accomplished through a process of disciplinary observation, or surveillance, which was aimed not only at the body but also at the subject's very soul (a term Foucault takes seriously to represent the psyche, personality, consciousness, and subjectivity of the individual). The quintessential model of surveillance is found in Jeremy Bentham's design for the panopticon prison, a circle of cells built around a central guard tower. In concept, each inmate is visible every moment. Of course, in practice every convict could not be under the guard's gaze at all times, but the possibility and illusion of constant surveillance would be sufficient to induce proper prison behavior. Here we have an inversion of visibility. In the days of the sovereign, it was the powerful that were most visible; now the subject is visible and power is hidden.

Such surveillance was hardly confined to prisons. Factories, hospitals, school classrooms, and military barracks are often designed precisely to maximize such disciplinary surveillance. The desired discipline is internalized and thus accomplished without recourse to violence. Paradoxically, however, although humans have in some ways turned themselves into machines, forced in the military to walk a certain way or stand at attention for long periods and on assembly lines to perform the same few actions endlessly, the purpose is not to create faceless automatons, but rather individuals. Only individuals can be ranked, judged, analyzed, and improved. Whereas in the past only rulers, heroes, and saints were individualized, now even the lowliest of men is a subject of minute record keeping. Individualization is accomplished partially via a process of normalization, in which a standard is set by a certain institution (the good soldier, the manly heterosexual, the worker who does his job well). Fall below the norm and one is punished; rise above, and one is promoted or rewarded.

What Foucault is doing in tracing these changes in approach to criminality is describing the *discourses* of different time periods. Foucault neither popularized the term "discourse" nor invented discourse analysis; what he did do is change the term's meaning to suggest a much more subtle and all-encompassing form of analysis. Previously discourse was a largely linguistic term that referred to a particular ideology, to ordinary conversation among a certain group or profession, or to social interaction. Foucault rejects all of these, and instead of perceiving discourse as a means of expression, he places it as the object of analysis. A comprehensive definition of the term, as used by Foucault, is difficult, because he himself uses it in different ways:

> Instead of gradually reducing the rather fluctuating meaning of the word "discourse," I believe that I have in fact added to its meanings: treating it sometimes as the general domain of all statements, sometimes as an individualizable group of statements, and sometimes as a regulated practice that accounts for a certain number of statements. . . . " (1972: 80)

Basically, and somewhat simplistically, a discourse is system of knowledge that determines the limits of thinking or acting—that is, it is a system of possibility that is specific to places and times; it is what allows us to make statements that are true or false. A discourse is comprised of a set of rules that is largely unconscious. In this sense, it resembles transformative grammar, in which a relatively small set of rules is capable of creating an infinite number of meaningful sentences. Unlike the rules governing language, however, discursive rules are those that determine what it is possible to know, perhaps even what is possible to conceive, and thus the rules that determine the limits of what we do as well as what we think. Among the rules underlying specific disciplines are those of exclusion (what cannot be included), classification (the ways in which we categorize things and their attributes), and order (the ways in which we relate things to each other). Rules also determine who can speak and who cannot; for example, only that body of credentialed experts designated "doctors" can get a hearing within the discourse of medicine. *All* discourses are historically specific; that is, they are related to particular historical conditions, and therefore there is no overall discourse that can claim ultimate truth (as is found, e.g., in the claims of science or religion). Critics have noted the lack of polemic in Foucault's writing, the dispassionate, nonjudgmental tone even when speaking of torture or madness. This is justified from his perspective on the grounds that it is impossible to judge one discourse as better than another, because there is no way to stand outside of discourse.

In a broad sense, it is possible to speak of Western discourse at a particular point of time. In his earlier works, Foucault uses the term "episteme" for such broad historical discourses. However, he uses the concept mostly to refer to systems of thought and action within specific institutions, such as prisons, hospitals, and Catholic confessionals, or to scholarly disciplines such as medicine, science, psychiatry, or sociology. Foucault's most important writings have focused on such circumscribed discourses as they have changed over time: madness, penology, medicine, and sexuality.

Foucault rejects liberal definitions of power as the ability to force people to do things through violence or the threat of violence. In addition, he does not view power as residing in individuals, classes, or—as Marx would have it—in those who own the means of production. Power is not a matter of conscious intention or decision making. Foucault (1980: 97) seeks to know "how things work at the level of on-going subjugation, at the level of those continuous and uninterrupted processes which subject our bodies, govern our gestures, dictate our behaviors, etc." Such all-pervasive power is inherent in discourse itself, because discourse determines what is true. Real power thus lies not in presidencies, police, and bureaucrats, but in the school system within which we are socialized, the medical profession that has control of our health, the psychiatric profession that determines what it is to be psychologically normal. Power cannot be separated from knowledge or vice versa—thus, *power/knowledge*. Claims to specialized knowledge are therefore claims to power, claims on the right to classify, to analyze, to observe, to experiment. In contrast to the ideology of Enlightenment liberalism in which truth is the enemy of power, truth, for Foucault, is a central aspect of power. Thus, instead of asking, "What is true?" he asks, "What discourse produces this particular set of truths?"

Discourses do exist outside the dominant discourse; however, they are subordinated and subjugated. Foucault has referred to his own writings as "fiction," not in the sense that he is telling made-up stories, but in the sense that his truth does not fit the dominant regimes of truth or the totalizing discourses of the day. In exposing the nature of power, he is offering a counter-discourse that invites marginalization.

DISCOURSE AND DEVELOPMENT

The direct application of Foucault's theories for anthropology are found in the discourse-analyses of "development," which became a virtual subdiscipline in itself in the mid-1990s. Arturo Escobar, in *Encountering Development: The Making and Unmaking of the Third World* (1995) seeks to deconstruct development, revealing it not as a beneficial process of modernization but as a "nightmare . . . [of] massive underdevelopment and impoverishment, untold exploitation, and oppression" (p. 4). President Truman, in the late 1940s, initiated a virtual development industry with his proclaimed goal of raising the living standards and levels of industrialization of the poorer countries to Western standards. "What does it mean," Escobar (p. 39) asks, "to say that development started to function as a discourse, that is, that it created a space in which only certain things could be said or even imagined?" The answer is that development, right from the beginning, relied exclusively on the knowledge system of the industrial democracies of the West. Alternative discourses—those of the peoples and cultures that would be affected—were ignored, marginalized, or subordinated.

The development discourse is fundamentally materialist—economic and technocratic. However, from the poststructuralist point of view, "The economy is not only, or even principally, a material entity. It is above all a cultural production, a way of producing human subjects and social orders of a certain kind" (p. 59). Thus, discourse analysis shifts the focus away from the targets of development—so-called "underdeveloped" nations and communities—to the agencies of development and the representations they make that do not so much reflect reality as constitute it. Within the normalizing discourse of development—the "normal" being Western capitalist industrialism—people are pigeonholed in various categories of abnormality: illiterate, underdeveloped, malnourished, landless peasants, and the like. The system assumes a superiority that negates even the possibility of any dialogue with inferior discourses. People are perceived as problems to be solved, and solutions are largely to be achieved through technology, conceived not only in its material sense, but also as a sort of moral force that will lead to an ethics of innovation and entrepreneurialism. Social life itself becomes a technical issue to be entrusted to technicians; that is, development professionals with specialized knowledge and the proper credentials. Prior to any intervention, the client populations are thus socially constructed by the development agencies as lacking something—technology, education, individualism, entrepreneurial values—that can then be supplied to them.

The "knowledge" of development agencies may have almost nothing to do with the people themselves, as is revealed in James Ferguson's (1994) analysis of the development industry's assault on Lesotho, a small landlocked country surrounded by South Africa. In 1979 alone, at least 26 countries donated $64 million in development assistance. The social history constructed by the World Bank to legitimize this huge intervention was a complete distortion of the country's past and present. Lesotho was portrayed as a typical underdeveloped peasant society, isolated from the market economy and in need of assistance in order to develop its resources. In reality, most of the agricultural land had been turned into plantations in the 1800s by Dutch colonists, displacing subsistence agriculturalists and forcing the men to migrate for wage labor jobs. Basically, the country is a labor reserve for South Africa. In Lesotho, according to Ferguson, development acts as an "anti-politics machine" that functions to displace discontent away from revolution against the state or the international system that maintains them in bondage.

The view that development constitutes a uniform discourse has been challenged even by those who adopt a Foucaultian methodology. Mark Hobart (1992: 12) argues for the coexistence of at least three different discourses in any development project: that of the developers, that of the target population, and that of the national government and local officials. Katy Gardner (1993: 134) observes that, although development may function hegemonically at one level, the development discourse is, in reality, created by many different agents with many different concepts of what constitutes their job. In her study of a long-term "Plantation Rehabilitation Project" in a country that she leaves unnamed (because she was hired as an advisor for the project), she found constantly changing discourses of development even within the donor agencies. In addition, power was not always centered in the hands of the donors; in this case, local plantation owners and government officials sometimes attained the upper hand. In addition, the workers, those at the bottom of the plantation hierarchy, often successfully made demands and challenged higher-level discourses. She concludes that discourse analysis and awareness of the knowledge/power nexus can be valuable, but only within limits. "Once we understand discourse as practice rather than as a systematized body of knowledge, we can see how it is produced through everyday conditions and activities and thus constantly subject to change and to the agency of individuals" (Gardner 1993: 154).

POSTMODERN ETHNOGRAPHY IN THE HEART OF DARKNESS

Postmodern writing runs the gamut from the highly general to the minutely particular, from Faulknerian density to Hemingwayic clarity, from the impersonal to the autobiographical. Thus, no single work could represent postmodernism's diversity. However, Michael Taussig's *Shamanism, Colonialism, and the Wild Man* (1987) embodies many of the dominant themes and styles common in postmodern ethnography: it is evocative rather than rationalist; its style is that of montage—fragmentary, self-contradictory, and disordered; it blends multiple disciplines including history, literature, anthropology, philosophy, poetry, and confessional biography; it explores Foucaultian notions of discourse, power, and knowledge; it gives voice to the subaltern while also quoting the writings of the colonizers; it is both self-reflective and self-referential; and, finally, it collapses categories and repeatedly disparages traditional anthropology's "magic of academic rituals of explanation" (p. xiv). His subject matter is "the politics of epistemic murk and the fiction of the real, in the creation of Indians, in the role of myth and magic in colonial violence as much as in healing, and in the way that healing can mobilize terror in order to subvert it" (p. xiii).

Taussig begins with a detailed rendering of the "culture of terror" that emerged out of colonialism in Latin America, and more specifically in the rainforests of the Putumayo River in southeastern Columbia. It was here, in the nineteenth and early twentieth centuries, within a context of routine murder and endemic torture, in this "space of death," that con-

queror and conquered, victimizer and victimized, were mutually transformed. The rubber boom required that Indians be converted into
laborers. Roger Casement, the British consul and close friend of Joseph
Conrad, who he had met in the Congo, reported the atrocities to a special
commission:

> The number of Indians killed either by starvation—often purposely
> brought about by the destruction of crops over whole districts or inflicted
> as a form of death penalty on individuals who failed to bring in their quota
> of rubber—or by deliberate murder by bullet, fire, beheading, or flogging
> to death, and accompanied by a variety of atrocious tortures, during the
> course of these 12 years, in order to extort these 4,000 tons of rubber,
> cannot have been less than 30,000 and possibly came to many more.
> (Casement, as cited in Taussig 1987: 20)

Casement bemoans such treatment, as well as the debt peonage—a blatant form of slavery—inflicted on Indians whom he viewed as "grown
up children." Perhaps, he opined, better wages would make all this
unnecessary (missing the point that Indians had no particular interest
in helping capitalist expansion no matter what). So much killing, dis-
memberment, and maiming, he noted, was hardly efficacious in a situation of acute labor shortage. Which, of course, missed the point that
terror was independent of the niceties of colonialism, that murder and
torture had their own logic in individual and group sadism, and that
the demands of power were independent of the rational calculations of
profit and loss.

Taussig's primary interests lie not in such econo-political analyses but
in the "mythic features, enclosed as they are in the synergistic relation
of savagery and business, cannibalism and capitalism" (1987: 73). Truth
in such a context does not emerge from the illusory, power-invested
objectivity of cross-checking facts but in paying serious attention to
myths and stories. "Far from being trivial daydreams . . . ," Taussig
observes, these stories and the imagination they sustained were a potent
political force without which the work of conquest and of supervising
rubber gathering could not be accomplished" (p. 121). Among the dominant motifs are the horror of the jungle and the horror of savagery,
especially cannibalism, which created a stark opposition between colo-
nizer and Other, but which, in the long run, was contagious, infecting,
and transformed conquerors and conquered alike. Ultimately, like Conrad's Kurtz in *Heart of Darkness,* colonial interlopers would succumb to
their own primordial savagery. Although Casement's shocked but real-
istic Foreign Office reports would create a factual Putumayo history for

the modern age, it would only be at the expense of masking a deeper "hallucinatory reality."

Whereas the first section of Taussig's book is a relatively straightforward evocation, through multiple and contradictory documents, of the Putumayo terror, the second and larger section is devoted more to this hallucinatory reality, expressed in the discourse of impoverished mestizos about Indians, in folk Catholic rituals, and above all, in the hallucinatory *yagé* experience of contemporary native healers and patients. It is through such a dialogue that one can feel the kaleidoscopic interconnections of wild and civilized, dominant and dominated, as it its expressed in the minutiae of everyday living.

According to legend—now rendered "true" in a booklet issued at the Church of La Merced in Cali, Columbia—in 1560, the lame Father Miguel de Soto had Indians carry him on their backs deep into the jungle to find a mythical vine-covered statue of Mary carrying the baby Jesus. The statue, known to the Indians as the Wild Woman of the Forest, was cut free and brought back to the church where, after performing many miracles, it stands today, conquered and tamed, its healing power brought under civilized control, transformed now into Our Lady of Remedies. Thus, "it is the Indian who is chosen by history to provide the civilized and conquering race with a miraculous icon. As a slave attends to the needs of the master, so the conquered redeem the conquerors."

However, it is in the *yagé* experience—including multiple personal journeys of the author—that is found the true voice of the Indian. *Yagé* is a powerful hallucinogenic drug that is employed in curing. Both shaman and patient take the drug and thus together enter into the intricate web of hybrid myths and stories, the deeply meaningful and reciprocal chaos that reaches beyond mere reason. A curious crossing may take place, a reversal of power, in which the Indian adopts mestizo imagery and the white man that of the Indian:

> In the lowland Indian's vision it is primarily the image of the splendor of the Columbian army in the highland city that provides the shaman with the powers to heal. . . . The image of the army is decisive. Its beauty, its gold, its arms, its music and dancing constitute a picture transforming evil. He tries to enter into this picture in order to sing and dance with the soldiers. . . .
>
> By contrast, the white colonist undergoes his transformative experience by means of the image of the shaman as devil. He dies at that point, ascending to the godhead of redemption. This process of death and rebirth swings on the pivot of wildness, as invested in the storming hurricane, light and shade, wild pigs, snakes coming into and out of oneself, and,

finally, the metamorphosing trinity of tiger-shaman-devil. (Taussig 1987: 327)

Taussig has little patience with rationalistic explanations of such experiences. He attacks the famous study of witchcraft among the African Zande by E. E. Evans-Pritchard (1937), in which sorcery is functionally interpreted as a means of explaining coincidence. Although there might be some truth to Evans-Pritchard's analysis, when weighed against the lived experience of shaman and patient, "such a formulation flattens our understanding of what their lives are about and what their invocation of sorcery does to what their lives are about. The clarity of the formula is misleading, and powerfully misleading at that" (p. 464).

Taussig wants no part of such distorting simplicities:

With his *yagé,* the colonially created wild man nourishes this chance against and in combination with the deathly reifications and fear-inspiring mysteries worked into the popular imagination by the official discourse of suffering, order, and redemption, institutionalized by the Church, the state, and the culture of terror. Working with and against the imagery provided by the Church and the conquest, *yagé* nights offered the chance, not to escape sorrow by means of utopic illusions, but rather the chance to combine the anarchy of death with that of carnival, in a process that entertains yet resists the seductive appeal of self-pity and redemption through suffering. (p. 467)

Although resolutely antidisciplinary, Taussig's book deserves to be included in the broad field of political anthropology because it is very much about power. However, the ways in which power is conceived, as inhering in historical documents, myth, folk beliefs, and the hallucinogenic experience, self-consciously offer a counter-discourse to political anthropology's traditional conceptualizations.

POSTMODERNISM: PROS AND CONS

Not long ago, anthropology was fairly neatly bifurcated along postmodern versus antipostmodern lines. This is not quite as true today. Much of postmodern thought has seeped into general anthropology, and beneficially so. Almost all fieldworkers have become reflexive about their inevitable ethnocentrism, their places within the societies they study, and about the specific point of view from which they are observing. There is a greater sensitivity to anthropology's history (although its colonial attachments can be exaggerated), and to the temporality of its paradigms. Postmodernism has successfully challenged once-rigid boundaries, not only among different academic disciplines but also within anthropology itself, questioning its perennial conceptualization of culture and community. Most important for political anthropology, postmodernism has pointed to the power inherent in knowledge itself, and the ways in which power permeates institutions previously considered neutral.

There are problems, however. It has been said that when a scientist is challenged he offers more data; when a postmodernist is challenged he offers more words. Although facetious, this observation does bring out a basic contradiction—actually two contradictions—inherent in the postmodern position. The first has to do with the criteria for determining truth or falsity, or, if that is too strong, for providing a convincing argument. If there is a general equivalence of discourse, one being as good as another, then why should that of postmodernism be preferable to that of more traditional anthropology? Given a "scientific" explanation and a postmodern one, what criteria can postmodernism provide to convince us to choose its side? Obviously it cannot be the accumulation of facts, or that the postmodern model fits the data better, because both of these criteria relate back to Enlightenment values that are specifically rejected. This would seem to suggest that the argument that wins is the one that *evokes* better, gives us a better *feeling* for what is being described, and is more *suggestive* or *subtler*—in other words, the criteria of literature. The postmodernist might argue that because the goal is not generalization but specification, not truth but interpretation, this criteria is perfectly legitimate; however, this merely begs the question: "Why choose this interpretation?"

With regard to ethnography, the answer would seem to be that the interpretation is based on thorough fieldwork and is convincingly argued. However, this brings out a second contradiction, or at least a paradox, in relation to the authority of the author. In traditional anthropology, in which the author is largely invisible, interpretation has tended to rest on data and methodology. One of the primary arguments—and a legitimate one—put forward by critical theorists is that the invisibility of the writer gives an illusion of objectivity and provides no sense of situatedness. However, in such writing, the implicit authority of the argument lies in the systematic accumulation and analysis of data and the use of the scientific method; if these are discounted, then virtually *all* of the weight of the argument falls on the author. After all, the author was there—she witnessed; she participated. However, this authority of the author is exactly what postmodernists reject, both in the "death of the author" sense that a work must be considered as a text, and in the sense that the power traditionally attributed to the author is distorting and illusory. The self-referential style of many postmodern works solves one problem—that of letting the reader in on the construction of the text, while amplifying another problem—rendering virtually all authority to the author. Some writers have tried to get around this by freely quoting and giving the natives a voice; however, if we are to believe Bourdieu, this can only provide surface information no matter how dramatic it might be; underlying meanings and structures must still be analyzed by the researcher. If culture or habitus or discourse or whatever is largely unconscious, the subaltern voice may be evidence but is hardly self-explanatory. Thus, we are back to the author's authority, and the question of why we should accept this particular interpretation.

Like Godel's Incompleteness Theorem—that axiomatic mathematical systems cannot prove themselves—postmodernism would seem to rest on a fundamental conundrum.

It is hard not to acknowledge the real contribution that has been made to anthropology—as well as history and literature—when postmodern authors are as interesting, imaginative, innovative, and stylistic as Taussig, or Carolyn Nordstrom, whose *A Different Kind of War Story* (1997) conveys the almost-unimaginable horror of the Mozambique conflict in a manner impossible in the more traditional "objective" ethnographic styles. The problem arises when claims are made that the postmodern approach is the *only* valid one and that it supercedes any attempt at a scientific anthropology that seeks to test or elaborate general theory. Such cosmic rejectionism turns postmodernism into exactly the type of meta-narrative it seeks to reject.

SUGGESTED READINGS

Bourdieu, Pierre, and Loïc J. D. Wacquant. *An Invitation to Reflexive Sociology* (Chicago: University of Chicago Press, 1992). It is rare that a major theoretician participates in an easy-to-read overview of his work. In Part I, Wacquant clearly summarizes Bourdieu's main concepts, such as habitus, cultural capital, and field. Part II is an edited version of a seminar with Bourdieu in Chicago, in which he answers questions from students. Part III is a transcript of a Paris workshop in which Bourdieu addressed students mainly on the subject of methodology.

Escobar, Arturo. *Encountering Development: The Making and Unmaking of the Third World* (Princeton, N.J.: Princeton University Press, 1995). Escobar applies Foucault's theories to an analysis of the discourse of development, revealing how Western conceptual patterns defined a process that has been destructive to non-Western societies throughout the world. A curious mixture of polemic and erudite scholarship, the book was influential in creating a virtual subdiscipline of antidevelopment literature.

Ferguson, James. *The Anti-Politics Machine: "Development," Depoliticization and Bureaucratic Power in Lesotho* (Cambridge: Cambridge University Press, 1994). Ferguson demonstrates how concepts such as "discourse" and "power/knowledge" can be fruitfully employed without succumbing to postmodern rejection of empirical methodology. The well-researched book focuses not on the targets of development in Lesotho, but on the discourses and practices of the enormous development industry that focused its attention on that tiny African country.

Foucault, Michel. *Discipline and Punish: The Birth of the Prison* (New York: Vintage, 1977). Foucault examines the emergence of different discourses of punishment and penology since the seventeenth century, revealing a movement from power centered in the sovereign to the form of power exercised today, in which the primary mechanisms of power are surveillance and discipline. Although Foucault's style is often dense, and his historical evidence minutely detailed, this is arguably the clearest exposition of his theory of power.

Kuzner, Lawrence. *Reclaiming a Scientific Anthropology* (Walnut Creek, Calif.: Altimira, 1997). The author is an unapologetic apologist for scientific anthropology. He describes and debunks recent challenges to scientific thinking, including postmodernism, and maps out his own program for putting the science back in social science. A good book to read in conjunction with Lemert, below.

Lemert, Charles. *Postmodernism Is not What You Think* (Malden, Mass., 1997). There are a number of books that explain postmodernism. This one by a sociologist convert to the cause is one of the clearest and most thorough. My only reservation is that a more accurate title would be: *Postmodernism Is Exactly What You Think*.

Nordstrom, Carolyn. *A Different Kind of War Story* (Philadelphia: University of Pennsylvania Press, 1997). This powerful study succeeds in going beyond traditional anthropological objectivism to evoke the horrors of the 15-year war in Mozambique, often through the voices of the people who experienced it. The first chapter, which provides a rationale for her technique, is a good introduction to the theory underlying postmodern ethnography.

Taussig, Michael. *Shamanism, Colonialism, and the Wild Man* (Chicago: University of Chicago Press, 1987). The brief outline of this book in this chapter barely touches on the rich historical documentation and native narration that Taussig uses to develop his argument for a complex dialectical blending of colonial and Indian worlds in the Putumayo River region of Columbia. The first section is a powerful description and analysis of the "culture of terror" of the rubber-tapping industry. The longer second section connects this historical material with present-day Indian concepts of healing.

Chapter 11

FROM MODERNIZATION TO GLOBALIZATION

Two major forces are in the process of transforming political anthropology. Postmodernism, discussed in the previous chapter, redistributes power away from individuals, classes, and state bureaucracies, embedding it in the fabric of discourse and knowledge. Globalization, the second major influence, is shifting power in other directions, both upward and downward, to global economic institutions such as the World Bank and the International Monetary Fund, and to nationalisms, ethnicities, and local-level nongovernmental institutions such as women's rights organizations and ecological groups. These changes are so profound that political anthropology is already a different discipline than it was only a decade ago and continues to change rapidly.

Within political anthropology's first 30 years or so, field-workers were able to generate their own categories, their own vocabularies, and their own theories without much reference to what was going on outside of the discipline. The functionalist studying the Nuer or the action theorist observing the political manipulations of an individual had little need for the megatheories even then emerging in the fields of economics and political science. During the 1970s and 1980s, however, it became impossible to ignore the fact that virtually all the societies that anthropologists researched were embedded in larger systems. Because the societies that anthropologists normally studied were within so-called "developing" countries, theories of development needed to be taken into account. Two

An American naval vessel in a Japanese harbor in the nineteenth century. The capitalist world economy was spread through trade and military might. Courtesy of the Library of Congress.

dominant perspectives evolved under the rubrics of *modernization theory* and *dependency theory*. By the 1990s, it was evident that neither of these was sufficient to explain an increasingly complex world, a world in some ways more integrated and in other ways more fragmented than could be accounted in either paradigm. Although globalization has not been articulated as a coherent theory (although there are myriad theories *about* globalization), the concept itself has been embraced as a way out of the theoretical impasse brought about by the increasingly evident insufficiencies of dependency theory.

MODERNIZATION THEORY

Until after World War II, there was little concept of what is today commonly known as the developing (or underdeveloped) world, because most of the countries now placed in that category were colonies. They weren't supposed to develop. Their goals were, quite overtly, to supply raw materials, cheap labor, and status to the mother countries of which they were extensions. As these countries gained their autonomy through the 1960s, the idea that they should "develop," at least in the sense of reducing poverty, became an article of faith in the First World. Aiding this process was partially altruistic, but, like the Marshall Plan that helped to rebuild Europe, it was also a matter of practicality; development would undercut the appeal of communism among the poor nations, as well as provide resources and markets for the United States.

The group that came to be known as "modernization theorists" used what at first appears to be a commonsense approach. Underdevelopment was perceived as a sort of primal condition; it was, virtually by definition, the normal situation of a society before it began to industrialize. It was observed that as countries began to develop a modern sector, they would become dual societies—one modernizing and one traditional. The modern sector would take off, leaving the traditional sector behind. Simon Kuznets (1955), with his Kuznets's Curve—a mathematical graph—demonstrated that income inequality would increase as the two sectors drew apart. However, based on historical data from the West, once per capita income reached about $700 (in 1960 dollars), there would be a decrease in inequality; income would become more evenly distributed as the poor began to participate in the modern sector. The challenge was to expand the modern sector until it engulfed the traditional sector; then the country would be developed.

So how was this to occur? To seek an answer, some scholars examined how the Western industrial democracies did it. Supposedly, if one could figure out the steps that Europe and the United States went through over the course of two hundred years, the process in developing countries could be deliberately speeded up. As articulated by W. W. Rostow (1960), development could be divided into five stages. First, there was traditional society, characterized by a low level of technology, a high concentration of resources in agriculture, and a low ceiling on productivity. In the second stage, the basic preconditions for development are set: an effective centralized national state and the spread of the belief in economic progress. During this transition period, capital is mobilized, trade increases, technology develops, and the government begins to support economic growth. In stage three, "take-off" occurs, and the society kicks into high gear. From there it will "drive to maturity" (stage four) of its own momentum until stage five, an "age of high mass-consumption" (maturity?), is attained. All this might sound uncomfortably familiar to anthropologists who recall nineteenth-century theories that postulated unilineal evolution leading from savagery to barbarism to civilization.

Although the causes of underdevelopment were seen as internal, the solutions would take place in the international marketplace. A country no longer had to wait for Rostow's stages to proceed of their own accord; the process could be helped along. After all, the developed countries had to invent all that machinery, amass all that capital, and create an entrepreneurial class out of nothing. If the First World could transfer those things to the Third World, the process of development would be enormously accelerated. Underdevelopment, from this point of view, is a matter of lacking something: the emphasis might be on technology, capital, education, entrepreneurial spirit, or administrative ability. Much theorizing became the search for the missing factor: what was it that developing countries *most* lacked? Whatever, if these deficiencies could be provided through foreign aid and the investments of multinational corporations, then the countries would develop. The theory relied heavily on classical economist David Ricardo's (1772–1823) concept of "comparative advantage," the idea that each nation should do what it does best—whether that is producing coffee or automobiles—and share in the expertise of other nations through trade. Because it would be the economic elite—that is, the owners and managers—who would belong to the modern sector, they would be the engines of development. Their profits would be put to work to create new production and new jobs, thus bringing the masses into the modern sector and raising their standard of living. Thus, modernization theory postulated a "trickle-down" process in which an increase in the wealth of the rich would raise the standard of living of those at the bottom.

Logically, it should have worked, and, indeed, it seemed to be work-ing. Between 1950 and 1975, hundred of billions of dollars and a great deal of expertise and technology were transferred to the Third World where, accordingly, per capita Gross National Product (GNP) grew at an average rate of 3.4 percent per year, far faster than the First World had developed (Morawetz 1977).

However, it gradually became evident that something was seriously wrong. A number of studies of income distribution revealed that the gap between the rich and the poor was widening, and in some cases the poor seemed to be getting poorer. This effect was seldom alleviated when the GNP reached some postulated level, as Kuznets (1955) had predicted (Brazil, with a per capita GNP of $1,640 by 1985, had achieved the dubious status of having the worst income distribution in the world). In a hypothetical country, a GNP growth of 5 percent in a given year might mean that the very rich increased their wealth by 15 percent while the income of the masses declined. Also, one goal of the modernization theorists was to close the gap between the First World and the Third World; in reality that gap has been widening at an extremely rapid rate.

Modernization theory may be defined in terms of its dichotomy be-tween tradition and modern, in which case it seems somewhat naive. However, if it is more broadly defined against later dependency theory, as the perception that the causes of underdevelopment are internal to the country, rather than located in the international sphere, then some fairly sophisticated analysis took place within this broad paradigm. Some mod-ernization theorists turned their attention to an empirical examination of the processes of change already visible within the Third World itself. Political sociologist S. N. Eisenstadt (1967, 1970) developed an alter-native model of modernization. Far from unilineal development, Third World countries reveal a remarkable variety of development patterns, some absolutely contradictory to the "stages" theory. For example, there is often a *negative* correlation between the degree of industrial devel-opment and literacy, mass media, education, and the like; in many coun-tries, development is so concentrated that only a handful of the population shares its benefits. According to Eisenstadt, the "common core" of modernization is *social differentiation* and *social mobilization.* The political sphere must be sufficiently differentiated from the religious sphere if the society is to be flexible enough to make the adjustments necessary to the constant change that is integral to the modernization process. In the Islamic countries, modernization has been severely re-tarded because of the identity of conservative religious tradition with politics. "Social mobilization" refers to the process by which traditional social and psychological loyalties are broken down so that new rearrangements of society and economy may become possible.

With regard to politics, administrative centralization and political elites are crucial elements of the modernization process. Centralization requires, first, an ideological transformation in which at least some local loyalties are shifted to a national government, or, more likely, one in which traditional groups begin to perceive the benefits accruing to them through support of a national government. This requires the establishment of symbols—for example, flags, national heroes, national origin myths, and national-level enemies—that are flexible enough to relate many diverse groups to the center. Centralized government, which requires some sort of bureaucratic framework, calls forth new organs of political competition (such as factions, special interest groups, and political parties) that must develop new rules of the political game. These rules can range from democratic voting to the Bolivian-style coup. Modernization invariably begins with some sort of elite center: rich landowners, an entrepreneurial class, or the military. All too often, both economic and political modernization will be restricted to this core group, resulting in a situation of *internal colonialism* in which a few small elites who are centered in one city exploit the rest of the country. In such "patrimonial states," common to Southeast Asia and Latin America, the elitist monopoly on modernization and political process is established as a permanent condition. If modernization is to expand beyond these elites, it must proceed through ever-widening political socialization, as new groups and new strata of society are brought into the political process.

DEPENDENCY THEORY

Was the Mayan civilization of Mexico "underdeveloped"? How about the precontact Eskimo, or the Bushmen of the Kalahari Desert of Africa who were hunter-gatherers until only a decade ago?

Such questions do not seem so much difficult to answer as simply absurd. Of course, people who are culturally intact, economically self-sufficient, and well adapted to their native environments are not "underdeveloped." However, this very absurdity reveals a fundamental problem with much modernization theory, which views underdevelopment as a primary condition characterized by a lack of technology, the entrepreneurial ethic, and capital. The Mayans, the Eskimo, and the Bushmen may be considered underdeveloped *today*, but only because they were all invaded by Europeans. "Underdevelopment," then, is not a thing, not some sort of natural state. It is a *relationship,* specifically a relationship with the "developed" countries, or as L. R. Stavrianos puts it in his massive history of the Third World, *Global Rift* (1981: 34–35):

> [T]he underdevelopment of the Third World and the development of the First World are not isolated and discrete phenomena. Rather they are organically and functionally interrelated. Underdevelopment is not a primal or original condition, to be outgrown by following the industrialization course pioneered by Western nations. The latter are overdeveloped today to the same degree that the peripheral lands are underdeveloped. The states of developedness and underdevelopedness are but two sides of the same coin.

This, in a nutshell, is dependency theory. The capitalist development of the First World *caused* the underdevelopment of the Third World.

Dependency theory is usually dated to the early 1970s and viewed as a reaction to modernization theory. To a great extent this is accurate. However, much of the initial formulation of dependency theory appeared as early as the 1940s when Raúl Prebisch and a group of economists from the United Nations Economic Commission for Latin America articulated a world system based on a *center* of industrialized countries and a *periphery* of underdeveloped countries. The Third World remained in poverty because of unequal exchange; the terms of trade in the international marketplace favored the developed countries. Far from benefiting from comparative advantage, poor countries had to sell raw materials at low prices to the rich countries, which then returned manufactured goods at a high price. Whereas it might take 25 tons of raw sugar to purchase a tractor in 1960, 20 years later it might require 110 tons to buy an equivalent tractor. Also, most productive resources were taken up by the export sector so that little was left to raise the standard of living of the poor. The effects of export dependency are most notable in agriculture, in which domestic food production declines as more and more food lands are employed in the production of cotton or coffee for export, and subsistence peasants are driven from their lands. At this point, the problem was not seen to be capitalism per se but rather a conflict between international and domestic capitalism. Third World countries were prevented from developing domestic industrial and manufacturing capabilities because their products could not compete with similar goods coming from the First World, which were invariably cheaper and of higher quality.

Throughout the 1960s, these studies would have a practical effect in influencing the economies of Latin American countries. Virtually all of these countries, and many others throughout the Third World, turned to import substitution as a means to control the international market. Import substitution is a policy by which goods manufactured inside the country cannot be imported at all, or can only be imported with the payment of prohibitively high tariffs; the idea is to encourage domestic investment, to develop indigenous entrepreneurs and skilled workers, and to reclaim the economy from foreign owners. Regional markets, based on the European Common Market, were established in Latin America to try to control trade. In retrospect, these policies were failures, although there is disagreement over why they failed. From the modernization perspective, they failed because they interfered with the underlying logic of capitalism, the free flow of goods based on supply and demand. From a dependency perspective, they failed because they did not go far enough. It might be noted that Taiwan and South Korea, two countries that have rapidly and successfully developed, both used import substitution and extensive government planning in the early stages, but they also employed a number of other strategies such as massive land reform, universal access to education, government ownership of key industries, and redistribution of wealth *before* industrialization (not to mention hefty foreign aid from the United States because they were threatened by communism). They opened to the global economy only after they had established strong domestic economies.

From the point of view of the later dependency theorists, most experiments in modernization failed because of the continuing faith that widespread development could take place within an international system dominated by capitalism. The new breed of dependency theorists were almost uniformly socialist (Chilcote 1984: 113), at least to the extent of believing that only through public ownership of major resources or through a degree of delinking from the capitalist system could real development take place.

The World Capitalist System

There is a lack of time depth, reminiscent of the structural-functionalists, in the writings of many of the early dependency theorists. Everyone, of course, recognized the economic distortions caused by colonialism, but few traced the system back farther, except in the general terms of Marxist theory. It was Immanuel Wallerstein (1974, 1980, 1989) who provided a minutely detailed account of the historical evolution of the World Capitalist System and popularized the vocabulary for its structure.

In describing the past, Wallerstein uses the term "world" in a peculiar way. He speaks of early "world-empires," such as those of Rome and China, that were based on conquest and exploitation through taxes and tribute. However, these were fundamentally different from the European-centered "world-economy," based on structures of trade, dependence, and an international division of labor that emerged during the sixteenth century. Unlike the world-empires of old, the new capitalist world-economy placed economic power not in the hands of the rulers, but in the hands of the owners of the means of production. Although the modern nation-state evolved at the same time as did modern capitalism and, for a while under mercantilism, competed with the capitalists for economic power, ultimately the state assumed a secondary position, serving the capitalist owners in three fundamental ways: controlling worker's demands and protecting property rights, safeguarding markets and the flow of resources internationally, and bringing new geographical areas into the system through conquest and intimidation.

The world system that emerged, through complex cycles of expansion and contraction, is divided into economic zones based on an international division of labor (Figure 11.1). The *core* countries are the economic and political centers of the system, and its main benefactors. At first, these were a handful of European countries, but after the Industrial Revolution the core became associated with the fully industrialized countries, including Europe, the United States, Canada, and Japan. These countries are relatively rich, capital intensive (reliant on machine labor), and focused on high-tech production.

The *periphery* includes those countries that historically have supplied unprocessed mining and agricultural products to the core. Production is labor intensive, and manufactured exports tend to be low-tech. The earliest periphery countries—that is, those first exploited for raw materials and cheap labor—were the countries of Eastern Europe, which happened to be closest to the core. Relatively quickly, the Americas were brought into the periphery, and by the early twentieth century, the system encompassed the entire world.

A third economic zone, the *semiperiphery,* partakes of characteristics of both core and periphery and mediates between the two. These countries, such as Argentina, Singapore, and South Korea, have more independence than do the peripheral countries, and often act as regional powers. Most are politically closely allied with the core.

Another element might be added to this structure—the so-called comprador or tributary elites (Shepherd 1987). These are the owners and managers within peripheral and semiperipheral countries, often educated

Figure 11.1
The Capitalist World System

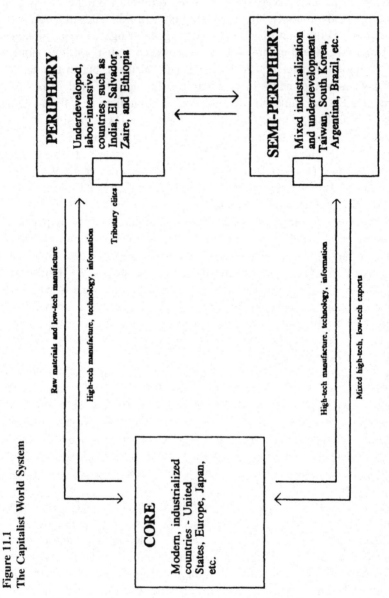

Source: Shepherd 1987 (on "tributary elites"); Wallerstein 1974.

in Europe or the United States, who through their ties and allegiances to transnational enterprises really represent the core.

As described by Wallerstein, the broad system boundaries are relatively stable, but there is considerable movement within them. Core countries can become peripheral and visa versa, and semiperiphery countries can move into the core.

The important thing about this perspective is that the world economy is seen as a *single* integrated system. However, there is no world political system. Political power is highly differentiated, consisting of numerous nation-states of varying degrees of autonomy and power, in competition with each other. The absence of a central political authority prevents the artificial restraints that would curtail capitalism.

Dependency theory in general, and world-system theory in particular, has been hotly criticized as simplistic in its neat division of the world and as economically deterministic, ignoring or slighting social, cultural, and political influences. One criticism was that dependency theory was postulated at such a high level of generalization that it tended to ignore the local-level and state-level conditions that promote underdevelopment. Hernando de Soto's *The Other Path* (1989) documented how in Peru a Kafka-esque labyrinth of laws created an impenetrable bureaucracy that made it extremely difficult and prohibitively expensive to participate in the legal economy. For this reason, the large majority of people lived in the informal economy of squatter housing, black market exchange, and gypsy transportation, where few taxes were paid, corruption was rampant, and the lack of enforceability of contracts prevented business growth. Although not really antithetical to a world-system perspective (as de Soto claimed), the data and analyses reveal a very significant *internal* component to ongoing poverty, a component as political and legalistic as economic. This suggests that some of the more sophisticated analyses of the modernization theorists, who focused on internal factors retarding development, might have considerable value even within a world-system framework.

"THE PEOPLE WITHOUT HISTORY"

In many ways, dependency theory and the world-system perspective were at odds with anthropological tradition, which focused on more or less clearly demarcated tribes, cultures, peoples, communities, and culture areas, either synchronically or within quite limited spans of time. Most ethnographers had difficulty relating their subjects to anything larger than a region or a state and seldom considered time periods of more than a few decades.

An important attempt to integrate anthropology and the world-system perspective is Eric Wolf's ambitious *Europe and the People Without History* (1982). Wolf points out that a negative effect of participant-observation fieldwork was to treat microcosms as wholes and thus to ignore the wider social and historical environment. There were, to be sure, attempts to reach beyond the particulars of time and place—notably diffusionism, neoevolutionism, and statistical cross-cultural comparisons—but none really exposed the crucial influences of European expansion.

Wolf categorically repudiates "the concept of the autonomous, self-regulating and self-justifying society and culture that has trapped anthropology inside the bounds of its own definitions" (p.18). He offers nothing less than "a new theory of cultural forms" (p. 19) that includes a historically based world perspective. Even the most remote of societies, he seems to be saying, can *only* be truly understood by reference to the global system.

The basis for Wolf's analysis is Marx's concept of "modes of production." Marx distinguishes between "work," the activity of individuals, and "labor," which is always social. Production is not simply a matter of people using nature to create goods; more importantly, production—which includes labor, technology, ownership, and transportation—determines the ways in which people relate to each other; that is, the ways in which societies are organized. A mode of production is, then, a way of deploying labor that has enormous consequences for the whole of society. Wolf delineates three fundamental modes of production:

- *The kin-ordered mode.* This mode—typical of bands, tribes and chiefdoms—is based on an opposition between those who "belong" to the group (e.g., a lineage or a clan) and those who do not. In addition, the division of labor considers gender, rank, and relations by marriage as well as blood relations. In other words, it is the kin group that determines the ways in which labor will be parcelled out. This mode depends heavily on symbolism, to the extent that kinship itself is a symbolic ordering of nature and to the extent that kinship systems are often legitimized by reference to the supernatural, such as ancestor spirits.

- *The tributary mode.* Although production in the kin-ordered mode is mainly a social and symbolic process, in the tributary mode it is a political process; that is, it is manifested through the exercise of power and domination. The tributary mode assumes two classes: a ruling elite of surplus takers and an underclass of surplus producers. The elite gains its ability to demand "tribute" either by controlling a strategic part of the production process (such as the land or irrigation works) and/or by possessing a means of coercion, such as a standing army. This mode encompasses a broad continuum, ranging from the tight centralized control of monarchs to the relatively weak control of local overlords (Wolf here combines two of Marx's modes of production, the "Asiatic" and the "feudal").

- *The capitalist mode.* Unlike Wallerstein, who views capitalism as a matter of exchange for profit, Wolf bases his definition on the buying and selling of human labor (in the tributary mode, the elites do not buy and sell labor, but only demand the products of labor). Marx's concept of "surplus value" explains how this works: that which workers produce above the value of their wages is a surplus that is transferred to the owners. Part of this surplus is sold back to the workers, in the form of goods, at a profit, and part is reinvested in new or expanded production. The two classes created by this system are the owners of the means of production at one pole and the labor force at the other. Competition among capitalists requires that they constantly reduce the costs of production, by cutting wages or some other means, while increasing output through technological change and greater efficiency. The process, then, involves three intertwined aspects: (1) capitalists control the means of production, (2) laborers must sell their labor to survive because they lack access to the means of production, and (3) there must be constant changes to increase production and cut costs. In contrast to kin-based systems, both the tributary and capitalist modes require an apparatus of coercion to protect the surplus-taking elites; this mechanism is the state.

In the year 1400, which Wolf employs as a convenient baseline, the kin-based mode was the most common in the area we now call the Third World. Outward expansion from Portugal, Spain, the Netherlands, France, and England spread European mercantilism to the far reaches of the world. Mercantilism, which superceded feudalism as the state gained control of local monarchies, was a system of state-encouraged and state-protected trade devoted to the enrichment of the state. The important thing about mercantilism for Wolf is that it is a tributary system. The spread of mercantilism thus shifted the kin-based mode of production to the tributary mode in native populations throughout the world, revolutionizing their social systems.

Tributary Transformation among the Plains Indians

The fur trade in North America reveals this process, as one culture after another was brought into the beaver trade, the buffalo trade, or the sea otter and seal trade. Few societies were altered as rapidly and as totally as were the Plains Indians—the Dakota, Cheyenne, Arapaho,

Mandan, and Pawnee, among many others. In prehorse days, they were woodland hunters and full-time horticulturalists living around the periphery of the Great Plains. Two influences combined to change their societies: the horse and commerce with Europeans.

The horse was introduced into the Americas in 1519 by Cortez during his conquest of Mexico, and was traded northward through a complex network. The Apache got horses around 1630; the Ute and Comanche around 1700, and the Blackfoot not until 1730. With the horse, the Plains tribes became full-time buffalo hunters. Even by the early 1800s, some tribes were not only hunting for their own benefit but also for that of the Europeans, supplying pemmican to explorers and traders; the Northwest Coast company needed almost 60,000 pounds of the preserved buffalo meat in a single year. Indians also supplied the frontier towns, such as St. Louis, with buffalo tongues and tallow. However, it was the virtual extermination of the beaver in the Northeast that created a new market for buffalo pelts on a massive scale. From the early nineteenth century, Indians supplied tens of thousands of skins per year to European traders (not mentioned by Wolf is the fact that female hides were preferred both for personal use and for trade, so female buffalo were killed at a ratio of 10 to 1, thus making the Indians major participants in the ultimate extinction of their own food supply).

These European influences touched every level of culture. With the adoption of the horse, group size—formerly small and relatively stable—became increasingly flexible. Buffalo dispersed into the mountains in the winter, requiring hunting by small bands or families, but came together in huge herds in the summer, permitting "tribal"-sized groups to coalesce. One result of the summer hunt was the expansion of the Sun Dance to the major yearly ritual, and its emphasis on the individual through a self-torture rite in which warriors skewered their chests and danced against rawhide thongs tied to a sacred pole. This new emphasis on individualism—a result of a requirement for personal prowess in hunting, trading, and warfare—challenged the old lines of authority. Ownership of the means of production, such as horses and weapons, was individualized, and this altered the old matrilineal and patrilineal kinship systems that depended on a collective ethic and collective ownership. A new bilateral emphasis arose, with kinship traced through the lines of both parents. New types of warfare emerged, mainly devoted to redistributing horses through theft. All of these changes were reinforced as the people became increasingly dependent on European trade in guns, ammunition, tools, cloth, and liquor. The most successful entrepreneurs, those with links to the white trading posts, sometimes became the important political and war leaders.

Capitalist Transformation in Mundurucú

Although the transformations implicit in the change from the kinship mode of production to the tributary mode were far reaching, the transformations required by the capitalist mode were much greater. Because of his focus on wage labor as the defining quality of capitalism, Wolf rejects Wallerstein's contention that capitalism emerged in the fifteenth century and was contemporaneous with mercantilism. For Wolf, capitalism emerged only with the mechanization of the textile industries in England at the end of the eighteenth century, and rapidly replaced mercantilism as it spread throughout the globe. Unlike other modes of production, in the capitalist mode, expansion is built into its internal logic; continuous capital accumulation combined with increases in productivity propel the owners of the means of production to constantly seek new sources of investment, new markets, and ever more resources. A fundamental difference between capitalism and mercantilism is that in the latter "merchants used money and goods bought with money to gain a lien on production, but they remained outside the process of production itself" (1982: 305). The capitalist, in contrast, takes complete control of the entire productive process, including, of course, the labor of the producers.

One major result of the spread of capitalism into the periphery was the emergence of the plantation, which employed a large labor force under strict supervision to produce a single cash crop for sale. Although this system had long been in use under the tributary system of slavery, now labor was purchased with wages. The system was rapidly extended to include "industrial crops." After the invention of vulcanization in 1839, rubber came to be used for raincoats, shoes, tires, condoms, and many other articles. Rubber tapping in Brazil reveals the effects of this capitalist mode on the Indians of the Amazonian Basin.

The Mundurucú Indians underwent a series of transformations from their encounter with Europeans. In the late eighteenth century, white settlers became allies with these horticultural people; a radical and previously unknown division of labor was effected as the women began to produce manioc for the settlers while the men became mercenaries against other Indians. This situation, in which the men were mobile and the women sedentary, brought about a curious change in kinship: the group remained patrilineal, but a matrilocal marriage rule emerged, in which the men moved in with their wives' families after marriage. The development of capitalist rubber tapping caused even greater changes. Entire highland villages disintegrated as people moved in household units to the riverside where the rubber trees were located. The rubber trader replaced the chief as the locus of production and exchange. Receiving wages in goods, the men became caught up in a system of debt bondage, in which they always owed more to the company than they could ever pay off. Their labor was now so little their own that they could not even move to another trader unless the new boss would agree to pay their debts.

Everywhere capitalism created a system in which labor was bought and sold as a commodity. Economic classes emerged where none had existed before and in many places the processes of cultural collapse, detribalization, and immigration were set into effect. Machines now set the pace of work, and wages determined the amount of time that an individual would have to work to provide subsistence for himself and his family. Supply and demand, often decided thousands of miles away, determined the availability of employment, and created massive waves of migration from country to country.

For Wolf, the typical ethnography that ignores these influences is anachronistic. In the transformations of social labor, cultures everywhere are "forever assembled, dismantled, and reassembled" (1982: 391).

GLOBALIZATION

Wolf's *Europe and the People Without History* anticipated current globalization studies. However, when it was published in 1982, the revolutionary flood of postmodernism and critical anthropology was sweeping away interest in such grand theory, with the result that there was little follow-up to Wolf's global vision. These same currents would leave dependency and world-system theory washed up on shores already cluttered with yesterday's theoretical enthusiasms. Such theories had, in any case, been expressed at too high a level to be of much use, even to those ethnographers who were sympathetic to them; the bird's-eye viewpoint was difficult to apply in the shantytowns and jungle communities where anthropologists reside.

Despite its apparent grandiosity, the concept of globalization offers an escape from this impasse. Unlike world-system or dependency theory, globalization does not necessarily focus on megastructures. Indeed, the primary aim of globalization studies is often expressed as the need to connect the global to the local, and visa versa. This is the stuff that anthropological dreams are made of: a new way of conceptualizing that ties the minutiae of daily life to a broader context. Because globalization is not really a grand theory or new paradigm (it can be these, but it can also be simply a context, like the setting for a play), those of a post-modern bent have felt quite at home with it. Postmodern concerns with identity, hegemony, shifting boundaries, fragmentation, media, popular culture, and power/knowledge have come to dominate anthropological globalization studies. At the opposite pole, more traditional economic and materialist anthropologists have discovered a wealth of possibilities in analyzing commodity chains (e.g., tracing supermarket grapes in Norway back to their source in Brazil) or showing how global capitalism is filtered and transformed at the local level.

Not surprisingly, there is little agreement about what globalization means. In the popular mind, and among some academics, globalization suggests homogenization, usually Westernization, of culture; most anthropologists, on the contrary, tend to emphasize differentiation and fragmentation as expressed in nationalisms, ethnicities, and diaspora communities. Some take a skeptical, so-what's-the-big-deal approach, seeing globalization more as media hype than a real issue, whereas others consider globalization to be the most significant cultural, political, and economic force of our time. Some view globalization in evolutionary terms as part of the gradual process of the working out of the internal dynamics of capitalism, whereas others take the position that globalization represents something entirely new, a quantum leap from what has gone before. There are enough facts and statistics to support the gamut of opinion; thus, no resolution to these conflicts can be expected.

No matter how globalization is conceived, one must come to terms with the fact that the present phase of globalization is characterized by neoliberal economics. "Neo*liberal*" aside, this is a politically and economically *conservative* ideology of the free market that was given its popular articulation by President Ronald Reagan and Prime Minister Margaret Thatcher at the 1983 economic summit in Cancun, Mexico. At the time, the economies of the vast majority of Third World countries, including the newly industrializing tigers of Southeast Asia, were characterized by extensive government intervention, state-owned industries, import substitution policies, price controls, subsidies on food and energy, laws strongly regulating multinational investment, and an emphasis on domestic development over integration into the world economy. The extremely rapid shift to neoliberal policies that took place mainly in the mid-1980s and especially after 1990 was, to a great extent, due to two major factors: the massive Third World debt crisis and the collapse of the Soviet Union. A major contributor to the debt crisis was the oil price increases that emerged from the Organization of Petroleum Exporting Countries (OPEC) takeover from British and American oil companies in retaliation for their support of Israel in the 1973 Arab-Israeli war. Enormous increases in the price of oil, combined with the promise of rapid economic development, led to extensive borrowing. Petrodollars flowing into the Middle East were recycled to private banks and multilateral lending institutions that, in turn, spread the wealth generously at floating interest rates. In order to keep from defaulting when the economic bubble burst in the 1980s, Third World countries turned to the International Monetary Fund (IMF) for loans that would help them pay off the interest on the debt (forget ever paying down on the principle). This placed in the hands of the IMF the power to regulate Third World economies through "contingency contracts"; the money would be doled out as countries made the proper neoliberal "structural adjustments," namely, selling off state-owned industries, doing away with subsidies and price controls, reducing tariffs, floating currencies, and opening investment to multinational corporations. In other words, economies shifted from a domestic focus to a global focus. Until 1990, the Soviet Union provided an alternate ideology, mostly for a small group of the poorest countries in the world, but the collapse of the Union of Soviet Socialist Republic removed the last vestige of serious opposition to global neoliberalism.

Thus, the present phase of globalization might be defined as the increasing flow of trade, finance, culture, ideas, and people brought about by the sophisticated technology of communications and travel, and by the worldwide spread of neoliberal capitalism. Any anthropological definition would also have to include the local-level resistances and adaptations to these processes (Lewellen 2002).

Globalization and Political Anthropology

The influence of postmodern concepts of power have had a profound impact on anthropological approaches to globalization. Whereas previously, power was conceived as centered in the state or in individual leaders, globalization may be giving way to variants of Gramsci's notion of *hegemony* as deriving from consent of the people to domination by a ruling elite. This hegemony is usually considered to be Western, manifested through global institutions such as the World Bank, the World Trade Organization, the IMF, and multinational corporations. Such a notion is often explicitly or tacitly combined with a Foucaultian sense of surveillant disciplinary power that is inherent in discourse and suffused through social institutions, such as development organizations. Conventional views that power is a matter of state monopoly on the legitimate use of force are flatly rejected. Rather, the state and its bureaucracies are only intermediate points of a power that are suffused through society, embedded in knowledge systems and in the institutions that dominate such knowledge (Foucault 1977, 1980). Such subtle analyses may reveal previously unanalyzed sources of power, but also may tend to underrate, trivialize, obfuscate, or ignore altogether more conventional manifestations of blatant guns-and-money power.

There are several other ways in which globalization awareness is bringing about significant reconceptualizations of the subject matter and theoretical perspectives of political anthropology. Among the most important are:

- The increasing diffusion and distancing of power, which is becoming invested in the closed deliberations of global lending institutions, multinational corporations, policy-making councils, and trade organizations, none of which are accessible to popular input except via the street theater of protest.

- The decline of state-centered authority with a concomitant shift of power not only to such global groups as those above, but also to local, regional, and international nongovernmental organizations.

- The widespread democratization that has accompanied neoliberal economics, especially during the 1990s, when numerous individual and one-party dictatorships gave way to at least the simulacrum of popular participation. Such democracies, which often legitimize rather than challenge inequities of wealth and power, should not be expected to function in the same way as in countries with long traditions of parliamentary government.

- The emergence of ethnic nationalisms and other interest groups that have come into existence as adaptations to or defenses against globalization (see chapter 9).

- The transnationalization and deterritorialization of power, as the "long-distance nationalism" of diaspora communities increasingly influences home policies.

- The emergence of powerful illegal politico-economic groups such as narcotics cartels and of only marginally ideological rebels, such as those focused on the diamond trade in Africa.

- The normalization of nonstate terrorism as a primary means of warfare.

Some of these issues have been dealt with elsewhere in this book. Two issues are focused on here: the decline of the centrality of the nation-state and the deterritorialization of the state through the process of transnationalism.

The Decline of the State

Many anthropologists see, as a primary aspect of globalization, the decline or demise of the current state-centric system, in which dominant power is vested in national governments. The idea of the nation-state is a recent invention, dating back only a few hundred years, and in a very real sense it was always a myth. The term combines two almost contradictory concepts: *nation,* which refers to a people with a common culture and heritage, usually speaking the same language; and *state,* which is the government of a bounded territory. Although some countries do seem to have large cultural majorities or dominant referent cultures to which immigrants are expected to assimilate over a few generations, as has been claimed for the United States (Spindler 1990: 37), the large majority of countries can claim little cultural cohesion. States whose boundaries were created by colonialism—that is, most of the Third World—normally embrace multiple and conflicting cultures. In many, if not most cases, one culture or ethnicity dominated the others, with the result that subordinated nations were being asked to subscribe to their own repression through the process of identifying with the nation state. Globalization has increased the pressure on the already fragile nation-state systems in two ways. First, during the Cold War, the United States and the Soviet Union provided massive military aid to repressive dictatorships that maintained a strained national unity through naked force, while the new democracies must allow multiple conflictive voices. Second, globalization has offered immigrants a degree of contact with the home country that greatly reduces the pressure to assimilate; the enormous growth of such communities leads to the increasing localization and even transnationalization of political identification (Glick Schiller, Basch, and Szanton Blanc 1992).

If the legitimacy of the nation-state is dependent on maintaining control of ideology and action within clearly defined physical borders, then transnationalism threatens such control. Not only have the constant movements of migrants, immigrants, tourists, and business personnel tended toward a deterritorialization of the state, but so has the international ubiquity of movies, television, radio, and the Internet (Appadurai 1996, 2000). Both multinational corporations and global economic institutions assume many of the powers over the economy once concentrated in state hands. Political scientist Samuel Huntington (1996) postulates that power is shifting from states to broad international "civilizations," such as Western, Islamic, and Latin American. In addition, the growth of regional political and economic institutions—OPEC, North

American Free Trade Agreement, Southeast Asia Treaty Organization, and the European Community—are further evidence of the ultimate demise of the state.

The problem with such theorizing is that it essentializes the nation-state within such a tight definition that it is an easy mark. In reality, the state has proved quite adaptable, and not particularly entrenched in its own physical borders. One need only consider the United States, which only a couple of centuries ago consisted of 13 small agrarian states crowded along the eastern seaboard. Today's multicultural postindustrial version—which extends a third of the way around the world, from Florida to the tip of the Aleutian Islands near Japan and north to well above the Arctic Circle—resembles that earlier nation in no manner except a continuity of constitutional government and the English language. The idea that such an adaptable behemoth should suddenly be threatened by Asian transnationals living in San Francisco, by the global spread of Wal-Mart, or by the World Bank is untenable. Even Third World countries that are newer and considerably more multicultural than is the United States, such as India or Indonesia, have been able to maintain a degree of nation-stateness because identity with the larger territorial political entity occupies a separate sphere from local or ethnic identity, a sphere reserved for national holidays, periods of external threat, national elections, or rites of unification such as the funerals of a statesmen. State boundaries are more secure today than at any time in the past; cross-border wars for the purpose of aggrandizing territory are extremely rare and are not well countenanced by the international community (as Iraq discovered when it invaded Kuwait). Large-scale migration can actually strengthen state power by dispersing potentially rebellious minorities and by providing remittances.

It is not clear what the "demise" of the state is supposed to lead to: Anarchy? World government? Rule by multinational corporations? Universal transnationalism? Meanwhile, the nation-state seems to be a structure quite amenable to globalization, although it needs to be reconceptualized in the sense that it is no longer the center of power it once was (or was thought to be), but rather one of a number of nodes of power that reach both above and below—to regional and global institutions, and to grassroots nongovernmental organizations.

Transnationalism and the Deterritorialized State

Transnationalism is a relatively new phenomenon that emerges from a flexible global labor market, from the technology for instantaneous communications such as satellite phone systems and e-mail, and the speed and relative inexpensiveness of long-distance transportation. Basically, transnationalism is the process of living across borders, in two or more countries at the same time. This gives rise to a curious form of hybrid identity in which assimilation in the country of settlement is no longer a goal; cultural maintenance within a diaspora community, reinforced by routine contact with the home country, can be maintained over generations. In South Africa, the end of apartheid opened the way for a flood of illegal immigrants, especially from Mozambique, who have found niches in the informal economy, usually as street salesmen and traders. They maintain regular contact with their countries of origin through trips back home, phone calls, and monetary transfers (Crush and McDonald 2000). Around the Pacific Rim, a network of well-off or wealthy Hong Kong Chinese business families have settled in multiple cities, maintaining their own language and culture. In San Francisco, such a group has established homes in one of the most exclusive housing areas (Ong 1999).

Transnationalism is of interest to political anthropologists for a number of reasons. Within the country of settlement, political exclusion based on racism or fear that foreigners are stealing jobs may bar access to assimilation and thus reinforce transnational community solidarity. On the other hand, such communities can form voting blocs and join with other political pressure groups that can influence politics. Leadership within transnational communities may provide a unique area of study, because appeal must be made both to the local situation and to homeland values and forms of legitimization. Most important, transnationals often continue to actively participate in their home country politics and may even occupy a protected niche of opposition against repressive governments as, for example, Chinese and Tibetan expatriate communities do in the United States.

Haiti and the Deterritorialized State

The successive dictatorships of Francois ("Papa Doc") Duvalier and his son Jean-Claude ("Baby Doc") Duvalier from 1957 to 1986 were so repressive and economically restrictive that thousand of Haitians of all classes emigrated, many of them to Miami or New York. This process was amplified by the wave of agribusiness and export-processing industries that transformed the countryside after 1960, stimulating even greater migration. Initially there was little transnationalism. Many migrants opposed the Duvalier regime, actively attempting to change the U.S. policy of support, and dared not return for fear of being imprisoned, tortured, or killed. Many remained illegally in the United States, overstaying visas, and thus feared bringing themselves to the attention of the Immigration and Naturalization Service. By the 1980s, there were over half a million Haitians living abroad—nearly 15 percent of the population.

The expulsion of Baby Doc opened a new era of transnationalism. Increasingly, both people and money flowed both ways, following long-established lines of kin, fictive kin, and united families. Families were conceived as networks of individuals and households that functioned as a unit in allocating labor and resources. A high value was placed on children as a means of elaborating and perpetuating these networks. Businesses emerged not only to bring Haitian foods and entertainment into the communities, but also to move people, money, videos, cassettes, and goods. The rigid class system was reproduced in the United States; the wealthy lived in upscale neighborhoods, whereas the poorest followed migrant agricultural jobs along the eastern seaboard. What united them was a continuing common identity as Haitians, the racial segregation of the United States that was based mainly on blackness, and either a refusal or inability to assimilate.

The election that brought Jean-Bertrand Aristide to the presidency of Haiti in 1990 represented the most significant popular participation in Haitian politics since the revolution of independence in 1804. Aristide's *Lavalas* movement, meaning "avalanche" or "flood," extended to expatriates, many of whom were active politically and economically in supporting him. Aristide was overthrown in a military coup a mere eight months after taking office. After a period of extreme repression, including the torture and killing of Aristide's supporters, he was returned to office as part of the U.S. invasion in 1994. Aristide recognized his foreign support by declaring those living abroad as the *Dizyèm Departman-an*, literally the Tenth Department, thus formally incorporating them into Haiti along with the country's border-bound nine states. The Chamber of Deputies, however, was opposed to any formal recognition of Haiti as a "deterritorialized state"; it refused Aristide's request to grant dual citizenship and blocked government and ambassadorial appointments to those who had become citizens of other countries. The United States has also opposed any kind of recognition of deterritorialization, fearing that the Haitian government would use it as an opportunity to involve itself in the political affairs of Haitian communities abroad (Basch, Glick Schiller, and Szanton Blanc 1994).

Haiti's transnational democratization has done little to bring about structural changes within the country. Indeed, much of Aristide's *Lavalas* platform was dissipated or diluted by U.S. demands that he subscribe to neoliberal policies. The class structure may actually be reinforced by its reproduction overseas. Leaders of the *Lavalas* movement emerged mainly from the technocratic, professional, and business strata, and their very dispersal might prevent them from becoming a unified challenge to the traditional aristocracy.

TOWARD THE FUTURE

The journey from Evans-Pritchard's *The Nuer* to postmodern studies of globalization is long and convoluted, but there is a certain logical inevitability to it. From its beginnings in relatively closed-system analyses of folk cultures, political anthropology has spread outward in every direction; there has been an increase in complexity and scope, in relation both to theory and to the societies studied. Predictably, this has led not only to greater breadth and depth in political studies, but also to increasing fragmentation. Once relatively cohesive, today political anthropology might be broken down into traditional (materialist, social scientific), postmodern, and synthetic theoretical approaches. Subject matter can be subdivided into identity politics, the state, gender, war and conflict, leadership, postcolonialism, globalization, and probably much more. Although such fragmentation might be the bane of writers of overview works (such as this one), it is also a healthy sign.

Predictions of the future have the agreeable attribute of being almost always wrong. However, certain trends are in evidence. One major trend is that the best ideas of postmodern theory—the fluidity of culture, the permeability of boundaries, the situatedness of the ethnographic observer—are being synthesized with the social *science* demands of more traditional anthropology. Globalization is another inevitable trend; political anthropologists simply cannot treat power as they did in the past, as manifest at purely local or state level. Beyond that, world realities will determine the direction of the political anthropology of the future: terrorism and the response to it; global warming; the shifting role of the state; the emergence of new forms of political mobilization; and, most important, that which we cannot even foresee today. Whatever these realities may be, political anthropology has developed the foundations and the flexibility to deal with them in an insightful manner.

SUGGESTED READINGS

Basch, Linda, Nina Glick Schiller, and Cristina Szanton Blanc. *Nations Unbound: Transnational Projects, Postcolonial Predicaments, and Deter-*

ritorialized Nation-States (Langhorne, Penn.: Gordon and Breach, 1994). This important book, at once a summary and elaboration of the three authors' multiple earlier works, provides a theoretical overview of the new field of transnational studies, with detailed examples of Haitian, Dominican, and Philippine transnationalism.

de Soto, Hernando. *The Other Path: The Invisible Revolution in the Third World* (New York: Harper and Row, 1989). An international best-seller, this book argues against dependency theory by showing how Peru's underdevelopment can be attributed to an unwieldy bureaucracy and an impenetrable maze of laws that forces most people into the informal economy.

Lewellen, Ted C. *The Anthropology of Globalization: Cultural Anthropology Enters the Twenty-First Century* (Westport, Conn.: Bergin and Garvey, 2002). An overview of anthropological approaches to globalization, including chapters on defining globalization, development, identity, transnationalism, diaspora, refugees, tribal cultures, and peasants.

Phillips, Lynne, ed. *The Third Wave of Modernization in Latin America: Cultural Perspectives on Neoliberalism* (Wilmington, Del.: Scholarly Resources, 1998). This anthology focuses on how global neoliberal economic policies have deeply affected the people of Latin America. Its subjects include Bolivian teachers, Peruvian Market women, and Mexican peasants.

Shannon, Thomas Richard. *An Introduction to the World-System Perspective* (Boulder, Colo.: Westview, 1989). Wallerstein's three-volume work on *The Modern World-System* can be overwhelming, making a clearly written overview valuable. This book includes details of Wallerstein's historical sequence in the evolution of the capitalist world-economy, including useful maps showing the extent of capitalism's spread at different times. The greatest value of the book, however, may not be its description but a long chapter on criticisms of the theory.

Wolf, Eric R. *Europe and the People without History* (Berkeley: University of California Press, 1982). Taking a Marxist orientation to the world system, at odds in many ways with Wallerstein, Wolf interprets mercantilist and capitalist expansion in terms of modes of production. This is a fundamentally anthropological view-from-the bottom perspective that is more interested in the effects of such expansion on indigenous peoples than on the policies of governments.

GLOSSARY

Action theory: A perspective within the **process approach** in which the focus is on the strategies of individuals for gaining and maintaining power.

Age-set system: In some societies, all those who undergo puberty initiation at the same time form a coherent group that passes through different statuses and roles together. In tribal societies, this can be an important pantribal sodality that overrides kinship loyalties and unites the wider group.

Arena: This term has no agreed-upon meaning, but in the **process approach** and **action theory**, it is often used to delimit a small area within the political **field** in which competition between a few individuals or factions takes place. In Bailey's **game theory**, it is an area in which teams that agree on a common set of rules compete.

Band: The least complex level of sociocultural integration, associated with hunting-gathering societies. Characterized by small, fluid groups; egalitarianism; informal leadership; and bilateral kinship.

Bivocal symbolism: According to Abner Cohen, all true symbols serve both existential and political ends; that is, they are felt in a deeply personal way, but at the same time they maintain political continuity through reaffirming common myths and values.

Cargo cult: A type of **revitalization movement** that seeks to gain access to Western trade goods ("cargo" in Pidgin English) by supernatural means.

Chiefdom: The least complex form of a centralized political system, usually found in cultures that base their subsistence on extensive agriculture or intensive fishing. Characterized by a ranking of individuals and lineages, inheritance of power within a dominant lineage, and maintenance of power through redistribution of wealth by a charismatic chief.

Complementary opposition: A system in which groups that are antagonistic at one level will unite at another level to counter a military threat.

Consensual power: Leadership that derives from the assent of the people, rather than force alone. This assent may be based on tradition, respect for an office, or faith in the personal qualities of a leader.

Corporatism: A model of the state in which the government functions through a limited number of monopolistic interest groups.

Cultural capital: For Pierre Bourdieu, anything that can be used in competitive struggles for status. Includes college degrees, professional licenses, artistic talent and the paintings produced by that talent, social skills, and so forth.

Dependency theory: A broad paradigm that views the underdevelopment of the Third World as a result of the capitalist expansion of the First World. In contrast to **modernization theory,** dependency theory puts the emphasis on *external* factors of underdevelopment.

Dependent power: Power that is granted, allocated, or delegated by someone who holds **independent power.**

Diachronic study: An analysis of a society "in time"; that is, in a historical or evolutionary context.

Discourse: A complex unit of analysis used in different ways by Michel Foucault. Roughly, a system of knowledge that determines the limits of thinking, perceiving, speaking, or acting for a particular group or within a particular historical period. The discourse contains the rules for designating a statement true or false.

Environmental circumscription: A theory by Robert Carniero that **primary states** arose when population growth and other pressures within areas bounded by mountains or desert forced increasingly complex modes of political and social organization.

Ethnicity: "A self-conscious . . . identity that substantializes and naturalizes one or more attributes—the usual ones being skin color, language, religion, and territory—and attaches them to collectivities as their innate possession and myth-historical legacy" (Tambiah 1996: 168).

Factions: Informal, leader-follower political groups organized for a particular purpose and disbanding when that purpose is accomplished or defeated. See also **pervasive factionalism** and **segmentary factional political system.**

Field: The basic unit of study in the **process approach.** Previous researchers tended to focus on a defined group, such as a tribe or community; a field, which is defined anew by each researcher, may cross the boundaries of different groups and may change over time. In Bailey's **game theory,** a "field" is more specifically defined as an area in which rival political structures interact, but without agreed-upon rules between them. For Pierre Bourdieu, a field is an area of competitive struggle over a particular type of **cultural capital.**

Game theory: Introduced into political anthropology by F. G. Bailey, this approach seeks to discover the **normative rules** and **pragmatic rules** of political manipulation. Politics is viewed as a game composed of "teams" competing for "prizes."

Gender: The culturally constructed aspect of sexual identity. "Sex" refers to the biological aspect.

General systems theory: A complex paradigm for the social sciences originally derived from cybernetics and biology. Systems are viewed as adapting to changes in their internal and external environments through feedback mechanisms (see **negative feedback** and **positive feedback**). This orientation has been especially useful in explaining the rise of primary states.

Globalization: The increasing flow of trade, finance, culture, ideas, and people brought about by the sophisticated technology of communications and travel, and by the worldwide spread of neoliberal capitalism. For anthropology, globalization also includes the local-level resistances and adaptations to these processes.

Habitus: A term coined by Pierre Bourdieu; the largely unconscious internalization of the objective norms and rules of society that suggest how we might act within any given situation.

Hybridity: A syncretism or compartmentalization of different culture traits in self-identity or social identity.

Hydraulic theory: A theory of state formation proposed by Karl Wittfogel. Canal irrigation required a division of classes into workers and administrators and tended to concentrate power in the hands of those who controlled the water supplies upon which the life of the community depended.

Independent power: A relation of dominance based on the direct capabilities of an individual, such as knowledge, skills, or personal charisma. In centralized societies, such power may attach to a particular office, such as that of king. See **dependent power.**

Institutionalization of leadership: A theory by Elman Service that the development of centralized political organization can be explained in terms of the perceived benefits of strong leadership and political continuity.

Intensification: As used by Marvin Harris, this refers to a fundamental process of cultural evolution by which population pressures combine with resource depletion to force improved means of producing food. Such technological changes in turn require new modes of social organization.

Legitimacy: A primary basis for **power** that derives from the people's expectations about the nature of power and how it should be attained, for example, by election in the United States or by holding redistributive feasts in Polynesia.

Male dominance: Control of productive resources and political power by men. Although widespread, cross-cultural studies suggest that male dominance is not universal.

Man-the-Hunter theory of evolution: The belief that the evolution of homo sapiens focused on the cooperative hunting of big game. The theory is presently disputed.

Matriarchy: Political control by women. Despite a widespread belief in primitive matriarchies, no such social system, either past or present, has ever been documented by anthropologists.

Mode of production: For Karl Marx, the way that production, especially labor, is organized. As reinterpreted by anthropologist Eric Wolf, there are three main modes of production: *the kin-ordered mode,* typical of bands, tribes, and chiefdoms; *the tributary mode,* in which an elite demands the products of labor as "tribute"; and *the capitalist mode,* which directly buys and sells human labor.

Modernism: In contrast to **postmodernism,** refers to Enlightenment values of progress through science and technology, the perfectibility of man and culture, rationalism, and the belief that reality is subject to articulation through grand theories or metanarratives.

Modernization theory: The assumption that the *internal* dynamics of a country are responsible for its development or underdevelopment. In some permutations, the emphasis is put on what a country is lacking, such as entrepreneurial spirit, technology, capital, and so forth. Other versions emphasize such dynamics as internal colonialism or the growth of a vast informal economy. Contrasted with **dependency theory.**

Nationalism: Group self-identification with a real or desired sovereign territory. *State nationalism* refers to an existing government's attempt to gain an overriding identification and loyalty from the subgroups that comprise the country. *Ethnonationalism* refers to the often-fervent desire of an ethnic group to attain or regain a homeland or sovereignty within a state.

Negative feedback: Deviation-minimizing processes. Change in a system will be limited by other elements of the system so that equilibrium is maintained (e.g., in hot weather, the body is cooled by sweating to maintain a constant temperature). See **positive feedback.**

Neo-evolutionism: A revival by Leslie White in the 1940s of nineteenth-century cultural evolutionary theory. Later theorists distinguished *general evolution*—broad changes in cultural complexity, such as from band to tribal society—from *specific evolution*—the observable adaptational changes of particular societies.

Normative rules: In F. C. Bailey's **game theory,** the political rules that are publicly professed, such as honesty, sportsmanship, and so forth. Contrasted with **pragmatic rules.**

Pervasive factionalism: A condition in which formal political structures have broken down or have become inoperative, and temporary **factions** arise to solve each problem as it appears.

Politics: One of those indefinable words that depends on the particular interests of the researcher. A good working definition is as follows: "The processes involved in determining and implementing public goals and . . . the differential achievement and use of power by the members of the group concerned with these goals" (Swartz, Turner, and Tuden 1966: 7).

Positive feedback: Deviation-amplifying processes. A slight "initial kick" will start a process of increasingly rapid change, which will be stopped only when the system attains a new level of equilibrium or collapses. See **negative feedback.**

Postmodernism: An overarching term for multiple theories dating from the 1970s that reject anthropology's scientific pretensions and all grand theory. Writings are often self-referential, emphasizing subjectivity, evocation, discourse, the subaltern voice, and the social construction of reality. Contrasted with **modernism.**

Power: In its broadest sense, "an ability to influence the behavior of others and/or gain influence over the control of valued actions" (R. Cohen 1970: 31). In its purely political aspect, such influence would be limited to the public domain. This amorphous term is better defined by breaking it into its component parts: **consensual power, dependent power, independent power, legitimacy,** and **support.**

Power/knowledge: In the works of Michel Foucault, the embedding of power within all **discourse.** Institutions determine what is normal or abnormal. Specialized knowledge, such as that of doctors or scientists, provides the power to classify, analyze, observe, and experiment and thus determine truth or falsity.

Pragmatic rules: In F. C. Bailey's **game theory,** those political rules that are concerned with gaining or maintaining power—that is, with winning the game, not with public display. Contrasted with **normative rules.**

Primary state: A state that developed independently of pre-existing states. This occurred in six areas: Mesopotamia, the Nile Valley, the Indus Valley of India, the Yellow River Valley of China, Mesoamerica, and Peru.

Process approach: Sometimes referred to as process theory, although it is too amorphous to constitute a coherent theory. Originally a reaction against **structural-functionalism,** this approach emphasizes change and conflict.

Retribalization: The tendency for some tribal groups to become *more* cohesive, to protect economic and political interests, during the process of modernization.

Revitalization movement: A deliberate attempt by a group, usually in a situation of cultural collapse and/or subjugation by a foreign power, to create a better society. Such movements may seek apocalyptic transformation through super-natural means, try to recreate a Golden Age of the past, or expel all foreign influences. A **cargo cult** is a type of revitalization movement.

Secondary state: Any state that came into existence through the influence of preexisting states.

Segmentary factional political system: A system either without formal political structures or in which such structures have broken down, so that competition between **factions** becomes the normal mode of political decision making.

Segmentary lineage: A unilineal system based on small, local, relatively auton-omous units that can be put together, building-block fashion, into increasingly larger structures for ritual or military purposes.

State: The most complex level of political integration. Found in societies whose subsistence is based on intensive agriculture, and characterized by leadership centered in an individual or elite group supported by a bureaucracy, supra-kinship loyalties, class structure, and economic redistribution based on tribute or taxation. Some **globalization** theorists view the state as in demise.

Structural-functionalism: The dominant theoretical orientation of British an-thropology during the 1930s and 1940s. **Synchronic analysis,** usually of groups treated as closed systems, showed how the various component insti-tutions contributed to the equilibrium of the whole.

Support: A broad concept, including virtually anything that contributes to or maintains political **power.** Two basic supports are coercion (force) and **legitimacy.**

Synchronic analysis: A type of analysis, typical of the structural-functionalists and French structuralists, that treats societies as though they are outside of time; that is, without reference to historical context.

Transnationalism: The process, made possible by **globalization,** of living in two or more countries at the same time. Immigrants do not assimilate into the new country but maintain close cultural, economic, and political ties with the home country through regular travel, media, e-mail, the Internet, and money transfers.

Tribe: A loosely defined term used to denote a wide range of social organizations that exist between hunting-gathering **bands** and centralized systems. Associ-ated with horticulture or pastoralism, charismatic leadership, unilineal kinship, and pantribal sodalities.

Tributary elites: The owners and managers of production, banking, and trade within periphery and semiperiphery countries who really represent the interests of the core. See **World Capitalist System.**

World Capitalist System: According to Immanuel Wallerstein, the expansion of capitalism outward from Europe beginning in the sixteenth century created a single world economy, consisting of a *core* of developed nations, a *periphery* of underdeveloped countries that supply raw materials and cheap labor to the core, and an intermediary group of *semiperipheral* countries.

BIBLIOGRAPHY

Abeles, Marc. 1997. "Political Anthropology: New Challenges, New Aims." *International Social Science Journal* 49 (3): 319–33.

Abrahamson, Mark. 1969. "Correlates of Political Complexity." *American Sociological Review* 34: 690–701.

Adams, Richard N. 1975. *Energy and Structure: A Theory of Social Power.* Austin: University of Texas Press.

———. 1977. "Power in Human Societies: A Synthesis." *In* R. D. Fogelson and R. N. Adams, eds., *The Anthropology of Power.* New York: Academic Press.

Adams, Robert McCormick. 1966. *The Evolution of Urban Society.* Chicago: Aldine.

Aigbe, Sunday A. 1993. *Theory of Social Involvement: A Case Study in the Anthropology of Religion, State, and Society.* New York: University Press of America.

Alonso, Ana María. 1994. "The Politics of Space, Time, and Substance: State Formation, Nationalism, and Ethnicity." *Annual Review of Anthropology* 23: 397–405.

Anderson, Benedict. 1983. *Imagined Communities: Reflections on the Origin and Spread of Nationalism.* Rev. ed. London: Verso.

Appadurai, Arjun. 1991. "Global Ethnoscapes: Notes and Queries for a Transnational Anthropology." *In* R. Fox, ed., *Recapturing Anthropology.* Santa Fe, N.Mex.: School of American Research.

———. 1996. *Modernity at Large: Cultural Dimensions of Globalization.* Minneapolis: University of Minnesota Press.

————. 2000. "Grassroots Globalization and the Research Imagination." *Public Culture* 12 (1): 12–19.

Aronoff, Myron J. 1983. "Conceptualizing the Role of Culture in Political Change." *In* M. J. Aronoff, ed., *Culture and Political Change: Political Anthropology.* Vol. 2. New Brunswick, N.J.: Transaction Books.

————. 1984a. "Gush Emunim: The Institutionalization of a Charismatic, Messianic, Religious-Political Revitalization Movement in Israel." *In* M. J. Aronoff, ed., *Religion and Politics, Political Anthropology.* Vol. 3. New Brunswick, N.J.: Transaction Books.

————. 1984b. "Introduction." *In* M. J. Aronoff, ed., *Religion and Politics, Political Anthropology.* Vol. 3. New Brunswick, N.J.: Transaction Books.

Bailey, F. G. 1960. *Tribe, Caste and Nation.* Manchester, U.K.: Manchester University Press.

————. 1968. "Parapolitical Systems." *In* M. Swartz, ed., *Local Level Politics,* Chicago: Aldine.

————. 1969. *Stratagems and Spoils: A Social Anthropology of Politics.* New York: Schocken Books.

————. 1970. *Politics and Social Change.* Berkeley: University of California Press.

Balandier, Georges. 1970. *Political Anthropology.* New York: Random House.

Banks, Marcus. 1996. *Ethnicity: Ethnological Constructions.* New York: Routledge.

Banton, Michael, ed. 1965. *Political Systems and the Distribution of Power.* London: Tavistock.

Barth, Frederick. 1959. *Political Leadership among the Swat Pathans.* London: Athalone.

Barth, Frederick, ed. 1969. *Ethnic Groups and Boundaries.* Boston: Little, Brown.

Basch, Linda, Nina Glick Schiller, and Cristina Szanton Blanc. 1994. *Nations Unbound: Transnational Projects, Postcolonial Predicaments, and Deterritorialized Nation-States.* Langhorne, Pa.: Gordon and Breach.

Baudrillard, Jean. 2001. *Jean Baudrillard: Selected Writings,* 2nd. ed. Ed. by M. Poster. Stanford, Calif.: Stanford University Press.

Block, Maurice, ed. 1975. *Political Language and Oratory in Traditional Society.* New York: Academic Press.

Boas, Franz. 1894. *The Social Organization and Secret Societies of the Kwakiutl Indians.* United States National Museum Annual Report 1894.

Bodley, John N. 1982. *Victims of Progress.* 2d ed. Palo Alto, Calif.: Mayfield.

Boserup, Esther. 1965. *The Conditions of Agricultural Growth: The Economics of Agrarian Change under Population Pressure.* Chicago: Aldine.

Bourdieu, Pierre. [1979] 1990a. *Distinction: A Social Critique of the Judgment of Taste.* Reprint, Cambridge, Mass.: Harvard University Press.

————. [1980] 1990b. *The Logic of Practice.* Translated by R. Nice. Reprint, Stanford, Calif.: Stanford University Press.

Bourdieu, Pierre, and Loïc J. D. Wacquant. 1992. *An Invitation to Reflexive Sociology.* Chicago: University of Chicago Press.

Briggs, Jean L. 1970. *Never in Anger: Portrait of an Eskimo Family.* Cambridge, Mass.: Harvard University Press.

Britan, Gerald M., and Ronald Cohen. 1980. "Toward an Anthropology of Formal Organizations." *In* G. M. Britan and R. Cohen, eds., *Hierarchy and Society: Anthropological Perspectives on Bureaucracy.* Philadelphia: Institute for the Study of Human Issues.

Britan, Gerald M., and Ronald Cohen, eds. 1980. *Hierarchy and Society: Anthropological Perspectives on Bureaucracy.* Philadelphia: Institute for the Study of Human Issues.

Brown, Donald. 1991. *Human Universals.* New York: McGraw-Hill.

Brown, Judith K. 1975. "Iroquois Women: An Ethnohistoric Note." *In* R. R. Reiter, ed., *Toward an Anthropology of Women.* New York: Monthly Review Press.

Buckley, Walter, ed. 1968. *Modern Systems Research for the Behavioral Sciences: A Sourcebook.* Chicago: Aldine.

Buenaventura-Posso, Elisa, and Susan E. Brown. 1980. "Forced Transition from Egalitarianism to Male Dominance: The Bari of Columbia." *In* M. Etienne and E. Leacock, eds., *Women and Colonization: Anthropological Perspectives.* New York: Praeger.

Bujra, Janet M. 1973. "The Dynamics of Political Action: A New Look at Factionalism." *American Anthropologist* 75: 132–52.

Burling, Robbins. 1974. *The Passage of Power: Studies in Political Succession.* New York: Academic Press.

Campbell, Bernhard G. 1979. *Humankind Emerging.* 2d ed. Boston: Little, Brown.

Carniero, Robert L. 1967. "On the Relationship between Size of Population and Complexity of Social Organization." *Southwestern Journal of Anthropology* 23: 234–43.

———. 1970. "A Theory of the Origin of the State." *Science* 169: 733–38.

———. 1978. "Political Expansion as an Expression of the Principle of Competitive Exclusion." *In* R. Cohen and E. Service, eds., *Origins of the State: The Anthropology of Political Evolution.* Philadelphia: Institute for the Study of Human Issues.

Castile, George Pierre, and Gilbert Kushner, eds. 1981. *Persistent Peoples: Cultural Enclaves in Perspective.* Tucson: University of Arizona Press.

Chagnon, Napoleon. 1968. *Yanomamo: The Fierce People.* New York: Holt, Rinehart and Winston.

Charles, Carolle. 1992. "Transnationalism in the Construct of Haitian Migrants' Racial Categories of Identity in New York City." *In* N. Glick Schiller, L. Basch, and C. Blanc-Szanton, eds., *Towards a Transnational Perspective on Migration: Race, Class, Ethnicity, and Nationalism Reconsidered,* 101–23. New York: Annals of the New York Academy of Sciences, Vol. 645.

Cheater, Angela, ed. 1999. *The Anthropology of Power: Empowerment and Disempowerment in Changing Structures.* London: Routledge.

Chilcote, Ronald H. 1984. *Theories of Underdevelopment.* Boulder, Colo.: Westview Press.

Childe, V. Gordon. 1936. *Man Makes Himself.* London: Watts.

———. 1946. *What Happened in History.* New York: Penguin.

Claessen, Henri J. M. 1978. "The Early State: A Structural Approach." *In* J. M. Claessen and P. Skalník, eds., *The Early State.* The Hague, The Netherlands: Mouton.

Claessen, Henri J. M., and Peter Skalník. 1978. "The Early State: Theories and Hypotheses." *In* J. M. Claessen and P. Skalník, eds., *The Early State.* The Hague, The Netherlands: Mouton.

Claessen, Henri J. M., and Peter Skalník, eds. 1978. *The Early State.* The Hague, The Netherlands: Mouton.

Clastres, Pierre. 1977. *Society against the State.* New York: Urizen Books.

Clifford, James. 1986. "Introduction: Partial Truths." *In* J. Clifford and G. E. Marcus, *Writing Culture: The Poetics and Politics of Ethnography.* Berkeley: University of California Press.

Clifford, James, and George E. Marcus. 1986. *Writing Culture: The Poetics and Politics of Ethnography.* Berkeley: University of California Press.

Codere, Helen. 1950. *Fighting with Property: A Study of Kwakiutl Potlatching and Warfare, 1792–1930.* Seattle: University of Washington Press.

———. 1957. "Kwakiutl Society: Rank without Class." *American Anthropologist* 59: 473–86.

Cohen, Abner. 1969a. *Custom and Politics in Urban Africa: A Study of Hausa Migrants in a Yoruba Town.* Berkeley: University of California Press.

———. 1969b. "Political Anthropology: The Analysis of the Symbolism of Power Relations." *Man* 4: 215–44.

———. 1974. *Two-Dimensional Man: An Essay on the Anthropology of Power and Symbolism in Complex Societies.* London: Routledge and Kegan Paul.

———. 1981. *The Politics of Elite Culture: Explorations in the Dramaturgy of Power in a Modern African Society.* Berkeley: University of California Press.

Cohen, Ronald. 1965. "Political Anthropology: The Future of a Pioneer." *Anthropological Quarterly* 38: 117–31.

———. 1970. "The Political System." *In* R. Naroll and R. Cohen, eds., *A Handbook of Method in Cultural Anthropology.* Garden City, N.Y.: Natural History Press.

———. 1978a. "Introduction." *In* R. Cohen and E. Service, eds., *Origins of the State: The Anthropology of Political Evolution.* Philadelphia: Institute for the Study of Human Issues.

Cohen, Ronald, and John Middleton, eds. 1967. *Comparative Political Systems: Studies in the Politics of Pre-Industrial Societies.* Austin: University of Texas Press.

Cohen, Ronald, and Alice Schlegal. 1968. "The Tribe as a Socio-Political Unit: A Cross-Cultural Examination." *In* J. Helm, ed., *Essays on the Problem of Tribe: Proceedings of the 1967 Annual Spring Meeting of the American Ethnological Society.* Seattle: University of Washington Press.

Cohen, Ronald, and Elman Service, eds. 1978. *Origins of the State: The Anthropology of Political Evolution.* Philadelphia: Institute for the Study of Human Issues.

Colson, Elizabeth. 1968. "Political Anthropology: The Field." *In* D. L. Sills, ed., *International Encyclopedia of the Social Sciences.* Vol. 12. New York: Macmillan and Free Press.

———. 1974. *Tradition and Contract: The Problem of Order.* Chicago: Aldine.

———. 1978b. "State Foundations: A Controlled Comparison." *In* R. Cohen and E. Service, eds., *The Origin of the State: The Anthropology of Political Evolution.* Philadelphia: Institute for the Study of Human Issues.

Coontz, Stephanie, and Peta Henderson. 1986. "Property Forms, Political Power, and Female Labour in the Origins of Class and State Societies." *In* S. Coontz and P. Henderson, eds., *Women's Work, Men's Property: The Origins of Gender and Class.* London: Verso.

Counts, Dorothy Ayers. 1984. "Revenge Suicide by Lusi Women: An Expression of Power." *In* D. O'Brien and S. W. Tiffany, eds., *Rethinking Women's Roles: Perspectives from the Pacific.* Berkley: University of California Press.

Crush, Jonathan, and David McDonald. 2000. "Transnationalism, African Immigration, and New Migrant Spaces in South Africa." *Canadian Journal of African Studies* 34 (1): 1–19.

Dahlberg, Frances. 1981. "Introduction." *In* F. Dahlberg, ed., *Woman the Gatherer.* New Haven, Conn.: Yale University Press.

Damas, David. 1968. "The Diversity of Eskimo Societies." *In* R. B. Lee and I. DeVore, eds., *Man, The Hunter.* Chicago: Aldine.

Danforth, Loring M. 1995. *The Macedonian Conflict: Ethnic Nationalism in a Transnational World.* Princeton, N.J.: Princeton University Press.

Davenport, W. 1969. "The Hawaiian Cultural Revolution: Some Political and Economic Considerations." *American Anthropologist* 71: 1–20.

Davis, Shelton H. 1977. *Victims of the Miracle: Development and the Indians of Brazil.* Cambridge: Cambridge University Press.

de Soto, Hernando. 1989. *The Other Path: The Invisible Revolution in the Third World.* New York: Harper and Row.

Deloria, Vine. 1969. *Custer Died for Your Sins.* New York: Avon.

di Leonardo, Micaela, ed. 1991. *Gender at the Crossroads of Knowledge: Feminist Anthropology in the Postmodern Era.* Berkeley: University of California Press.

Diamond, Jared. 1999. *Guns, Germs, and Steel: The Fates of Human Societies.* New York: Norton.

Draper, Patricia. 1985. "Two Views of Sex Differences in Socialization." *In* R. L. Hall, ed., *Male-Female Differences: A Bio-Cultural Perspective.* New York: Praeger.

Drucker, P., and Robert F. Heizer. 1967. *To Make My Name Good: A Reexamination of the Southern Kwakiutl Potlatch.* Berkeley: University of California Press.

Duley, Margot I., and Karen Sinclair. 1986. "Male Dominance: Myth or Reality?" *In* M. Duley and M. Edwards, eds., *The Cross-Cultural Study of Women.* New York: The Feminist Press.

Dumond, D. E. 1965. "Population Growth and Cultural Change." *Southwestern Journal of Anthropology* 21: 302–24.

Earle, Timothy. 1997. *How Chiefs Come to Power: The Political Economy in Prehistory.* Stanford, Calif.: Stanford University Press.

Easton, David. 1953. *The Political System.* New York: Knopf.

———. 1959. "Political Anthropology." *Biennial Review of Anthropology, 1958.* Stanford, Calif.: Stanford University Press.

Edelman, Marc. 1999. *Peasants against Globalization: Rural Social Movements in Costa Rica.* Stanford, Calif.: Stanford University Press.

Eisenstadt, S. N. 1959. "Primitive Political Systems: A Preliminary Comparative Analysis." *American Anthropologist* 61: 200–20.

———. 1963. *The Political Systems of Empire.* Glencoe, Ill.: Free Press.

———. 1966. *Modernization: Protest and Change.* Englewood Cliffs, N.J.: Prentice Hall.

———. 1967. "Transformation of Social, Political, and Cultural Orders in Modernization." *In* R. Cohen and J. Middleton, eds., *Comparative Political Systems.* Austin: University of Texas Press.

———. 1970. "Social Change and Development." *In* S. N. Eisenstadt, ed., *Readings in Social Evolution and Development.* Oxford, U.K.: Pergamon Press.

———. 1973. "Varieties of Political Development: The Theoretical Challenge." *In* S. N. Eisenstadt and S. Rokkan, eds., *Building States and Nations.* Beverly Hills, Calif.: Sage.

Ekern, Stener. 1998. *Street Power: Culture and Politics in a Nicaraguan Neighborhood.* Bergen, Norway: Norse.

Engels, Frederick. [1891] 1972. *The Origin of the Family, Private Property and the State.* Reprint, New York: International Publishers.

Escobar, Arturo. 1995. *Encountering Development: The Making and Unmaking of the Third World.* Princeton, N.J.: Princeton University Press.

Esman, Milton J. 1994. "Ethnic Identity as Political Force: The Scope of the Inquiry." *In* M. J. Esman, ed., *Ethnic Politics.* Ithaca, N.Y.: Cornell University Press.

Esman, Milton J, ed. 1994. *Ethnic Politics.* Ithaca, N.Y.: Cornell University Press.

Estioko-Griffin, Agnes, and P. Bion Griffin. 1981. "Woman the Gatherer: The Agta." *In* F. Dahlberg, ed., *Woman the Gatherer.* New Haven, Conn.: Yale University Press.

Evans-Pritchard, E. E. 1937. *Witchcraft, Oracles and Magic among the Azande.* Oxford, U.K.: Clarendon Press.

————. 1940a. *The Nuer.* Oxford, U.K.: Oxford University Press.

————. 1940b. "The Nuer of the Southern Sudan." *In* M. Fortes and E. E. Evans-Pritchard, eds., *African Political Systems.* Oxford, U.K.: Oxford University Press.

————. 1965. *The Position of Women in Primitive Societies and Other Essays in Social Anthropology.* London: Faber and Faber.

Faron, L. C. 1967. "The Mapuche Reservation as a Political Unit." *In* R. Cohen and J. Middleton, eds., *Comparative Political Systems.* Austin: University of Texas Press.

Ferguson, James. 1994. *The Anti-Politics Machine: "Development," Depoliticization and Bureaucratic Power in Lesotho.* Cambridge: Cambridge University Press.

Flannery, Kent. 1968. "Archeological Systems Theory and Early Mesoamerica." *In* B. Meggers, ed., *Anthropological Archeology in the Americas.* Washington, D.C.: Anthropological Society of Washington.

Fogelson, R. D., and Richard N. Adams, eds. 1977. *The Anthropology of Power: Ethnographic Studies from Asia, Oceania, and the New World.* New York: Academic Press.

Fortes, Meyer, and E. E. Evans-Pritchard, eds. 1940. *African Political Systems.* Oxford, U.K.: Oxford University Press.

Foucault, Michel. 1972. *The Archeology of Knowledge and The Discourse on Language.* New York: Pantheon.

————. 1977. *Discipline and Punish: The Birth of the Prison.* New York: Vintage.

————. 1980. *Power/Knowledge: Selected Interviews and Other Writings 1972–1977.* New York: Pantheon.

Fox, Robin. 1967. *Kinship and Marriage.* Middlesex, U.K.: Penguin.

Frazer, James G. [1890] 1900. *The Golden Bough.* 3 vols. Reprint, London: Macmillan.

Freeman, L. C., and R. F. Winch. 1957. "Societal Complexity: An Empirical Test of a Typology of Societies." *American Journal of Sociology* 62: 461–66.

Fried., Morton H. 1967. *The Evolution of Political Society.* New York: Random House.

————. 1968. "On the Concepts of 'Tribe' and 'Tribal Society.' " *In* J. Helm, ed., *Essays on the Problem of Tribe: Proceedings of the 1967 Annual Spring Meeting of the American Ethnological Society.* Seattle: University of Washington Press.

————. 1978. "The State, the Chicken, and the Egg: Or, What Came First?" *In* R. Cohen and E. Service, eds., *Origins of the State.* Philadelphia: Institute for the Study of Human Issues.

Friedl, Ernestine. 1975. *Women and Men: An Anthropologist's View.* New York: Holt, Rinehart and Winston.

————. [1978] 1990. "Society and Sex Roles." *In* J. Spradley and D. W. McCurdy, eds., *Conformity and Conflict: Readings in Cultural Anthropology*. 7th ed. Reprint, Glenview, Ill.: Scott, Foresman.

Friedman, Jonathan. 1994. *Cultural Identity and Global Processes*. London: Sage.

Fulton, Richard. 1972. "The Political Structure and Function of Poro in Kpelle Society." *American Anthropologist* 74: 1218–33.

Gailey, Christine Ward. 1987. *Kinship to Kingship: Gender Hierarchy and State Formation in the Tongan Islands*. Austin: University of Texas Press.

García Canclini, Néstor. 1995. *Cultural Hybridity: Strategies for Entering and Leaving Modernity*. Minneapolis: University of Minnesota Press.

Gardener, Katy. 1993. "Mixed Messages: Contested 'Development' and the 'Plantation Rehabilitation Project.' " *In* M. Hobart, ed., *An Anthropological Critique of Development: The Growth of Ignorance*. London: Routledge.

Geertz, Clifford. 1973. *The Interpretation of Cultures*. New York: Basic Books.

Georges, Eugenia. 1992. "Gender, Class, and Migration in the Dominican Republic: Women's Experiences in a Transnational Community." *In* N. Glick Schiller, L. Basch, and C. Blanc-Szanton, eds., *Towards a Transnational Perspective on Migration: Race, Class, Ethnicity, and Nationalism Reconsidered*. New York: Annuls of the New York Academy of Sciences, Vol. 645.

Gilroy, Paul. 1993. *The Black Atlantic: Modernity and Double Consciousness*. Cambridge, Mass.: Harvard University Press.

Gledhill, John. 2000. *Power and Its Disguises: Anthropological Perspectives on Politics*. 2d ed. London: Pluto Press.

Glick Schiller, Nina, Linda Basch, and Cristina Blanc-Szanton. 1992. "Transnationalism: A New Analytic Framework for Understanding Migration." *In* N. Glick Schiller, L. Basch, and C. Blanc-Szanton, eds. *Towards a Transnational Perspective on Migration: Race, Class, Ethnicity, and Nationalism Reconsidered*. New York: Annals of the New York Academy of Sciences, Vol. 645.

————. 1995. "From Immigrant to Transmigrant: Theorizing Transnational Migration." *Anthropological Quarterly* 68 (1): 48–63.

Gluckman, Max. 1940. "The Kingdom of the Zulu of South Africa." *In* M. Fortes and E. E. Evans-Pritchard, eds., *African Political Systems*. Oxford, U.K.: Oxford University Press.

————. 1960. *Order and Rebellion in Tribal Africa*. Glencoe, Ill.: Free Press.

————. 1965. *Politics, Law and Ritual in Tribal Society*. Oxford, U.K.: Basil Blackwell.

————. 1969. *Custom and Conflict in Africa*. New York: Barnes and Noble.

Gluckman, Max, and Fred Eggan. 1965. "Introduction." *In* M. Banton, ed., *Political Systems and the Distribution of Power*. London: Tavistock.

Goody, Jack, ed. 1966. *Succession to High Office*. Cambridge: Cambridge University Press.

Graham, Elspeth, Joe Doherty, and Mo Malek. 1992. "Introduction: The Context and Language of Postmodernism." *In* J. Doherty, E. Graham, and M. Malek, eds., *Postmodernism and the Social Sciences.* New York: St. Martin's Press.

Gramsci, Antonio. 1971. *Selections from the Prison Notebooks of Antonio Gramsci.* Translated by Q. Hoare and G. N. Smith. New York: International Publishers.

Gupta, Akhil, and James Ferguson, eds. 1997. *Anthropological Locations: Boundaries and Grounds of a Field Science.* Berkeley: University of California Press.

Haas, Jonathan. 1982. *The Evolution of the Prehistoric State.* New York: Columbia University Press.

Hall, John R. 1985. "Apocalypse at Jonestown." *In* A. C. Lehmann and J. E. Meyers, eds., *Magic, Witchcraft, and Religion: An Anthropological Study of the Supernatural.* Palo Alto, Calif.: Mayfield Publishing.

Hall, Stuart. 1990. "Cultural Identity and Diaspora." *In* J. Rutherford, ed., *Identity, Community, Culture, Difference.* London: Lawrence and Wishart.

Hammond, Dorothy, and Alta Jablow. 1976. *Women in Cultures of the World.* Menlo Park, Calif.: Cummings Publishing.

Harner, Michael. 1970. "Population Pressure and the Social Evolution of Agriculturalists." *Southwestern Journal of Anthropology* 26: 67–86.

Harris, Marvin. 1968. *The Rise of Anthropological Theory.* New York: Thomas Crowell Co.

———. 1974. *Cows, Pigs, Wars and Witches.* New York: Vintage.

———. 1977. *Cannibals and Kings: The Origins of Culture.* New York: Vintage.

Harvey, David. 1990. *The Condition of Postmodernity.* Cambridge, Mass.: Blackwell.

Helm, J., ed. 1968. *Essays on the Problem of Tribe: Proceedings of the 1967 Annual Spring Meeting of the American Ethnological Society.* Seattle: University of Washington Press.

Hobart, Mark. 1993. "Introduction: The Growth of Ignorance." *In* M. Hobart, ed., *An Anthropological Critique of Development: The Growth of Ignorance.* London: Routledge.

Hoebel, E. Adamson. 1940. *The Political Organization and Law Ways of the Comanche Indians.* American Anthropological Association Memoir 54.

———. 1960. *The Cheyenne: Indians of the Great Plains.* New York: Holt, Rinehart and Winston.

Hopkins, Terence, and Immanuel Wallerstein, eds. 1982. *World System Analysis: Theory and Methodology.* Beverly Hills: Sage.

Horowitz, Irving Louis. 1984. "Religion, the State, and Politics." *In* M. J. Aronoff, ed., *Religion and Politics, Political Anthropology.* Vol. 3. New Brunswick, N.J.: Transaction Books.

Huizer, Gerrit, and Bruce Mannheim, eds. 1979. *The Politics of Anthropology: From Colonialism and Sexism toward a View from Below.* The Hague, The Netherlands: Mouton.

Hunt, Eva, and Robert C. Hunt. 1978. "Irrigation, Conflict and Politics: A Mexican Case." *In* R. Cohen and E. Service, eds., *Origins of the State.* Philadelphia: Institute for the Study of Human Issues.

Huntington, Samuel. 1996. The *Clash of Civilizations: Remaking of the World Order.* New York: Simon and Schuster.

Izmirlian, Harry, Jr. 1969. "Structural and Decision-Making Models: A Political Example." *American Anthropologist* 71: 1062–73.

Janssen, Jacobus J. 1978. "The Early State in Ancient Egypt." *In* H. J. M. Claessen and P. Skalník, eds., *The Early State.* The Hague, The Netherlands: Mouton.

Jolly, Clifford J., and Fred Plog. 1976. *Physical Anthropology and Archeology.* 2d ed. New York: Knopf.

Kearney, Michael. 1996. *Reconceptualizing the Peasantry: Anthropology in a Global Perspective.* Boulder, Colo.: Westview.

Kertzer, David I. 1988. *Ritual, Politics and Power.* New Haven, Conn.: Yale University Press.

Kimura, Doreen. 2002. "Sex Differences in the Brain." *Scientific American Special Edition: The Hidden Mind* 12 (1): 32–35.

Kojiian, Raffi. 2002. "Armenian Genocide." Available at: http://www.cilicia.com/armo10.html. Accessed June 4, 2002.

Kottak, Conrad Phillip. 1983. *Assault on Paradise: Social Change in a Brazilian Village.* New York: Random House.

Kuper, Adam. 1973. *Anthropologists and Anthropology: The British School, 1922–1972.* New York: Pica Press.

Kurtz, Donald V. 2001. *Political Anthropology: Paradigms of Power.* Boulder, Colo.: Westview.

Kuzner, Lawrence. 1997. *Reclaiming a Scientific Anthropology.* Walnut Creek, Calif.: Altimira.

Kuznets, Simon. 1955. "Economic Growth and Income Inequality." *American Economic Review* 45 (March): 1–28.

Lampere, Louise, Helena, Ragoné, and Patricia Zavella, eds. 1997. *Situated Lives: Gender and Culture in Everyday Life.* New York: Routledge.

Lane, Jeremy F. 2000. *Pierre Bourdieu: A Critical Introduction.* London: Pluto Press.

Lanternari, Vittorio. 1963. *The Religions of the Oppressed: A Study of Modern Messianic Cults.* New York: New American Library.

Leach, Edmund R. 1954. *Political Systems of Highland Burma.* Boston: Beacon Press.

———. 1961. *Rethinking Anthropology.* London: Athlone Press.

Leacock, Eleanor B. 1979. "Lewis Henry Morgan on Government and Property." *In* M. B. Leons and F. Rothstein, eds., *New Directions in Political Economy: An Approach from Anthropology.* Westport, Conn.: Greenwood Press.

Leacock, Eleanor B., ed. 1981. *Myths of Male Dominance: Collected Articles on Women Cross-Culturally.* New York: Monthly Review Press.

Leibowitz, Lila. 1975. "Perspectives on the Evolution of Sex Differences." *In* R. R. Reiter, ed., *Toward an Anthropology of Women.* New York: Monthly Review Press.

Lemert, Charles. 1997. *Postmodernism Is not What You Think.* Malden, Mass.

Levinson, David, and Martin J. Malone. 1980. *Toward Explaining Human Culture: A Critical Review of the Findings of Worldwide Cross-Cultural Research.* New Haven, Conn.: HRAF Press.

Lewellen, Ted C. 1978. *Peasants in Transition: The Changing Economy of the Peruvian Aymara.* Boulder, Colo.: Westview Press.

———. 1979. "Deviant Religion and Cultural Evolution: The Aymara Case." *Journal for the Scientific Study of Religion* 18: 243–51.

———. 1981a. "Political Anthropology." *In* S. Long, ed., *The Handbook of Political Behavior.* Vol. 3. New York: Plenum.

———. 1981b. "Types of Preindustrial Political Systems," *Micropolitics* 1 (4): 321–43.

———. 1989a. "Holy and Unholy Alliances: The Politics of Catholicism in Revolutionary Nicaragua." *Journal of Church and State* 31: 15–33.

———. 1989b. "Penny Corporatism: Control and Autonomy in Neighborhood Political Organization in Revolutionary Nicaragua." Paper presented at the American Anthropological Association Annual Meeting, Washington, D.C., November 1989.

———. 1995. *Dependency and Development: An Introduction to the Third World.* Westport, Conn.: Bergin and Garvey.

———. 2000. "What's Hot? What's Not? in Anthropology." *Anthropology News* March 2000, 80.

———. 2002. *The Anthropology of Globalization: Cultural Anthropology Enters the Twenty-First Century.* Westport, Conn.: Bergin and Garvey.

Lewis, Herbert S. 1968. "Typology and Process in Political Evolution." *In* J. Helm, ed., *Essays on the Problem of Tribe: Proceedings of the 1967 Annual Spring Meeting of the American Ethnological Society.* Seattle: University of Washington Press.

———. 1993. "Jewish Ethnicity in Israel: Ideologies, Policies, and Outcomes." *In* J. Toland, ed., *Ethnicity and the State.* New Brunswick, N.J.: Transaction Books.

Little, Kenneth. 1965. "The Political Function of Poro." *Africa* 35: 349–65.

Lloyd, Peter C. 1965. "The Political Structure of African Kingdoms: An Explanatory Model." *In* M. Banton, ed., *Political Systems and the Distribution of Power.* London: Tavistock.

Logan, N., and W. Sanders. 1976. "The Model." *In* E. Wolf, ed., *The Valley of Mexico.* Albuquerque: University of New Mexico Press.

Lomax, Alan, and C. M. Arensberg. 1977. "A Worldwide Evolutionary Classification of Cultures by Subsistence Systems." *Current Anthropology* 18: 659–708.

Lomax, Alan, and Norman Berkowitz. 1972. "The Evolutionary Taxonomy of Culture." *Science* 177: 228–39.

Lomnitz, Claudio. 2001. *Deep Mexico, Silent Mexico: An Anthropology of Nationalism.* Minneapolis: University of Minnesota Press.

Lott, Bernice. 1987. *Women's Lives: Themes and Variations in Gender Learning.* Monterey, Calif.: Brooks/Cole Publishing.

Lowie, Robert H. [1927] 1962. *The Origin of the State.* Reprint, New York: Russell and Russell.

———. [1920] 1970. *Primitive Society.* Reprint, New York: Liveright.

Lyotard, Jean-François. 1984. *The Postmodern Condition.* Minneapolis, Minn.: University of Minneapolis Press.

MacCormack, Carol P. 1980. "Nature, Culture and Gender: A Critique." *In* C. P. MacCormack and M. Strathern, eds., *Nature, Culture and Gender.* Cambridge: Cambridge University Press.

Maine, Henry. [1861] 1987. *Ancient Law: Its Connection with the Early History of Society and Its Relation to Modern Ideas.* Reprint, London: J. Murray.

Mair, Lucy P. 1962. *Primitive Government.* Baltimore: Penguin.

Malinowski, Bronislaw. 1922. *Argonauts of the Western Pacific.* New York: Dutton.

Marcus, George E., and Michael M. J. Fischer. 1986. *Anthropology as Cultural Critique: An Experimental Moment in the Human Sciences.* Chicago: University of Chicago Press.

Marquet, Jacques. 1971. *Power and Society in Africa.* New York: McGraw-Hill.

Marshall, Lorna. 1967. "!Kung Bushman Bands." *In* R. Cohen and J. Middleton, eds., *Comparative Political Systems.* Austin: University of Texas Press.

Mascia-Lees, Frances E., and Nancy Johnson Black. 2000. *Gender and Anthropology.* Prospect Heights, Ill.: Waveland.

Mason, J. Alden. 1957. *The Ancient Civilisations of Peru.* Middlesex, U.K.: Penguin.

McGlynn, Frank, and Arthur Tuden, eds. 1991. *Anthropological Approaches to Political Behavior.* Pittsburgh, Pa.: University of Pittsburgh Press.

McLean, John. 1889. "The Blackfoot Sun Dance." *Proceedings of the Canadian Institute,* ser. 3, vol. 4: 231–37.

Middleton, John. 1960. *Lugbara Religion: Ritual and Authority among an East African People.* London: Oxford University Press.

———. 1966. "The Resolution of Conflict among the Lugbara of Uganda." *In* M. Swartz, V. Turner, and A. Tuden, eds., *Political Anthropology.* Chicago: Aldine.

Middleton, John, and David Tate, eds. 1958. *Tribes without Rulers.* London: Routledge and Kegan Paul.

Mitchell, Clyde. 1964. "Foreword." *In* J. van Velsen, ed., *The Politics of Kinship: A Study of Social Manipulation among the Lakeside Tonga.* Manchester, U.K.: Manchester University Press.

Mooney, James. [1896] 1973. *The Ghost Dance Religion and Wounded Knee.* Reprint, New York: Dover Publications, Inc.

Moore, Henrietta. 1988. *Feminism and Anthropology*. Minneapolis: University of Minnesota.

Morawetz, David. 1977. *Twenty-Five Years of Economic Development 1950 to 1975*. Baltimore.: John Hopkins University Press.

Morgan, Lewis Henry. 1877. *Ancient Society*. New York: Henry Holt.

Morgen, Sandra. 1989. "Gender and Anthropology: Introductory Essay." *In* S. Morgen, ed., *Gender and Anthropology: Critical Reviews for Research and Teaching*. Washington, D.C.: American Anthropological Association.

Mountcastle, Amy. 1997. *Tibetans in Exile: The Construction of Global Identities*. PhD diss. (Anthropology), State University of New Jersey, New Brunswick.

Mukhopadhyay, Carol C., and Patricia J. Higgens. 1988. *Annual Review of Anthropology 1988* 17: 461–95.

Murdock, George Peter. 1949. *Social Structure*. New York: Macmillan.

———. 1959. "Evolution in Social Organization." *In* B. Meggers, ed., *Evolution and Anthropology: A Centennial Appraisal*. Washington, D.C.: Anthropological Society of Washington.

———. 1973. "Measurement and Cultural Complexity." *Ethnology* 12: 379–92.

Murdock, George Peter, and Suzanne F. Wilson. 1972. "Settlement Patterns and Community Organization: Cross-Cultural Codes 2." *Ethnology* 11: 254–95.

Murra, John V. 1958. "On Inca Political Structure." *Systems of Political Control and Bureaucracy in Human Societies: Proceedings of the 1958 Annual Spring Meeting of the American Ethnological Society*. Seattle: University of Washington Press.

Nicholas, Ralph W. 1965. "Factions: A Comparative Analysis." *In* M. Banton, ed., *Political Systems and the Distribution of Power*. London: Tavistock.

———. 1966. "Segmentary Factional Political Systems." *In* M. Swartz, V. Turner, and A. Tuden, eds., *Political Anthropology*. Chicago: Aldine.

Nietzsche, Friedrich Wilhelm. [1883] 1976. *Thus Spake Zarathustra*. Translated by W. Kaufmann. Reprint, New York: Penguin.

———. [1887] 1989. *On the Genealogy of Morals*. Translated by W. Kaufmann. Reprint, New York: Vintage.

Nordstrom, Carolyn. 1997. *A Different Kind of War Story*. Philadelphia: University of Pennsylvania Press.

O'Brien, Denise. 1984. " 'Women Never Hunt': The Portrayal of Women in Melanesian Ethnography." *In* D. O'Brien, and S. W. Tiffany, eds., *Rethinking Women's Roles: Perspectives from the Pacific*. Berkeley: University of California Press.

Ong, Aihwa. 1999. *Flexible Citizenship: The Cultural Logics of Transnationality*. Durham, N.C.: Duke University Press.

Ornstein, Henry. 1980. "Asymmetrical Reciprocity: A Contribution to the Theory of Political Legitimacy." *Current Anthropology* 21: 69–91.

Ortner, Sherry B. 1974. "Is Female to Male as Nature Is to Culture?" *In* M. Z. Rosaldo and L. Lamphere, eds., *Woman, Culture and Society.* Stanford, Calif.: Stanford University Press.

Ortner, Sherry B., and Harriet Whitehead. 1981. "Introduction: Accounting for Sexual Meanings." *In* S. Ortner and H. Whitehead, eds., *Sexual Meanings: The Cultural Construction of Gender and Sexuality.* Cambridge, U.K.: Cambridge University Press.

Otterbein, Keith P. 1971. "Comment on 'Correlates of Political Complexity.' " *American Sociological Review* 36: 113–14.

Paige, Jeffrey M. 1974. "Kinship and Polity in Stateless Societies." *American Journal of Sociology* 80: 301–20.

Parker, Seymour, and Hilda Parker. 1979. "The Myth of Male Superiority: Rise and Demise." *American Anthropologist* 18: 289–309.

Patterson, Thomas C. 1971. "The Emergence of Food Production in Central Peru." *In* S. Struever, ed., *Prehistoric Agriculture.* Garden City, N.Y.: Natural History Press.

Petersen, Glenn. 1989. "Ponapean Chieftainship in the Era of the Nation-State." *In* P. Skalník, ed., *Outwitting the State: Political Anthropology.* Vol. 7. New Brunswick, N.J.: Transaction Publishers.

Pfeiffer, John E. 1977. *The Emergence of Society: A Prehistory of the Establishment.* New York: McGraw Hill.

Phillips, Lynne. 1998. "Conclusion: Anthropology in the Age of Neoliberalism." *In* L. Phillips, ed., *The Third Wave of Modernization in Latin America: Cultural Perspectives on Neoliberalism.* Wilmington, Del.: Scholarly Resources.

Philp, Mark. 1985. "Michel Foucault." *In* E. Skinner, ed., *The Return of Grand Theory in the Human Sciences.* Cambridge, U.K.: Cambridge University Press.

Price, Barbara J. 1978. "Secondary State Formation: An Explanatory Model." *In* R. Cohen and E. Service, ed., *Origins of the State.* Philadelphia: Institute for the Study of Human Issues.

———. 1979. "Turning States' Evidence: Problems in the Theory of State Formation." *In* M. B. Icons and F. Rothstein, eds., *New Directions in Political Economy: An Approach from Anthropology.* Westport, Conn.: Greenwood Press.

Radcliffe-Brown, A. R. 1940. "Preface." *In* M. Fortes and E. E. Evans-Pritchard, eds., *African Political Systems.* Oxford, U.K.: Oxford University Press.

Ramos, Alcida Rita. 1998. *Indigenism: Ethnic Politics in Brazil.* Madison: University of Wisconsin Press.

Rappaport, Roy. 1968. *Pigs for the Ancestors: Ritual in the Ecology of a New Guinea People.* New Haven, Conn.: Yale University Press.

Rapport, Nigel, and Joanna Overing. 2000. *Social and Cultural Anthropology: Key Concepts.* London: Routledge.

Reyna, S. P., and R. E. Downs, eds. 1999. *Deadly Developments: Capitalism, States, and War.* Amsterdam: Gordon and Breach.

Robbins, Richard, H. 2002. *Global Problems and the Culture of Capitalism.* Boston: Allyn and Bacon.

Rosaldo, Michelle Z. 1974. "Women, Culture and Society: A Theoretical Overview." *In* M. Z. Rosaldo and L. Lamphere, eds., *Woman, Culture and Society.* Stanford, Calif.: Stanford University Press.

Rosenau, Pauline Marie. 1992. *Post-Modernism and the Social Sciences: Insights, Inroads, and Intrusions.* Princeton, N.J.: Princeton University Press.

Rostow, W. 1960. *The Stages of Economic Growth.* Cambridge, U.K.: Cambridge University Press.

Sacks, Karen. 1979. *Sisters and Wives: The Past and Future of Sexual Equality.* Westport, Conn.: Greenwood Press.

Sàenz, Candelario. 1999. "Insurrection in the Texas Mexican Borderlands: The Plan of San Diego." *In* S. P. Reyna and R. E. Downs, eds., *Deadly Developments: Capitalism, States, and War.* Amsterdam: Gordon and Breach.

Sahlins, Marshall. 1969. "The Segmentary Lineage and Predatory Expansion." *American Anthropologist* 63: 332-45.

Sahlins, Marshall, and Elman Service. 1960. *Evolution and Culture.* Ann Arbor: University of Michigan Press.

Sahliyeh, Emile. 1993. "Ethnicity and State-Building: The Case of the Palestinians in the Middle East." *In* J. Toland, ed., *Ethnicity and the State.* New Brunswick, N.J.: Transaction Books.

Schapera, Isaac. 1967. *Government and Politics in Tribal Societies.* New York: Schocken Books.

Schlegel, Alice. 1977. "Toward a Theory of Sexual Stratification." *In* A. Schlegel, ed., *Sexual Stratification: A Cross-Cultural View.* New York: Columbia University Press.

Schröder, Ingo W., and Bettina E. Schmidt. 2001. "Introduction: Violent Imaginaries and Violent Practices." *In* I . S. Schröder and B. E. Schmidt, eds., *Anthropology of Violence and Conflict.* London: Routledge.

Schwartz, Norman B. 1969. "Goal Attainment through Factionalism: A Guatemalan Case." *American Anthropologist* 63: 332–45.

Scott, James C. 1985. *Weapons of the Weak.* New Haven, Conn.: Yale University Press.

Seaton, S. Lee. 1978. "The Early State in Hawaii." *In* H. J. M. Claessen and P. Skalník, eds., *The Early State.* The Hague, The Netherlands: Mouton.

Seaton, S. Lee, and Henri J. M. Claessen, eds. 1979. *Political Anthropology: The State of the Art.* The Hague, The Netherlands: Mouton.

Seligman, Linda J. 1998. "Survival Politics and the Movements of Market Women in Peru in the Age of Neoliberalism." *In* L. Phillips, ed., *The Third Wave of Modernization in Latin America: Cultural Perspectives on Neoliberalism.* Wilmington, Del.: Scholarly Resources.

Service, Elman R. 1962. *Primitive Social Organization: An Evolutionary Perspective.* 2d ed. New York: Random House.

————. 1975. *Origins of the State and Civilization: The Processes of Cultural Evolution.* New York: W.W. Norton.

————. 1978. "Classical and Modern Theories of Government." *In* R. Cohen and E. Service, eds., *Origins of the State: The Anthropology of Political Evolution.* Philadelphia: Institute for the Study of Human Issues.

Shannon, Thomas Richard. 1989. *An Introduction to the World-System Perspective.* Boulder, Colo.: Westview.

Sharp, Henry S. 1981. "The Null Case: The Chipewyan." *In* F. Dahlberg, ed., *Woman the Gatherer.* New Haven, Conn.: Yale University Press.

Shepherd, George W., Jr. 1987. *The Trampled Grass: Tributary States and Self-Reliance in the Indian Ocean Zone of Peace.* Westport, Conn.: Greenwood.

Shore, Cris, and Susan Wright. 1997. *Anthropology of Policy: Critical Perspectives on Governance and Power.* London: Routledge.

Shumway, David R. 1992. *Michel Foucault.* Charlottesville: University Press of Virginia.

Siegel, B. J., and A. R. Beals. 1960. "Pervasive Factionalism." *American Anthropologist* 62: 394–417.

Silverblatt, Irene. 1988. "Women in States." *Annual Review of Anthropology 1988* 17: 427–460.

Skalník, Peter. 1989. "Outwitting the State: An Introduction." *In* P. Skalník, ed., *Outwitting the State: Political Anthropology.* Vol. 7. New Brunswick, N.J.: Transaction Publishers.

Slocum, Sally. 1975. "Woman the Gatherer: Male Bias in Anthropology." *In* R. R. Reiter, ed., *Toward an Anthropology of Women.* New York: Monthly Review Press.

Smith, Michael G. 1968. "Political Anthropology: Political Organization." *In* D. L. Sills, ed., *International Encyclopedia of the Social Sciences.* Vol. 12. New York: Macmillan and the Free Press.

Southall, Aidan W. 1953. *Alur Society.* Cambridge, U.K.: W. Heffer and Sons.

————. 1965. "A Critique of the Typology of States and Political Systems." *In* M. Banton, ed., *Political Systems and the Distribution of Power.* London: Tavistock.

————. 1974. "State Formation in Africa." *In* B. J. Siegel, ed., *Annual Review of Anthropology.* Vol. 3. Palo Alto, Calif.: Annual Reviews, Inc.

Southwold, Martin. 1966. "Succession to the Throne in Buganda." *In* J. Goody, ed., *Succession to High Office.* Cambridge, U.K.: Cambridge University Press.

Spier, Leslie. 1921. *The Sun Dance of the Plains Indians: Its Development and Diffusion.* American Museum of Natural History Anthropological Papers, Vol. 16, Pt. 7.

Spindler, George and Louise. 1990. *The American Cultural Dialogue and Its Transmission.* Bristol, Penn.: Falmer Press.

Spiro, Melford E. 1965. "A Typology of Social Structure and the Patterning of Social Distributions: A Cross-Cultural Study." *American Anthropologist* 67: 1097–119.

Stavrianos, L. S. 1981. *Global Rift: The Third World Comes of Age.* New York: William Morrow.

Stem, Bernhard J. 1931. *Lewis Henry Morgan: Social Evolutionist.* Chicago: University of Chicago Press.

Stevenson, Robert R. 1968. *Population and Political Systems in Tropical Africa.* New York: Columbia University Press.

Steward, Julian. 1949. "Cultural Complexity and Law: A Trial Formulation of the Development of Early Civilizations." *American Anthropologist* 51: 1–27.

———. 1955. *Theory of Culture Change: The Methodology of Multilinear Evolution.* Urbana: University of Illinois Press.

Swartz, David. 1997. *Culture and Power: The Sociology of Pierre Bourdieu.* Chicago: University of Chicago Press.

Swartz, Marc. 1968. *Local-Level Politics.* Chicago: Aldine.

Swartz, Marc, Victor Turner, and Arthur Tuden, eds. 1966. *Political Anthropology.* Chicago: Aldine.

Tambiah, Stanley J. 1996. "The Nation-State in Crisis and the Rise of Ethnonationalism." *In* E. N. Wilmsen and P. McAllister, eds., *The Politics of Difference: Ethnic Premises in a World of Power.* Chicago: University of Chicago Press.

Taussig, Michael. 1987. *Shamanism, Colonialism, and the Wild Man.* Chicago: University of Chicago Press.

Textor, Robert B. 1967. *A Cross-Cultural Summary.* New Haven, Conn.: HRAF Press.

Toland, Judith D, ed. 1993. *Ethnicity and the State: Political and Legal Anthropology Series.* Vol. 9. New Brunswick, N.J.: Transaction Books.

Tuden, Arthur, and Catherine Marshall. 1972. "Political Organization: Cross-Cultural Codes 4." *Ethnology* 11: 436–64.

Turner, Victor. 1957. *Schism and Continuity in an African Society.* Manchester, U.K.: Manchester University Press.

U.S. Census Bureau. 2002. "Profile of General Demographic Characteristics, 2000." Available at: http://censtats.census.gov/data/US/01000.pdf. Accessed on June 16, 2002.

Upham, Steadman. 1990. "Analog or Digital?: Toward a Generic Framework for Explaining the Development of Emergent Political Systems. *In* S. Upham, ed., *The Evolution of Political Systems.* Cambridge, U.K.: Cambridge University Press.

van Dyke, Rijk. 1998. "Pentecostalism, Cultural Memory and the State: Contested Representations of Time in Postcolonial Malawai." *In* R. Werbner, ed., *Memory and the Postcolony: African Anthropology and the Critique of Power.* London: Zed.

van Velsen, J. 1964. *The Politics of Kinship: A Study in Social Manipulation among the Lakeside Tonga.* Manchester, U.K.: Manchester University Press.

Vincent, Joan. 1978. "Political Anthropology: Manipulative Strategies." *In* B. J. Siegal, ed., *Annual Review of Anthropology.* Vol. 7. Glencoe, Calif.: Annual Reviews, Inc.

———. 1990. *Anthropology and Politics: Visions, Traditions, and Trends.* Tucson: University of Arizona Press.

———. 2002. *The Anthropology of Politics: A Reader in Ethnography, Theory and Critique.* Malden, Mass.: Blackwell.

Voget, Fred W. 1975. *A History of Ethnology.* New York: Holt, Rinehart and Winston.

Wallace, Anthony F. C. 1972. *The Death and Rebirth of the Seneca.* New York: Vintage.

———. 1985. "Nativism and Revivalism." *In* A. C. Lehmann and J. E. Meyers, eds., *Magic, Witchcraft, and Religion: An Anthropological Study of the Supernatural.* Palo Alto, Calif.: Mayfield Publishing.

Wallerstein, Immanuel. 1974. *The Modern World-System I: Capitalist Agriculture and the Origins of the European World-Economy in the Sixteenth Century.* New York: Academic Press.

———. 1980. *The Modern World-System II: Mercantilism and the Consolidation of the European World-Economy, 1600–1750.* New York: Academic Press.

———. 1989. *The Modern World-System III: The Second Era of Great Expansion of the Capitalist World-Economy, 1730–1840s.* New York: Academic Press.

Weatherford, J. McIver. 1981. *Tribes on the Hill.* New York: Rawson, Wade.

Webster, Paula. 1975. "Matriarchy: A Vision of Power." *In* R. R. Reiter, ed., *Toward an Anthropology of Women.* New York: Monthly Review Press.

Wenke, Robert I. 1980. *Patterns in Prehistory: Mankind's First Three Million Years.* New York: Oxford University Press.

Werbner, Richard, ed. 1998. *Memory and the Postcolony: African Anthropology and the Critique of Power.* London: Zed.

Weyer, E. M. 1959. "The Structure of Social Organization among the Eskimo." *In* R. Cohen and J. Middleton, eds., *Comparative Political Systems.* Austin: University of Texas Press.

White, Leslie. 1943. "Energy and the Evolution of Culture." *American Anthropologist* 45: 335–56.

———. 1949. *The Science of Culture.* New York: Grove.

———. 1959. *The Evolution of Culture.* New York: McGraw-Hill.

Whyte, Martin King. 1978. *The Status of Women in Preindustrial Societies.* Princeton, N.J.: Princeton University Press.

———. 1980. "Bureaucracy and Anti-Bureaucracy in the People's Republic of China." *In* G. M. Britan and R. Cohen, eds., *Hierarchy and Society:*

Anthropological Perspectives on Bureaucracy. Philadelphia: Institute for the Study of Human Issues.

Wilmsen, Edwin N. 1996. "Introduction: Premises of Power in Ethnic Politics." In E. N. Wilmsen and P. McAllister, eds., *The Politics of Difference: Ethnic Premises in a World of Power.* Chicago: University of Chicago Press.

Wilmsen, Edwin N., and Patrick McAllister, eds. 1996. *The Politics of Difference: Ethnic Premises in a World of Power.* Chicago: University of Chicago Press.

Winkler, Edwin A. 1970. "Political Anthropology," *Biennial Review of Anthropology, 1969.* Stanford, Calif.: Stanford University Press.

Wirsing, Rolf. 1973. "Political Power and Information: A Cross-Cultural Study." *American Anthropologist* 75: 153–70.

Wissler, Clark. 1918. *The Sun Dance of the Blackfoot Indians.* Anthropological Papers of the American Museum of Natural History, Vol. 16, Pt. 3.

Wittfogel, Karl. 1957. *Oriental Despotism: A Comparative Study of Total Power.* New Haven, Conn.: Yale University Press.

Wolf, Eric R. 1982. *Europe and the People Without History.* Berkley: University of California Press.

———. 2001. *Pathways of Power: Building an Anthropology of the Modern World.* Berkeley: University of California Press.

Wolf, Eric R., and Edward Hansen. 1972. *The Human Condition in Latin America.* New York: Oxford University Press.

Worsley, Peter M. 1985. "Cargo Cults." In A. C. Lehmann and J. E. Meyers, eds., *Magic, Witchcraft, and Religion: An Anthropological Study of the Supernatural.* Palo Alto, Calif.: Mayfield Publishing.

Wright, Henry T. 1977. "Recent Research on the Origin of the State." In B. J. Siegel, ed., *Annual Review of Anthropology,* 1977. Palo Alto, Calif.: Annual Reviews, Inc.

———. 1978. "Toward an Explanation of the Origin of the State." In R. Cohen and E. Service, eds., *Origins of the State: The Anthropology of Political Evolution.* Philadelphia: Institute for the Study of Human Issues.

Yanagisako, Sylvia, and Carol Delaney, eds. 1995. *Naturalizing Power: Essays in Feminist Cultural Analysis.* New York: Routledge.

Zenner, Walter P. 1996. "Ethnicity." In D. Levinson and M. Ember, eds., *The Encyclopedia of Cultural Anthropology.* New York: Henry Holt.

About the Author

TED C. LEWELLEN is Professor Emeritus of Anthropology at the University of Richmond. He is presently retired and living in Grand Junction, Colorado.

INDEX

CPSIA information can be obtained
at www.ICGtesting.com
Printed in the USA
BVOW03s1922020917
493714BV00001B/52/P